The Motivation Factor

The Motivation Factor

A Theory of Personal Investment

Martin L. Maehr
University of Illinois
at Urbana-Champaign

Larry A. Braskamp
University of Illinois
at Urbana-Champaign

Lexington Books
D.C. Heath and Company/Lexington, Massachusetts/Toronto

Library of Congress Cataloging-in-Publication Data

Maehr, Martin L.
    The motivation factor.

    Bibliography: p.
    Includes index.
    1. Employee motivation. 2. Achievement motivation.
I. Braskamp, Larry A. II. Title.
HF5549.5.M63M34   1986   658.3′ 14   85-45158
ISBN 0-669-11226-7 (alk. paper)

Published simultaneously in Canada
Printed in the United States of America
International Standard Book Number: 0-669-11226-7
Library of Congress Catalog Card Number: 85-45158

The paper used in this publication meets the minimum requirements of American National Standard for Information Sciences—Permanence of Paper for Printed Library Materials, ANSI Z39.48-1984.

The last numbers on the right below indicate the number and date of printing.

10   9   8   7   6   5   4   3   2   1

95   94   93   92   91   90   89   88   87   86

Contents

List of Figures   ix

List of Tables   xi

Foreword   xv

Acknowledgments   xvii

1. Introduction   1

   Motivation and Behavior   2
   Motivation and Personal Investment   6
   Personal Investment Defined   8
   The Outcomes of Personal Investment   12
   Conclusion: A Look Ahead   15

2. What Motivates People? An Overview of Possible Causes   17

   Motivation as a Personal Trait   17
   Situational Causes of Motivation   27
   Cognition and Motivation   35
   What Causes Motivation: An Interpretive Summary   43

3. Toward a Theory of Personal Investment   45

   Basic Elements of a Theory of Personal Investment   45
   The Central Role of Meaning   47
   On the Meaning of Meaning   48
   The Nature, Function, and Variety of Personal Incentives   49
   The Nature of Selfhood   58
   Perceived Options   61
   Antecedents of Meaning   62
   Conclusion   70

4. **Assessing Meaning and Personal Investment and Their Causes   71**

Assessing Motivation in Adulthood   72
The Inventory of Personal Investment   76
The Inventory of Work Investment   82
An Interpretive Summary   90

5. **Meaning and Personal Investment: An Exploration of Relationships in Field Settings   93**

Characteristics of People Who Excel   95
Meaning and Vocation   101
Meaning and Work Investment   106
Implications: A Step Beyond the Data and a Look Ahead   122

6. **Organizational Culture, Meaning, and Personal Investment   125**

The Concept of Organizational Culture   126
Defining Culture   127
The Culture of the Organization   130
Assessment of Organizational Culture   131
The Influence of Organizational Culture on Personal Investment   146
The Individual in the Organization   151
Conclusion   153

7. **Age and Personal Investment   155**

Personal Investment and "The Seasons of a Man's Life"   156
Does the Motivation to Achieve Decrease with Age?   157
Age, Meaning, and Personal Investment   160
High Achievement and Age   174
Some Concluding Thoughts about Motivational Changes throughout the Life Span   177

8. **Sociocultural Context, Meaning, and Personal Investment   183**

The Sociocultural Matrix   184
Cross-Cultural Differences in Achievement-Related Meanings   193
The United States Versus Japan: A Cross-Cultural Study of Personal Investment Meanings   202
Gender Differences in Meanings and Personal Investment   212
Meaning and Personal Investment in the Cultural Context   213

9. **Managing Personal Investment   215**

A Personal Investment Perspective   216
A Perspective on Management   218
Strategies for Enhancing Motivation and Personal Investment   219
Conclusion   246

10. A Final, Unscientific Postscript   247

    In Retrospect   248
    Vive la Work Ethic!   249
    Quality of Work Life   251
    Beyond the World of Work   252
    Conclusion   253

Appendix A: Summary of Discriminant Analyses for Testing Differences
              among Selected Vocational Groups   255

References   259

Index   273

About the Authors   285

List of Figures

1-1. An Outline of the Motivational Process 10

1-2. Motivational and Other Factors that Affect Work Performance 11

1-3. The Personal Investment–Product–Evaluation Triangle 12

2-1. An Outline of McClelland's Interpretation of Weber's Protestant Ethic–Spirit of Capitalism Hypothesis 21

2-2. Causal Relationships Explored in McClelland's *The Achieving Society* 23

2-3. Model of Situational/Contextual Factors that Influence Motivation 28

3-1. An Outline of the Factors Leading to Personal Investment 49

3-2. Hypotheses Associated with Risk-Taking and Challenge-Seeking under Personal Incentive Conditions 58

3-3. Antecedents of Meaning and Personal Investment 63

5-1. Pictorial Representation of the Focal Hypothesis of Chapter 5 94

5-2. Profiles of High Achievers and Others in the Sample 99

5-3. Profiles of Mercantilists and Academics 103

5-4. Profiles of College and University Faculty Members 104

5-5. Profiles of "Indians" and "Chiefs" 106

5-6. Pictorial Summary of Causal Relationships and Indices 109

6-1. Average Scores of Employees in Six Organizations on Organizational Culture and Saliency Scales 138

6-2. Average Scores of Employees in Six Organizations on Personal Incentives Scales 141

6–3. Average Scores of Employees in Six Organizations on Job Opportunities Scales 143

6–4. Average Scores of Executives and Managers on Organizational Culture and Saliency Scales 144

6–5. Average Scores of Executives and Managers on Job Opportunities Scales 145

7–1. Average Scores of U.S. Adults on Four Personal Incentives Scales, by Age Group 162

7–2. Average Scores of U.S. Adults on Four Personal Incentives Scales, by Age Group 163

7–3. Average Scores of U.S. Adults on the Goal-Directedness Scale, by Age Group 165

7–4. Average Scores of U.S. Adults on Four Job Opportunities Scales, by Age Group 166

7–5. Average Scores of U.S. Adults on Four Job Opportunities Scales, by Age Group 167

7–6. Average Scores of U.S. Adults on the Advancement Scale, by Age Group 169

7–7. Average Scores of U.S. Adults on the Marketability Scale, by Age Group 170

7–8. Average Scores of U.S. Adults on Task Incentive and Opportunities Scales, by Age Group 172

7–9. Average Scores of U.S. Adults on Power Incentive and Opportunities Scales, by Age Group 173

7–10. Average Scores of U.S. Adults on Recognition Incentive and Opportunities Scales, by Age Group 174

7–11. Average Scores of U.S. Adults on Financial Incentive and Opportunities Scales, by Age Group 175

7–12. Average Scores of U.S. Adults on the Job Satisfaction Scale, by Age Group 176

7–13. Average Scores of U.S. Adults on the Organizational Commitment Scale, by Age Group 177

9–1. Pressure Points for Changing Personal Investment in an Organization 219

List of Tables

3–1. Personal Incentive Categories   51

3–2. Components of Sense of Self   59

4–1. Secretarial Behaviors That Illustrate the Nature and Level of Personal Investment   74

4–2. Classification of Individuals Taking the IPI   78

4–3. Description of Inventory of Personal Investment Factors   79

4–4. Intercorrelations and Reliabilities of IPI Scales   80

4–5. Theoretical Classification of IPI Factors   81

4–6. Dimensions Measured by the Inventory of Work Investment (IWI)   83

4–7. Organizations in the IWI Sample   84

4–8. IWI Respondents Classified by Organizational Unit in Six Organizations   84

4–9. Examples of IWI Items Used to Assess Each of the Eight Personal Incentives   85

4–10. Examples of IWI Items Used to Assess the Three Sense-of-Self Factors   85

4–11. Descriptions of Marketability and Organizational Advancement Scales and Sample Items   85

4–12. Description of Job Opportunities Scales and Sample Items   86

4–13. Reliabilities and Correlations among the Eight Job Opportunities Scales   87

4–14. Descriptions of the Four Organizational Culture Scales and Sample Items   88

4–15. Description of the Organizational Saliency of Culture Scale and Sample Items 88

4–16. Reliabilities and Correlations among the Four Organizational Culture Scales and the Saliency of Culture Scale 89

4–17. Descriptions of the Four Job Satisfaction Scales and Sample Items 89

4–18. Description of the Organizational Commitment Scale and Sample Items 90

4–19. Reliabilities and Correlations among the Four Job Satisfaction Scales 90

5–1. Correlations between Personal Incentives and Job Opportunities and Organizational Culture on the Same Dimensions 111

5–2. Correlations between Job Opportunities and Job Satisfaction and Organizational Commitment 112

5–3. Correlations among Job Satisfaction, Organizational Commitment, Marketability, and Organizational Advancement 112

5–4. Significant Personal Incentive and Sense-of-Self Predictors of Job Satisfaction and Organizational Commitment 113

5–5. Significant Predictors of Satisfaction and Commitment Based on Personal Incentives, Sense of Self, and Advancement 115

5–6. Significant Predictors of Satisfaction and Commitment Based on Personal Incentives, Sense of Self, and Marketability 116

5–7. Correlations of Discrepancies between Organizational Culture/Personal Incentive and Job Satisfaction/Organizational Commitment 117

5–8. Significant Congruency and Component Variables for Predicting Job Satisfaction 118

5–9. Significant Congruency and Component Variables for Predicting Organizational Commitment 120

5–10. Significant Predictors of Satisfaction and Commitment 121

6–1. Summary Descriptions of Six Sample Organizations 137

6–2. Significant Differences in Organizational Culture among Six Organizations 139

6–3. Correlations among Organizational Culture, Saliency, Commitment, Marketability, Advancement, and Job Satisfaction 140

6–4. Correlations between Job Opportunities and Organizational Culture on Similar Dimensions 142

6–5. Differences in Perceptions of Organizational Culture among Groups in Three Organizations 146

6–6. Personal Incentives, Job Opportunity, and Organizational Culture Scales that Are Significant Predictors of Job Satisfaction and Organizational Commitment 148

6–7. Correlations of Organizational Culture Items with Organizational Commitment, Job Satisfaction, and Saliency 150

7–1. Differences in Personal Incentives at Different Life Stages 161

7–2. Correlations between Time in the Organization and Personal Incentives and Job Opportunities 168

8–1. General Indices for 30 Language/Culture Communities 194

8–2. Concepts Chosen to Reflect Achievement Meanings 195

8–3. Cross-Cultural Factors of Achievement 196

8–4. Achievement Concepts Most Associated with Affective Goals 197

8–5. Achievement Concepts Most Associated with Abstract Goals 197

8–6. Achievement Concepts Most Associated with Achievement Options: Instrumental Behavior 198

8–7. Achievement Concepts Most Associated with Achievement Options: Interpersonal Style 199

8–8. Achievement Concepts Most Associated with Achievement Situations 200

8–9. Achievement Concepts Most Associated with Sex Role 201

8–10. Achievement Concepts Most Associated with the I-Myself Concept: Sense of Self 202

8–11. Achievement Concepts Most Associated with Internality-Externality: Sense of Self 202

8–12. Profile of 522 Japanese Adults in Sample 204

8–13. Comparison of U.S. and Japanese Adults by Occupational Group 205

8–14. Standardized Beta Weights in Regression Equation to Predict Country from Personal Incentives and Sense of Self 211

Foreword

Everyone deals with aspects of motivation. Parents talk about their children's interest in sports, music, school or certain television programs. Business managers are concerned about American workers' lack of motivation for high productivity and quality; workers describe boring jobs; teachers complain about lazy students; and we all bemoan the desire to wield a big stick on the part of our own, or other countries', political leaders. Motivation has thus been a central concern of human beings and of psychologists as well. Psychological theorists, however, have sometimes tried to leave out motivational constructs as they developed biological, environmental, learning, cognitive, and behavioral concepts intended to account for psychological phenomena.

But motivation is a hardy and persistent field; it pops up again and again because both in folk psychology and scientific psychology we recurrently find that a parsimonious explanation needs to give attention to desires, feelings, goals, and values—the arena over which motivation theories range.

One of the prime concerns, both of those looking to psychologists for help and of the curious scientist, is motivation for work and achievement. Why do some people happily work 60, 80, or 90 hours a week while others go to their jobs with the intent to avoid as much work as possible? What drives people to strive for success, for promotion to a more demanding job, for a more nearly perfect performance?

These are the questions addressed by this book. The key theoretical construct is "personal investment", a term which is certainly metaphorical—but metaphorical in the best sense, because it communicates to students and other non-psychologists an immediate intuitive sense of what the authors are describing. And the metaphor's surplus meaning also has nice heuristic value to the theorists in pointing to questions for their theories about value, or payoff, of personal investments and of the trade-offs (or synergism) between different investments.

Maehr and Braskamp's theory has a nice balance of behavioristic and cognitive approaches. While they emphasize that motivation is always inferred from *behavior*, the concept of personal investment clearly requires a cognitive explanation of how and why personal investments have acquired the meanings which result in changes in the ongoing stream of behavior.

The balance between theory, research, and application is also appealing. The book has a strong research-based theoretical foundation, but in reading each chapter I got some ideas I could apply—sometimes directly suggested in the text and sometimes inferences and insights stimulated by the text.

In short, I look forward to continued companionship with this book. I hope you will too.

Wilbert McKeachie
University of Michigan

Acknowledgments

This volume represents most immediately the culmination of five years of research. More generally, it is based upon our concerns with issues of motivation, achievement and management which we have explored throughout our careers. It is also a book that could not have been produced without the help of numerous colleagues, students—and the support of our families. As most authors, we are indebted to many, but can only list a few. In mentioning our special indebtedness to our colleagues, Del Harnisch, Jack Kelly, Bill McKeachie, and John Nicholls, we are fearful that we will offend many others who also contributed significantly. We will offend no one by expressing our thanks to our families. That amazing octogenarian and perceptive psychologist in his own right, Dr. Martin J. Maehr, was not only a model for excellence and a source of encouragement, he also assisted us in gathering data and interpreting it. Our wives, Jane and Judi, more deeply involved in the real world of work than we, not only encouraged us, but put our ideas to the test. For this, and many other reasons, we thank them. Even our children at times got into the act, serving as research assistants in recording data, obtaining desired computer output—and in being only a healthy distraction. An all too often unsung hero in our research has been Ms. Joyce Wolverton who not only assisted us in administering the several research projects on which this book was based but somehow also managed to get this report into typewritten form.

To all: Thank you!

Martin L. Maehr
Larry A. Braskamp

1
Introduction

A s we write these words, the United States seems to be undergoing an agonizing self-appraisal of what it is, what it can do and be. Gone are the illusions of unlimited power and achievement; the former left with Vietnam, the latter with the loss of sales to the Japanese. What has happened to our productivity, to the quality of our efforts, to our dedication to accomplish great and mighty things? What has happened to the "achieving society" we thought we had?

There may be many or no answers to these questions. There may be many or no solutions to the problems described. A proposed answer, however, is contained in the following excerpt from the *New York Times* Business Section ("Motivation Factor," 1983, p. 1):

> Lester Thurow, an economist from the Massachusetts Institute of Technology and adviser to Democrats, can rattle off a list of proposals to open the way to a sustained economic recovery. But for him, any proposal pales compared with the need to do something to upgrade and adjust the American workforce to the imperatives of world competition.
>
> "All that counts is the highly motivated workforce and you'll make it," he said at the Philadelphia conference. "You can have no natural resources and your country blown up," Mr. Thurow said, referring to Japan, "and if you have a workforce you'll make it." He pointed to Argentina which he says probably has more natural resources per capita than any other country, "But it has still a lousy economy."

A motivational answer to a nation's presumed malaise is by no means novel (cf. Inkeles, 1980; Steers, 1981; Yankelowich, 1979). However, it is by no means clear that it poses a solution either, yet it is regularly cited as important, if not critical.

The possible role of motivation in a society is hardly an issue to be ignored. Even harder to ignore is the role of motivation in individual lives. Over the past several years, we have talked to thousands of people about their work, achievement, and productivity. In some cases, these discussions have focused on managing others. In other cases, the problems involved managing oneself.

We listened to a recently appointed president of a small corporation who has worried about motivational problems in his sales force: "How can I be sure I've got a real 'dynamo' rather than just another 'dud'? What incentive system should I employ? How can I prevent this infernal turnover problem?" We listened to a member of a "million-dollar club" describe how he sold insurance: It was all motivation—his own and that of his clients, but mostly his own. Indeed, what he told us sounded more like religion than business, or even motivation as psychologists talk about it. But *he* saw motivation as the critical ingredient that guides sales and lives.

We also listened to people struggling with what they saw as their own motivational problems. A young mother of three described her motivation (often, lack of motivation) as she struggled to complete an MBA so that she could resume her role in the world of work. A friend described beginning a law career in earnest—enthusiastic about 10-hour workdays and proud of working through weekends and vacations—only to drop it all and move to a 160-acre farm precisely at the point when all the effort was about to pay off in fame and fortune.

Such examples abound. They are often the topic of conversation at late-afternoon social hours. Motivating others and motivating ourselves are repeated demands, often perplexing problems. Personal interests and national concerns require a serious consideration of motivation, particularly as it relates to work, achievement, and productivity. The writing of this book was prompted by such problems, questions, and concerns. This is a book about motivation and achievement in the adult years. It is concerned, first, with the world of work—an achievement domain of personal importance in adulthood and a major concern of society. But our interest does not stop with the issues of effectiveness, productivity, and achievement. We are also concerned with how work and achievement accord with establishing a meaningful and satisfying existence through the adult years. Thus, this is a book about *personal investment*.

Motivation and Behavior

Few would ignore the importance of motivation in human affairs. Yet while agreeing that motivation is important, they are likely to disagree about what it is. Psychological folklore, at least, would have it that motivation has something to do with inner states of the person, such as needs, drives, and psychic energies. Certainly, in talking about motivation, most of us use that kind of language a good deal of the time. But these are inferences that are made from observing certain behavioral patterns. Perhaps the disagreement and confusion about the nature of motivation stems, in part, from not looking first at the behavior that is to be explained. We suggest that any discussion of motivation should begin with a description of the behavior to be observed and later move to possible inferences, generalizations, and suggestions regarding antecedents. What do we *see* that leads us to conclude that a person is motivated? What does a work force *do* that merits the label "motivated"?

Talk about motivation seems to refer to a wide variety of activities. On closer examination, however, the behavior on which motivational inferences are based is more limited. We suggest that most motivational talk arises from observations about variation in five behavioral patterns, which we label direction, persistence, continuing motivation, intensity, and performance. In themselves, these labels may suggest the behavioral basis for motivational inferences, but further explanation is clearly in order.

Direction

The apparent *choice* among a set of action possibilities is a first indicator of motivation. When an individual attends to one thing and not another, we are likely to infer that he or she is motivated in one way but not another. The choices individuals make between behavioral alternatives suggest motivational inferences. When a salesman gives up a weekend with friends and family to carry through on a major project, we can draw motivational inferences. Similarly, when one worker attends to a task while a fellow worker "goofs off," we can use the term *motivation*. More broadly, changes in career direction are examples of apparent choices that prompt motivational inferences. Sometimes the changes are dramatic: The career change of Martin Luther perhaps changed the course of Western History, as did that of the apostle Paul. More often, however, career changes occur with less fanfare and effect—as when an executive who has gone about as far as he can go in the organization begins investing more of his time and energy in leisure pursuits.

It is the *observation* of change in direction that occasions the inference that motivation of some kind is involved. Strictly speaking, choice is not a simple behavioral observation; it is an inference that is drawn from the observation that a person does one thing when other possibilities were open to him or her. Thus, the designation or attribution of choice among alternatives prompts motivational inferences.

Persistence

Persistence is the second behavioral pattern that forms the basis for motivational inferences. When an individual concentrates attention on the same task or event for a greater or lesser period of time, observers are likely to infer the existence of a greater or lesser degree of motivation. When we see a person put in 12–15-hour work days and occasionally work through a weekend, we are likely to infer that she is "highly motivated." One may wonder about why she does this and debate the motives, but it is the observation of this pattern that prompts the wonder and stimulates the debate.

Similarly, when a 65-year-old retired dockworker sits at his worktable for hours repairing and refurbishing antique clocks, most observers would agree that motivation is involved. Of course, many such examples could be cited in regard to almost any area of human activity. The point is that observations concerning persistence sum up to a critical indicator of motivation. It is worth noting, however, that persistence may be viewed as an instance in which the same direction of behavior is retained. In other words, the person repeatedly chooses the same (or closely similar) behavioral alternatives while simultaneously rejecting other alternatives. In an important sense, then, the behavioral pattern of persistence is really just another example of a choice that is made or a behavioral direction that is taken.

Continuing Motivation

What we have come to call continuing motivation is a pattern that is strikingly suggestive of motivation (Maehr, 1976). We first became aware of the importance of this pattern in education when we observed some schoolchildren using a free moment to return to a previously encountered task on their own, without any externally imposed reason for doing so (Fyans, Kremer, Salili, & Maehr, 1981; Maehr & Stallings, 1972; Salili, Maehr, Sorensen, & Fyans, 1976; Sorensen & Maehr, 1976). It seemed that, in many ways, the child who proceeded to use a free moment to do additional problems, check out an extra book from the library just to learn a bit more about insects, or try out a physics experiment in his father's workshop is "really motivated." We remain impressed with the importance of continuing motivation in a wide array of educational activities (Maehr, 1983, 1984a), but we are becoming increasingly aware that not only is continuing motivation important for students in school, it is at least as important for adults at work.

Workers who, in some sense, take their work home with them intrigue us. Professionals who not only tote briefcases home at night but also engage in continuing education to improve their work skills are thought of as truly professional, dedicated, highly motivated. Each of us has known someone who "lives" his or her work—a description that is apparently based on observations of what we have labeled continuing motivation.

The continuing motivation pattern can be differentiated from the persistence pattern. Whereas persistence relates to continuous activity, the focus of continuing motivation is on the return to a task after an interruption of some kind. It is almost as if a certain tension exists when a task is left incomplete; the person simply cannot leave it alone (cf. Zeigarnik, 1927). Continuing motivation and persistence may both be viewed as particular examples of choice and decision situations. At this point, however, it seems appropriate to reflect a wide array of different patterns that might lead to inferences before summarizing and abstracting them into general categories.

Intensity

The intensity with which a given task is performed is a fourth index of motivation. Intensity refers generally to the amount of energy expended and is tied most directly to indices of sheer physical action. *Activity level* is a prime indicator of the exertion of physical effort. Any person's activity level varies over time, as is obvious in the normal working and sleeping cycles. Nearly as obvious are the differences observed in people's tendencies to become less active as they become older. Some people also seem to be more active than others; they sleep less, they do more, and they appear to work at a faster pace. Intensity may also be indicated by other measures of energy output, but the point we wish to make is that, in many ways, intensity level is a more complex and less reliable indicator of motivation than choice and persistence. Physiological factors are likely to be implicated much more than they are in the three previous patterns. Moreover, in most work situations, the motivation pattern is not so much one of intensity as of direction—luckily for managers, employers, and those who are in the business of motivating persons. There is often little that one can do about intensity level, because it is controlled by factors largely external to the immediate situation. Yet it is important to take this pattern into account in the wider scheme of things.

Performance

The final behavioral pattern that characteristically prompts motivational inferences is variation in performance. If variation in performance cannot be explained in terms of variation in competence, skill, or physiological factors, then a motivational inference is frequently drawn. Employers can readily cite instances in which "good workers" slump and do below-standard work as well as examples of "poor workers" who "get serious" and increase their efficiency and output. Sometimes, these slumps and jumps can be related to the acquisition of a necessary skill; sometimes, physiological factors such as illness are involved. However, when such explanations are found wanting for one reason or another, a motivational explanation is likely to be invoked.

Performance level is not a pure measure of motivation. It is a product of acquired skills, ability, and a combination of the behavioral patterns already reviewed. Thus, choice, persistence, and intensity are all likely to be reflected in performance. One might even argue that performance level is, at best, a very crude measure of motivation. Yet it is a behavioral pattern that is taken seriously in the discussion of motivation, perhaps because it is often the bottom line in the rationale for studying motivation. In any event, because variation in performance level often leads to motivational inferences, this pattern of behavior has its place in the present taxonomy.

These clearly overlapping behavioral patterns may or may not be all-inclusive. Moreover, they represent not "pure observations" but, rather, judgments about behavior in specific instances. For the moment, they suffice to suggest what we are talking about when we say that people or groups are or are not motivated. The consideration of motivational issues begins with the observation of the behavioral patterns outlined here. For example, when managers or supervisors ask how they can motivate employees, they are probably asking how they can direct employees to do one thing and avoid other things. Further, they are concerned with some degree of persistence at these activities and they especially hope that the activities are performed not only when the supervisor is present but also when the employees are left on their own. Moreover, these managers expect—and rightly so—that persistence in attending to the "right" activities will result in increased levels of performance. In other words, it can be argued that the behavioral patterns defined here are, in fact, what laypersons and professionals alike are talking about when they talk about motivation. Identifying motivation with certain behavioral patterns not only has theoretical value; it also accords with practical demands placed on motivation theory.

Motivation and Personal Investment

On the surface, at least, these varied behavioral patterns may seem diverse and disparate. They all reflect motivation, however, and in that way they are similar. More generally, they all indicate how and the degree to which individuals are *investing* themselves in a given activity. As we observe individuals apparently making choices, persisting at tasks, and exhibiting varying levels of intensity, a convenient metaphor comes to mind. People can and do invest their money in a variety of ways. They also can and do invest their personal resources of time, talent, and energy in a variety of ways. Observations of a person's choices and persistence, in particular, might suggest that the person involved is, in effect, investing his or her personal resources in a certain way. Observations of intensity might suggest not only direction but also the amount of investment. In this context, the term *personal investment* seems apt, because it captures the underlying meaning of the disparate behavioral patterns commonly associated with motivation.

Resource Distribution

It can be effectively argued that, for most purposes, motivational problems are problems of resource distribution. The issue is really not *whether* a person is motivated but, rather, how, to what ends, and in what ways the person is motivated. The assumption is that all people are motivated to do something;

the question is *what* they are motivated to do. As an example, consider our friend Frank, who is a plumber. He is also a good auto mechanic. Most of all, however, Frank is a person with a variety of avocations, hobbies, and interests. He is a fascinating conversationalist and a great consultant on various home repair projects. He is not particularly noteworthy, however, as a plumber. He does his job well enough when he gets around to it, but he typically puts only limited effort into this enterprise. No one would describe Frank as ambitious, energetic, or even hardworking. He carries out his assignments methodically and with skill—but hardly with speed. Indeed, his slow pace might be—and often has been—taken as a *lack* of motivation. But this is only one side to Frank. If one considered all the other things Frank is doing, one would not in any sense see him as lacking in motivation. He has simply chosen to invest himself at least as much in his various avocations as in his vocation. Frank is not so unusual. When we observe certain workers on the job, it is often easy to label them "unmotivated" when we might better view them as investing their resources in other ways than on the job. It is all the same, you say? Well, not exactly. Labeling a person "unmotivated" suggests that the person is simply lacking in something and that nothing can be done about it. Viewing the same situation from the perspective of personal investment, one begins to ask what there is about the work situation that is not attracting the worker's best efforts. Why is he or she investing himself or herself elsewhere? Perhaps the work situation cannot be changed to attract the best efforts of certain workers—but perhaps it can. Indeed, as we subsequently illustrate (see chapter 9), there are several ways in which one can change the degree to which people shift their personal investment to the work sphere. The point to be made now, however, is conceptual. Motivation can be properly thought of as a process whereby people take certain available resources—their time, talent, and energy—and distribute them as they choose.

This perspective is useful in a number of ways. There are perhaps few situations in which motivation is as major a problem as in the case of workers whose backgrounds differ from that of the employer or supervisor. It may be a problem of managing former bedouins in the oil fields of the Middle East or supervising the work of so-called hard-core unemployed in the United States. In such cases, the manager or supervisor is probably wise to avoid assuming too quickly that an employee is simply lacking in motivation and to consider that something about the work situation is not eliciting the workers' investment. It is self-defeating to pass off a person's behavior as merely a lack of motivation when this implies the lack of a special ingredient in his or her personal makeup. It is often also incorrect, in that it reflects a lack of knowledge or appreciation of the backgrounds of the workers involved and the broader sphere in which they live. The concept of personal investment suggests that we examine more closely the way individuals choose to invest themselves and then ask what it is about the task that may preclude or discourage them from investing time, talent, and energy in this particular context. Of course, one cannot always change the job to fit the person—nor should one attempt to do so—but assuming at the outset that people either are or are not motivated leaves only the option of hiring or firing them. In some cases, the only option is hiring them and living with a bad situation. Viewing motivation as personal investment, however, suggests that one can consider motivation not only as an enduring trait of individuals or groups but as a direct product of the situation in which the person or group is placed. And situations are usually easier to change than people.

Resource Availability

Just as individuals may choose to invest their time, talent, and energy—*themselves*—differently, they may also have more or less to invest. Certainly, some people have greater amounts of ability, skill, and knowledge. It seems possible, also, that individuals and groups could vary in energy level as well. From there on, however, the matter becomes a bit more complicated. It is common to attribute the achievements of great persons to great energy. Edmund Morris (1979) repeatedly described Theodore Roosevelt as someone who seemingly possessed boundless energy, exhibited intensity in most of what he did, and maintained a high activity level. Robert Massie (1980) described Peter the Great in a similar fashion, and numerous other examples could be cited. But even descriptions of the less than great—those who do well in their various organizations—commonly mention their *energy*. It seems that certain people simply have greater motivational resources. This may be true, but we caution against making too much of this point. First, the relationship between the physiological conditions that might produce high energy levels and motivational interests in social behavior is by no means clear—except perhaps in extreme instances. Illness, malnutrition, and psychological depression are obviously related to reduced intensity. But in most cases, motivational intensity seems to vary as much with the situation as with the person and cannot be readily attributed to specific physiological characteristics. Moreover, we have observed that, in most cases, the *availability* of motivational resources is not really the issue; the *allocation* of resources is. When employers, teachers, or parents worry about motivation, it is generally safe to assume that the issue is not whether the person has the requisite energy but, rather, how this energy is invested (cf. Maehr, 1974a).

Thus, the concept of personal investment both implies the possibility of greater motivational resources and emphasizes the different ways of distributing these resources. In this book, the stress will be clearly on the latter. It is an area in which we know more, and it is an area in which we can do more.

Personal Investment Defined

The term *personal investment* appears to serve well in labeling the behavioral patterns that are at the heart of social motivation. Not only does it describe behavior in the work setting, it is also applicable to leisure (Kelly, 1982a) and to the wider realm of human affairs (see, for example, Kuhlen, 1964). It is indeed a convenient metaphor—a felicitous term—for talking about how individuals live out their lives. In this book, it is even more than that. It is also a technical term, a theoretical construct, around which a theory is based and measurement procedures are developed. Therefore, we must define more specifically what we mean by personal investment.

Personal Investment in the Motivational Process

Personal investment is most readily defined as a course of action rather than as a psychological state. It is a concept that appears to integrate a collection of behavioral patterns, all of which reflect a degree of attraction toward something. But the emphasis is on something that is done that is observable, objective, and quantifiable. One can see people persist and measure how long they do so. Personal investment is really the bottom line, the hard data, the object of our final concern when we talk about motivation. But one cannot define personal investment without recognizing that this bottom line is part of a larger process. The use of the term *personal* suggests that more is involved than simply the observation of investment choices. At the least, there are likely to be cognitive and affective correlates of these behavioral patterns. Personal investment must also be viewed as part of a chain of events, and a theory of personal investment must specify this process as well as the factors that initiate and modify it.

Figure 1–1 provides an outline of the full motivational process as we envision it. It is a sketch that will have to be filled in later but is sufficient for now, to suggest the essential elements of the motivational process. Personal investment appears in the figure as the end of the process. As we have suggested, it is the ultimate issue in considering motivation. Preceding it are two types of causal factors. First are certain factors external to the person that are likely to influence personal investment. The nature of the task is certainly one of these factors. Everyone knows that certain tasks are simply more interesting than others, and what will be interesting to whom, when, and why are significant questions in motivational theory and research. Other factors—such as payoffs, rewards, and punishments—also determine interest or personal investment. Between such external factors and personal investment there is the person. Later (in chapter 3), we will show that external factors seldom, if ever, operate directly to determine personal investment. Rather, the effects of external events are modified by internal psychological factors—the person's thoughts, perceptions, and feelings. Thus, in many respects, the portion of the diagram encompassed by a broken line in figure 1–1 (the internal factors) is the most important. It refers to how individuals perceive, construct, and transform external events around them—crucial steps in the motivational process. One must know something about the *meaning* of situations to people before one can understand how and why they choose to invest themselves.

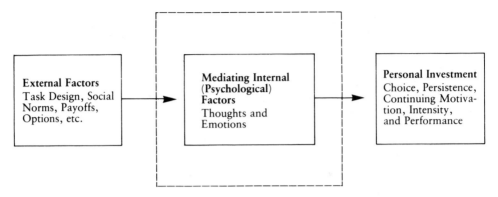

Figure 1–1. An Outline of the Motivational Process

Motivation and Personal Investment in Context

It may be easy to assume that motivation is everything, but it is not. It is only one of several facets of behavior that are important in any given setting. In the work setting, for example, whether the worker is or is not motivated is not the only factor that affects performance. Skill is involved in most cases, and the quality of interpersonal relationships among co-workers may also affect performance when the task requires some degree of cooperation and social interaction. Certainly, the organization of the task is also important. Even highly motivated workers might be very inefficient if they don't have the appropriate skills or tools or if it is unclear what they are to do and how. Their motivation will also be to little avail if they are forced to spend an inordinate amount of time covering for an alcoholic co-worker, working around an incompetent supervisor, or resolving personality clashes. Work motivation—as motivation of any kind—must be understood in a wider context.

Figure 1–2 outlines the wider context of work behavior and suggests where motivation fits in. As indicated in the figure, an individual comes to the job not only with a certain level of skill and ability but also with an existence outside of and beyond the job. For most people, there is life after work; their personal investments in family, friends, and associations are important to them. Within the specific job context, one may distinguish two categories of influence. First, there are the specific attractions of the job itself—its definition, demands, and rewards. Second, a job exists in an organizational setting; thus, the company, not just the job, plays a role. All in all, figure 1–2 anticipates a major point to be made in our ensuing discussion: Motivation, achievement, and satisfaction must always be considered in a wider context.

Motivation and Personal Investment as a Dynamic Process

It is important to remember that motivation is a *dynamic* process. Personal investment occurs as part of a continuous stream of ever-changing events.

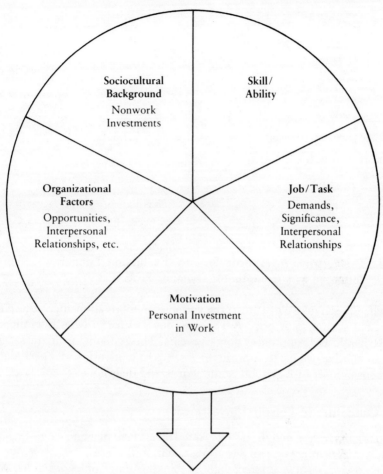

Job Performance, Absenteeism, Turnover, Skill Development, etc.

Figure 1–2. Motivation and Other Factors That Affect Work Performance

Choosing to do something and then doing it initiates a set of interactions with other people, machines, animate and inanimate entities that affect what the person does. People not only believe, they act; and their action results in feedback. Feedback—responses to and outcomes of action taken—is especially important in determining the continuing flow of events. In this regard, we have found it especially useful to keep in mind that a product–evaluation cycle is characteristically embedded in the flow of behavior. The essence of such a cycle is portrayed in figure 1–3. As most such portrayals, it is a less than perfect picture of how events occur in the real world. What it is meant to suggest is that personal investment is both a product and a producer of dynamic interaction with a variety of persons, situations, and events. The effects of one's personal investment feed back to affect the continuing investment of

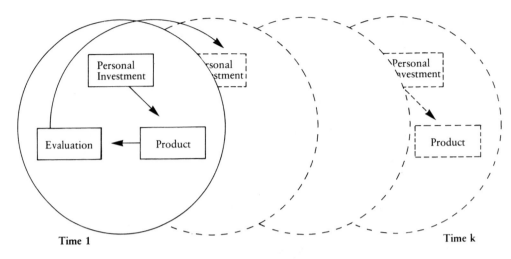

Figure 1–3. The Personal Investment–Product–Evaluation Triangle
Portrayed as a Continuous, Dynamic Process

oneself. We can take a picture of the variables in motivation at any given moment, but such a static portrayal seldom does justice to what in reality is a very dynamic and continuous flow of events. This is an important message to keep in mind as we try to capture the essence of motivation and personal investment in a set of inevitably static words and diagrams.

The Outcomes of Personal Investment

The term *motivation* and the term *personal investment* place no value judgment on how a person uses his or her time, talent, and energy. However, we can scarcely use the term *investment* without thinking of outcomes or results. What comes from a certain distribution of one's personal resources? Is it good or bad? If one or the other, is it equally so from different perspectives—the person's own as well as society's? As we have defined personal investment, one could readily apply it to absorption in computer games, square dancing, or gardening as well as work, education, or career development. Because different investments have different effects, however—on ourselves and on others—they are likely to have differential values. Thus, it is important not only to describe when, how, and under what conditions individuals invest themselves but also to determine the effects of different investment patterns. This is not a simple issue, but one can readily think of three possibilities. We shall describe each of these briefly to illustrate the point that not all personal investments lead to the same end.

Achievement

Achievement is the first type of outcome from personal investment that might come to mind. Having said that, however, it is necessary to amplify a bit what is meant by the ubiquitous and elusive concept of achievement. When educators worry publicly about decreasing SAT scores, they seem to mean one kind of thing—school achievement. When the captains of industry worry about achievement, they seem to mean something else—economic productivity. Historians, too, have a stake in all this as they wonder about why societies wax and wane. And the international community continually confronts the dilemma of governments, officials, and laborers who resist development, preferring the old ways to the new and apparently lacking a capacity to make the most of their opportunities.

Clearly, achievement means many different things, and one should not define it in a way that ignores such a wide array of meanings. Defining achievement so as to embrace such a variety of behavior is a tall order, but fortunately, there are some precedents to advise us (Maehr, 1974a, 1974b; McClelland, 1961, 1985a). First, achievement is usually thought of in terms of successes and failures in accomplishing things that society deems valuable. School achievement is a case in point, as is achievement in a career. Further, achievement is something done *by* a person or group; it is not something that happens *to* persons or groups. The issue of responsibility is crucial. When the person is thought to be responsible for the outcome, the outcome is labeled "achievement." Finally, achievement involves performance when the outcome is not a foregone conclusion. An outcome whose results were never in question is not an achievement. Achievement occurs only when the results are uncertain at the outset. Thus, habitual and repetitive acts are not labeled "achievements."

In summary, achievement involves a personal accomplishment—something that is attributed to one's ability and effort. But it is an accomplishment that is not only valued by the person; it also has social significance. We can imagine one investing oneself totally in computer games with some degree of "success," but only in special instances would we associate this investment with achievement. Indeed, much human capital is invested in ways that really yield little in the way of achievement as we have defined it. This does not necessarily imply that such activity is good or bad. It suggests only that it will be differentially valued. Possibly implied as well is that a given society can or will tolerate only so much of it. Each society, for survival's sake, demands that human resources yield a certain level of what we have called achievement.

Personal Growth

Personal growth is a second possible outcome of personal investment. Personal investment can lead to an enhancement of one's ability, skill, or competence. Children and adults do not necessarily freely choose tasks that enhance their competence. Individuals are more or less likely to invest themselves in activities and tasks that enhance their ability, and certain situations may encourage or discourage such investment. For example, three attorneys may use their free time quite differently. One may enroll in a MBA program, hoping not only to upgrade his or her skills but also to move his or her career along. The result that person has in mind is what we have termed achievement. Another may choose to enroll in a course in ceramics, just because he or she finds fulfillment in doing things with his or her hands. The third attorney may take every chance to sail, simply because this challenges his or her courage and skill. Enhancement of ability may be involved in each case, but clearly the goal in the first case is achievement, whereas in the other two it is personal growth. Yet another attorney might spend his or her free time fishing, with little evident payoff and little interest in enhancing skills or abilities. Certainly, all these activities can have their place, but just as certainly, they may have different effects on the course of a person's life—they may pay off quite differently.

Life Satisfaction

The third possible outcome of personal investment involves life satisfaction and general well-being. How does a pattern of personal investment affect the quality of one's life? Does a certain pattern of personal investment yield a greater or lesser sense of well-being? Personal investment patterns that lead to personal growth may seem desirable, and personal investment patterns that yield achievement may be highly valued by our society—but what makes a person feel satisfied? It is clear that a discussion of motivation and personal investment must consider the outcomes in the broader context of the quality of life.

An acquaintance of ours, when told of the outstanding achievements of someone else, almost invariably remarks, "But is he happy?" Such comments can sometimes be passed off as "sour grapes," yet underlying such comments are important concerns. Does investing oneself in such a way as to excel in an area carry with it a certain price in terms of life satisfaction? A recent study of highly talented and gifted performers indicates that it might. Bloom (1982a, 1982b) and his colleagues have been studying "world-class" performers in music (pianists), art (sculptors), sports (tennis players, swimmers) and science (mathematicians, neuroscientists). Although many facets of the study are intriguing, one particularly fits in with the present point: Some price in family solidarity and satisfaction was paid by these individuals, but in no sense did this extreme investment in achievement seem to result in deep regret, severe dissatisfaction, or serious neurotic symptoms. Such findings, of course, only tempt us to pursue the matter further, which is why we cite them in the first chapter.

Just as we may ask about the price paid for having invested oneself heavily in any activity, so may we ask about people who appear to invest little or who perhaps have few alternatives for investment. This may be at the heart of job or career satisfaction and (in extreme instances) psychological depressions (cf. Klinger, 1977). Perhaps popular descriptions of career plateauing and job burnout may relate to the foreclosure of personal investment options.

Questions relating to the quality of life necessarily arise as we consider personal investment in work and achievement. Although we do not intend to focus on quality of life, neither will we ignore issues related to it. We do intend to exhibit an awareness of these issues and present a reasonable review of their importance in the consideration of motivation and adult development.

Conclusion: A Look Ahead

Achievement, personal growth, and life satisfaction are possible outcomes of personal investment patterns. Other outcomes are also possible, and we can assume that, in most cases, people experience all three cited here and a few others as well. The salient point, however, is twofold: (1) different patterns of investment may have different effects on a person, and (2) these effects may be valued differently by different individuals, groups, and societies.

By now, it should be quite clear that this book is about motivation and personal investment. It may be equally clear that the world of adults is our focus and that we will concern ourselves especially with work orientations and career patterns. After all, adults do spend much of their time in work settings, and no society can afford to ignore questions of worker motivation. Certainly, adult development must be viewed in a broader context; even the personal investment one makes in one's work and career can be understood only in this broader context. To understand the investment in work—or the relative lack of such investment—the wider sphere of life must be considered.

We believe these issues demand the attention of a wide variety of individuals. This book is directed primarily at those who are concerned with managing motivation, including managers and human resource professionals of various types. We also hope that the issues discussed here are relevant to fellow researchers. Only as practice, theory, and research interact can progress be made on what may be some of the more important questions confronting the societies of the world.

2
What Motivates People? An Overview of Possible Causes

Why do people invest their time, talent, and energy in various ways? To answer this question, we must weave together a variety of research results on the nature and nurture of human motivation into a meaningful whole—a theory of motivation and personal investment. The burden of this chapter is to examine certain options on the way toward developing such a theory.

Generally, two approaches can be taken in studying motivation. We can focus on the *person* and ask whether there is anything about the person's previous experience and behavior that would lead us to predict how he or she would approach a situation. Or we can focus on the *situation* and concern ourselves with factors external to the person that might affect motivation. These two points of focus are by no means mutually exclusive. Indeed, a full understanding of human motivation necessarily involves the consideration of both, because the behavior we see is characteristically a product of both sets of causes. However, it is convenient to divide the subject matter in this manner, especially because studies tend to focus on only one aspect. Moreover, it is difficult to concentrate on both aspects simultaneously.

Motivation as a Personal Trait

Perhaps the most common assumption about motivation—particularly motivation that leads to achievement—is that some people have it and some don't. In other words, some people have a built-in personality trait (or traits) that is likely to lead them to exhibit a greater or lesser effort.

We once heard this point of view stated succinctly by a friend who was chief executive officer of a large corporation: "There are good guys and bad guys, and I hire the good guys." Upon reflection, we wondered about our friend's possible gender bias, his overconfidence in knowing good from bad, and his apparent belief that job performance could be explained so simply. That aside, the notion is common that motivation is best thought of as an inherent trait of the person that exhibits itself in a wide array of activities. This notion not only figures strongly in decisions about personnel but also guides the development of policy in government, business, and education.

A number of years ago, one of us traveled fairly regularly to Iran. The trips usually were occasions for making interesting acquaintances. On one such trip, the new acquaintance was an automotive executive who was returning from Tehran after concluding negotiations for establishing a new assembly plant. After an obviously successful trip, this executive was enthusiastic about the potential of Iran. This was in the early 1970s, and it was easy to be optimistic about Iran. What was interesting, however, was the rationale that this relativley insightful and reasonably sophisticated person gave for his beliefs and expectations. He spoke little of financial resources or stability of the government; rather, he concentrated almost exclusively on the "character" of the people. He claimed to sense a vibrant nature, a high energy level, and a will to move the country forward. In that pre-oil cartel era, "the personality of the people" was his primary reason for initiating a major business venture. His attitude is not unique. It is a common belief that motivation revolves largely around "character"—the nature of the person involved. Some people have it and some people don't, whatever this magical "it" may be .

The Work of David McClelland

Anecdotes aside, there is solid scientific evidence in support of the notion that people's enduring and inherent traits have a pervasive effect on how they choose to invest themselves in any given situation. Perhaps no one has made this point with greater clarity and emphasis than David McClelland and his colleagues and students, working initially at Wesleyan University and later at Harvard (McClelland, 1985a, 1985b). McClelland not only has made the strongest case for the role of personality in motivation but has also raised most of the basic questions that must be asked and answered in the study of personal investment. We do not always agree with him, but it is difficult—and would be foolish—to ignore him. For a number of reasons, then, it is useful to begin this review of theoretical perspectives with his work.

Development of Assessment Procedures. In the 1940s, McClelland and his students initiated a systematic study of human motivation (McClelland, 1942, 1951; McClelland, Atkinson, Clark, & Lowell, 1953). At the time, there was much talk about motivation but little scientific research. As a result, there was little agreement about how motives should be defined and few guidelines for measuring them. Thus, at the outset, McClelland and his colleagues set for themselves the task of developing an appropriate assessment procedure. It does little good to say that a person is highly motivated to achieve, is power hungry, has an affiliation drive, or the like, if one cannot assess these presumed motivational orientations beyond actually observing the person achieving, exerting power, or affiliating. How does one identify the motivational orientations of a prospective employee, a person one barely knows, a person with little job experience?

Following Freud, McClelland and his associates initially assumed that motives exhibit themselves most reliably in a person's fantasy life—dreams, idle thoughts, and casual reflections on things and events. Perhaps in these unguarded moments, a person's true self emerges. Perhaps thoughts that are very relevant to us and that have the greatest controlling influence on our affairs are most likely to be exhibited when external constraints on our thinking are minimized. Thus, the McClelland group proceeded as if fantasy were the key to assessing motives and developed a standardized procedure for eliciting fantasy samples from people on the basis of the work of Henry Murray (1938). Essentially, this procedure involved presenting an ambiguous series of pictures to individuals and asking them to make up stories that described what was going on. By design, the pictures were open to a variety of interpretations. What people chose to see in the pictures should reflect a personal bias and perhaps suggest an enduring and characteristic orientation toward life. In other words, it was assumed that the stories would reveal something very basic about the people who wrote them. Thus, if an individual were strongly motivated by an achievement motive, he would be expected to construct a story that not only would reflect this dominant theme in his life but would reveal his own feelings about success and failure.

McClelland and his colleagues then proceeded to define empirically and systematically the kind of language, content, and imagery that represented a variety of motivational orientations. Specifically, they related fantasy to behavior in both laboratory and field settings and began to answer the question of whether their fantasy measure of motives in fact predicted what people would do (see, for example, Atkinson, 1958; McClelland, 1985a). In short, they began to establish the validity of their approach. In so doing, they also produced descriptions of motivational patterns that seemed to be pervasively important. In the main, McClelland has focused his efforts on three patterns of motivation: need for achievement (*n* Achievement), need for power (*n* Power), and need for affiliation (*n* Affiliation). Certainly, these three patterns have greatest utility in understanding behavior in work organizations.

Achievement Motivation. McClelland and his group concentrated first on the role of an underlying achievement motive (*n* Achievement) in determining achievement behavior. Once they had devised a method for systematically scoring achievement themes, they proceeded to determine whether or not such dreaming was related to the complex behavior that is called achievement. Early research indicated that people who differed in achievement fantasy did indeed exhibit different patterns of behavior in achievement situations.

When given a choice, the "fantasy achievers" exhibited a clear preference for achieving situations. They seemed to welcome putting their competence on the line. Fantasy achievers also seemed to show an altogether different orientation toward achievement. They were likely to take moderate risks in competitive and gamelike situations, seemingly welcoming a challenge. They were also more likely to work on their own, with success at the task as the only reward. And, in general, they seemed willing and able to delay gratification and to work energetically and independently to live up to a standard of excellence. In short, they possessed the kinds of habits that would lead to achievement in most contexts. Above all, they could be characterized by an overall proclivity toward attaining success. Indeed, the initial research efforts indicated quite clearly that the fantasy achievers were more than dreamers—they were doers as well. The fantasy measure apparently did identify people who not only dreamed about achievement but actually achieved (Heckhausen, 1967; Kornadt, Eckensberger, & Emminghaus, 1980; McClelland, 1961, 1985a). At least, they characteristically demonstrated patterns of behavior that were clearly important to some forms of achievement.

The Achieving Society. Successfully identifying a personality trait of relative stability and of some predictive value was no minor achievement, but McClelland's research did not stop there. Following the early preliminary work on the nature and assessment of achievement motivation, the research took an important new direction. A bold hypothesis was proposed that was concerned with the role of achievement motivation in bringing about economic growth. The hypothesis focused especially on how motivated people could change society.

It is obvious that societies and cultural groups differ in economic growth and general productivity. Part of the explanation for these differences undoubtedly lies in the variable opportunities presented to groups and societies and in their capacities to capitalize on them. Intuitively, it would seem that part of the explanation would also lie in the motivational realm. In *The Achieving Society*, McClelland (1961) gave this intuition some basis in empirical fact. Basically, McClelland's hypothesis was that a society shows economic growth when it fosters the development and use of achievement-motivated people. In other words, McClelland proposed a variant of the "great person" theory of history; special people—not events—determine the course of history.

McClelland was actually proposing a variant of an older hypothesis originally suggested by the German sociologist Max Weber (1904/1930). In *The Protestant Ethic and the Spirit of Capitalism*, Weber observed that Roman Catholic and Protestant European countries tended to differ in economic productivity and development, and he attributed this difference to the religious ethic espoused. Thus, he suggested that the "Protestant ethic" promoted self-reliance, denial of personal pleasure, and the evaluation of work as good in itself. Moreover, the emphasis on predestination presumably created some inclination for people to establish themselves as successful in order to achieve concrete, here-and-now assurance that they were indeed among "the elect." In short, Weber argued that the Protestant ideology led, if not inevitably at least rather directly, to capitalism and, more generally, to increased economic productivity.

McClelland suggested more specifically how ideology might result in a changed economy as well as in changed people. The essence of McClelland's suggestion is diagrammed in figure 2–1. As can be seen in the diagram, this suggestion really consists of several hypotheses. First, it is hypothesized that an ideology such as the Protestant ethic fosters a certain characteristic pattern of child-rearing and, subsequently, different kinds of personalities. That is, the Protestant ethic particularly emphasizes self-reliance, independent mastery, and individual competence. Assuming that Protestant parents follow the accepted ideology in rearing their children, they should typically provide the ideal circumstances for creating highly achievement-oriented children. There is some evidence (Heckhausen, 1967; Rosen, 1982; Rosen & D'Andrade, 1959; Winterbottom, 1953, 1958) that McClelland is right—that achievement training is a precursor to an achievement orientation. Moreover, it is achievement *training*, not just *talk* about the value of achievement, that is important. Although parents may discuss the importance of achievement a great deal and extol its value, the initiation of direct achievement training is crucial; communication of an ideology is not sufficient. This achievement training especially involves presenting the child with opportunities for independent and successful action in challenging and socially significant tasks. Only as children accomplish something successfully and on their own do they acquire an increased interest not only in continuing to do that something but also in attempting other tasks. A certain amount of uncertainty is involved in attempting to do something one has never done before—to try a new thing, to master a new skill. According to McClelland and his colleagues, child-rearing practices can produce children who are oriented toward such risks as well as children who shrink from them. More specifically, child-rearing practices that emphasize independence training and mastery produce people who are high in achievement motivation.

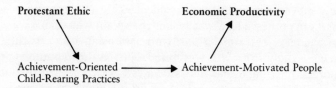

Figure 2–1. An Outline of McClelland's Interpretation of Weber's Protestant Ethic–Spirit of Capitalism Hypothesis

The next major assertion implicit in the McClelland theory is that when ideology and practice favor achievement-motivated individuals to any important extent, a "spirit of capitalism" will result—simply because more highly achievement-motivated people are contributing to the society. This spirit is most likely to occur when these highly motivated people are given the opportunity to fill leadership positions in the society. It is always possible, of course, that societal leadership may be vested in the hands of a minority that is not characterized by achievement motivation. Although there may be many highly achievement-motivated people in other segments of the society, they may be prevented, at least temporarily, from exercising any controlling influence. For a society to exhibit the spirit of capitalism in the sense of economic growth and productivity, however, achievement-motivated people must be allowed access to leadership positions.

In *The Achieving Society*, McClelland (1961) tested this intriguing hypothesis, with interesting and important results. Briefly summarized, he conducted a series of cross-cultural and cross-national studies that essentially related earlier child-rearing experiences to later economic growth in the society, along the lines suggested in figure 2–1. The McClelland group assumed that the current leaders of any given country had been subjected to critical achievement training approximately 25 years earlier. They further assumed that the nature of this training could be most accurately indexed by considering the nature of classroom reading materials used during that earlier period. Through these textual materials, McClelland attempted to recapture the past experiences of the current leaders and to determine whether achievement was a dominant theme in their early training. He assumed that any correlation between reading materials of 25 or 50 years ago and current achievement would be difficult to attribute to a third factor, particularly if there were little or no correlation between current reading material and level of achievement. In other words, a time-lag correlational analysis was conducted that simulated the determination of causation in more rigorously controlled experiments. The outline of this analysis is presented in figure 2–2, along with a summary of the hypothesis tested.

An interesting feature of this research is that there are many reasons why a correlation between the significant variables might not emerge. For example, wars, unusual climatic conditions, or discoveries of new resources could conceivably subvert any motivational tendencies created in the populace. Only McClelland's hypothesis, however, seems to explain why such a correlation is found. In extensive research, a positive relationship between child-rearing practices and economic growth was found—just as the hypothesis predicted. Furthermore, McClelland and his associates have continued to find such a relationship, not only among a limited set of highly developed Western societies but also among societies of almost every clime and time. There does, indeed, seem to be something to the notion that societies stand, fall, grow, or

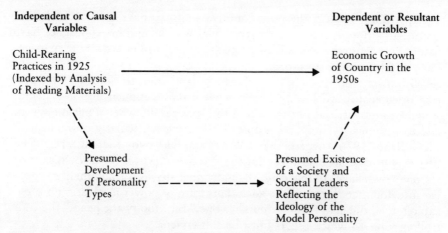

Figure 2–2. Causal Relationships Explored in McClelland's *The Achieving Society*

deteriorate according to their concern with the development of character in their children. Specifically, as societies give children training that leads to achievement motivation, so they ensure their economic future.

Motivation Within an Organizational Context. Clearly, McClelland's early research emphasizes that certain enduring (personality) motivational characteristics are an important resource for society. One is moved immediately to conclude that they would be a resource for certain organizations as well. If the availability of people with high achievement motivation enhances productivity in the society, one might expect that these same people will have effects on productivity in various organizations. This might logically lead one to suggest that organizations should select high achievement-motivated people for leadership roles if they wish to be achieving organizations. McClelland's subsequent research, as well as that of others, indicates that this is true only to a limited degree. As McClelland and his colleagues began to explore other motives, it became increasingly clear that one must consider different motive patterns in selecting effective managers, staff members, and workers. Moreover, it also seems wise to consider a profile of motive patterns, rather than concentrating on the existence of one particular motivational characteristic. Therefore, in addition to achievement motivation, McClelland and his co-workers have paid special attention to what is called the *power motive* and have also considered *affiliation motives*.

Power Motivation. Next to achievement motivation, power motivation has been most extensively researched by McClelland and his colleagues (McClelland,

1975, 1985a). Indeed, the power motive seems to have held McClelland's special attention in recent years, particularly as he and his colleagues have focused on defining the kinds of people who perform effectively in management and leadership positions.

By power motivation (*n* Power), McClelland refers to a motivational pattern oriented toward having impact—particularly, influencing others. Presumably, motivational satisfaction in this case results when a person has an effect on things, events, and people. In focusing particularly on managers, McClelland (1976) suggests that *n* Power can take two different forms. The first may be described as a love for the exercise of power for its own sake or for one's own sake. In this case, the individual strives for dominance simply because dominance itself is the goal. This form of power motivation is often exploitative; the goal is to be "number one," the "top of the heap," the controlling force to which others must be subservient.

In contrast, the *institutionalized-power* manager is less concerned with personal dominance and more concerned with working with and through an organization. In this form, the need to exert power is exhibited through the development of an effective organization. Individuals who fall in this category sublimate their power needs to the larger organization; their control occurs as they manage others and produce outcomes through them.

It is clear that those who are effective or comfortable in leadership positions within an organization would be characterized by a power motivation, particularly of the institutionalized-power type—much as described by McClelland. Generally, power motivation seems to be a necessary complement to achievement motivation in the profile of the effective manager. A work organization needs a leader who not only has high standards of excellence and is willing to take moderate risks and push for excellence but also has the inclination to manage and direct the behavior of others. Independent achievement is not necessarily expected of managers, but achievement through others is.

Affiliation Motivation. Finally, McClelland's (1985a, chap. 7) work calls attention to the importance of affiliation motives in the general realm of work behavior. Generally, the affiliation need (*n* Affiliation) is defined as a desire for companionship and social assurance. Again, as in the case of *n* Achievement or *n* Power, these needs are expressed through the kinds of themes exhibited in fantasy. The critical element is not primarily whether or not a person describes social encounters; rather, the stress is on the emotion expressed in relating to others. Further research has indicated that individuals who are high in *n* Affiliation are more often found in social contexts. They are especially responsive to social approval—more responsive, for example, than to information on competence and progress toward attaining a standard of excellence. The opportunity for satisfactory social interaction on the job is especially important for people who are high in the affiliation motive. Presumably, their productivity and work satisfaction can be maintained or enhanced through a cooperative and socially supportive work environment. Moreover, it seems that certain jobs are better filled by people who are high in *n* Affiliation rather than in *n* Power or *n* Achievement. Jobs that call especially for the initiation of social interaction should be attractive to people who are high in *n* Affiliation. For example, a good receptionist in an office ought to be high in *n* Affiliation rather than in *n* Power or *n* Achievement.

Leadership. But what about effective leaders and managers? As McClelland has defined the three motives, one might expect that some combination of *n* Power and *n* Achievement should be basic to effective management—that effective managers would be inclined to exert power and that they might be reasonably high in achievement motivation. It is doubtful, however, that they would be characterized by high affiliation motivation for a variety of reasons. Principal among these, perhaps, is that effective managers must make hard decisions that facilitate the overall well-being of the company but that may not enhance a sense of solidarity with their employees. If managers need to be liked, they might avoid the tough decisions they must make.

In their most recent research, McClelland and his colleagues have found that certain combinations of motives are important for different roles in work organizations. A study of the careers of AT&T managers is interesting in this regard (McClelland & Boyatzis, 1982). These managers had been administered the usual fantasy measures at the beginning of their career, and their patterns of advancement were tracked over a 16-year period. Those who were characterized by high *n* Achievement tended to advance quickly in those segments of the company where individual skill, creativity, and desire were required, such as in the engineering and development areas. But their careers tended to peak at a level lower than those who were characterized by a combination of high *n* Power, low *n* Affiliation, and high activity inhibition (also a score derived from the Thematic Apperception Test). This so-called leadership syndrome was associated with a rise to top management. McClelland (1985a) explained this by suggesting that top management does not require individual achievement so much as it requires achievement through the exertion of power over others. People who possess the so-called management syndrome presumably have no difficulty in doing this. They enjoy power (high *n* Power), and they are not constrained by feelings toward others (low *n* Affiliation) as they make hard decisions, but they do not blatantly exploit for their own personal advantage (high activity inhibition). That is, they exercise power according to organizational guidelines and in the service of organizational goals.

This general characterization is more pertinent in larger organizations, in which general management situations are more common, than in organizations in which technical expertise is given great credibility and importance.

Cornelius and Lane (1984) concluded from their study of managerial success in technical/professional settings that "both the need for power and the willingness to exert power may be important for managerial success only in situations in which technical expertise is not critical" (p. 38). They, like McClelland and Boyatzis (1982), obtained no relationship between managers' need to achieve and managerial success in a bureaucracy.

Clearly, what is seen in McClelland's work is a progression from examining individual motives to defining motivational profiles that may explain behavior in any given situation. Achievement motives remain important in explaining achievement, but motivation in most work settings must also take account of power and affiliation motives. Moreover, this does not seem to be the end of the line in defining the motivational profile; other motives are likely also important. The emphasis remains on enduring, traitlike characteristics that a person brings to a situation, but there is an awareness of a range of motives that interact in determining behavior in particular contexts.

Personality and Motivation: Some Conclusions

It is not difficult to accept the idea that a person's behavior typically exhibits consistency over time and that individuals characteristically approach each new situation with an orientation or bias. Furthermore, it is obvious that individuals differ in such orientations and biases. These and other factors give rise to the basic notion that motivation can be properly viewed as an enduring, perhaps unique, trait of the person—that there is something about individuals that allows us to predict what they will do in certain situations. McClelland defines this something as an acquired, affectively based, and largely unconscious drive. Whether or not one accepts that formulation, there does appear to be some basis for stressing that each person brings a package of motivational predispositions, predilections, and biases to each new situation. This package is formed through past experiences and thus is different for each person. Moreover, these patterns are not unlike habits in that people tend to exhibit them regularly and across a wide variety of situations. The power of this set of conclusions is illustrated in a particularly dramatic way in the work of David McClelland.

Multiple Motivational Determinants of Behavior. McClelland has been concerned with a variety of motives that may be operative in determining the behavior we observe. People are not only characterized as high in achievement motivation; they can also be characterized simultaneously in terms of power, affiliation, and other orientations. Personal causes of motivation might best be viewed in terms of a profile of motives. If one wishes to predict how a person will invest himself or herself in a given situation, one should consider the varying strengths of motives in that person. Thus, in McClelland's more recent research on managerial success, the emphasis is on a motivational profile of successful managers. Where the manager's role primarily involves influencing and controlling the behavior of other people, the successful manager will likely be high in power motivation and low in affiliation motivation—that is, inclined toward exercising control but remote enough from personal ties to make it easy to make hard decisions affecting staff.

Motivational Change. Insofar as motivation is a personal trait, motivational change is not an easily resolved problem. If motives are a stable product of early experiences, what can one do to enhance motivation? Presumably, enhancing motivation could involve revising a lifetime of experience—hardly an attractive course of action in many cases. It is not surprising, then, that the focus on personality and motivation has spawned an interest in selecting the right people for jobs. Given an emphasis on personal motivational traits, the primary way to obtain a high level of motivation in any work group is to select motivated people. Thus, measurement and personnel selection become the major focus of activity in the effort to initiate motivational change according to a personality theory approach to motivation. It is interesting, however, that even McClelland, who is committed to the notion of personality as a critical cause of motivation, argues for the possibility of motivational change throughout the life span (see Arnoff & Litwin, 1971; Heckhausen & Krug, 1982; McClelland, 1978; McClelland & Winter, 1971; Yukl, 1981). However, changing enduring motivational traits does not appear to be easy.

Situational Causes of Motivation

Although discussions of motivation generally focus on the person as the causal source, it is clear that whether a person does one thing or another is probably also determined by situational factors. Sometimes, the situation is overwhelmingly important (Maehr, 1974a, 1974b, 1978; Maehr & Nicholls, 1980; Spenner & Featherman, 1978).

An extensive literature deals with the role of situations in affecting motivation (see Mitchell, 1982; Staw, 1983). This literature is varied and diverse, and it is difficult to identify any particular theory or theoretical point of view that fully incorporates all the varied factors of situations that may be important. Many theories deal with one or another aspect of the situation—job design (Hackman & Oldham, 1980), rewards/reinforcement (Deci, 1980; Lawler, 1977; Staw, 1974), goal setting (Latham & Yukl, 1975; Locke, Staw, Saari, & Latham, 1981), group influence (Porter, Lawler, & Hackman, 1975) and leadership (Yukl, 1981)—but no single theory summarizes or integrates all the critical variables. Thus, rather than describing a representative theory, we will present a taxonomy that we have found useful. This taxonomy is outlined in figure 2–3, and our review of situational factors involved in motivation is organized around the categories identified there.

Figure 2–3 identifies two basic variables—or facets—that must be taken into account: group membership, with attendant *social expectations*, and the nature of the *task* itself. Associated with each of these major categories are several subcategories, which will be discussed in turn.

Group Membership and the Expectations of Others

People do not act in isolation from the social groups in which they hold membership. To a significant degree, social groups determine for individuals what

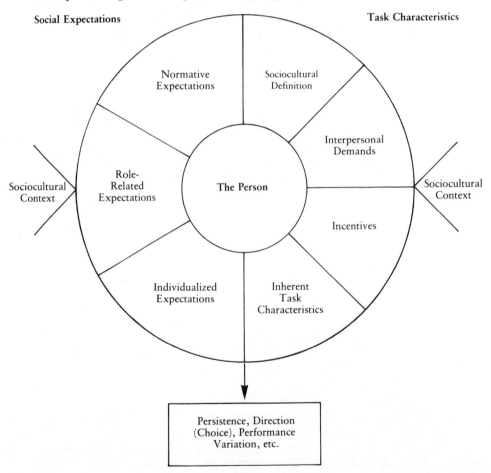

Figure 2–3. Model of Situational/Contextual Factors That Influence Motivation

is generally worth doing and what is expected of them personally. An individual's "reference group"—or "significant others"—conveys to the individual the basic pattern that his or her behavior should and must take. Moreover, there is considerable evidence that individuals typically conform to such social expectations (Maehr, 1974a). The chairman of the board of a medium-sized company put it this way: "Whatever I've done, I've done it to make my family proud of me." Not all people are so family-centered, but each person has his or her own reference groups. The expectations that exist within these groups are powerful controlling forces. They define where, how, and to what degree people will invest their time, talent, and energies. They do so principally by presenting possibilities for such investment (Maehr, 1974a, 1978). When we ask why an individual happens to invest himself or herself in this or that activity, we should ask, first, what the available options were. These available options are systematically determined by the social groups of which a person is a member. Both work and extra-work groups are important in this regard. Basic guidelines for action are established by family, school, and other social institutions. Consider, for example, the pursuit of a career in medicine. This involves accepting the value of schooling and hard work and also placing family ties in a secondary role—often establishing a nuclear family that is physically and psychologically remote from an extended family. Such sacrificing of family to career is differentially sanctioned and approved in various family, social, and cultural groups.

Even relatively transient groups have effects. For example, work groups also set guidelines for action, formally or informally. Some of the research on work behavior points to the important role of these work groups (Homans, 1950; Pfeffer, 1982; Van de Ven & Astley, 1981). Thus, a person's membership in any group automatically means that something is expected of the person. The price of membership is conformance to these expectations to some degree.

At least three kinds of expectations exist for the individual as a participant in a social group: *normative, role-related*, and *individualized* expectations. Each of these types of expectations relates not only to *what* should be done but also to *how* it should be done.

Normative Expectations. The term *normative expectations* refers to the expectations that exist for all members in a given group. The existence of a social group inevitably involves the development of general behavioral norms for all who hold membership in the group. Families, clubs, schools—even play groups—cannot exist without some minimal agreed-upon set of expectations regarding how members should behave or even think and believe. Work groups are no exception. The group expectations refer to all aspects of life; they also define work patterns, guide career striving, and direct achievement. In the broadest sense, they specify the options available for personal investment.

Within one's circle of family and friends, there are likely to be general expectations regarding both what *can* be done and what is *worth* doing. The norms of a social group deal with the general range of possible or allowable behavior; they describe acceptable and preferred options. Thus, not every job is equally acceptable.

Normative expectations also refer to *how* something can or should be done. For example, the popular media are currently flooded with stories about the cooperative approach to work and achievement in Japan (Hatvany & Pucik, 1981; Ouchi, 1981; Pascale & Athos, 1981). The Japanese approach is often contrasted with the more interpersonally competitive approach that presumably characterizes the United States. Whether or not such comparisons are justified, different groups seem to expect work and achievement to occur in different ways and to be directed to different ends (Fyans, Salili, Maehr, & Desai, 1983).

Generally, social groups have normative expectations for most significant life domains, and particularly for work and achievement. That is, within a social group, there are beliefs and expectations about what is worth doing and what can and should be accomplished. Certain groups consider some tasks and activities inferior or unworthy for the membership to perform. The plan of work and the pattern and goals of achievement in relationship to family and leisure are also significantly prescribed. Within various work groups, there are formal and informal expectations regarding how hard to work, how faithful to be, and, generally, how to behave. Consequently, one can often predict the choices individuals make when one knows a bit about the groups in which they hold membership (Salancik & Pfeffer, 1978). Particularly when one knows the norms or generalized expectations for the members of these groups, one can describe a range of options from which persons must choose in investing their efforts.

Role-Related Expectations. Role expectations are particularized expectations—expectations that apply especially to individuals who happen to occupy a specific position in a group. An example is the set of expectations that exists for an individual who happens to be the leader of a group. There is a rich literature on the effects of role expectations on behavior (see, e.g., Biddle, 1979); but the important point to consider here is whether occupying a particular position in a social group affects the individual's motivation. There is considerable evidence to indicate that it does. After a comprehensive analysis of relevant studies, Klinger and McNelley (1969) concluded that role and status changes do eventuate in significant changes in achievement motivation. Indeed, they suggested that the behavior exhibited by people described by McClelland and his colleagues as high in achievement motivation is, to a considerable degree, a role-associated behavior. That is, people act that way when they are in a certain position and play a certain role.

In this regard, a most interesting and illustrative study was conducted by Zander and Forward (1968). In this study, subjects were first identified as high or low in achievement motivation according to usual procedures. Subsequently, they participated in a three-person group performance situation in which leader and follower roles were rotated. What is most intriguing about the results is that, while in the leadership role, the low achievement-motivated subjects exhibited the same achievement patterns as the high achievement-motivated subjects. Apparently, the high achievement motivation patterns were a part of their repertoire; they required only the right eliciting conditions. In this case, the temporary switch in social roles was sufficient to change their style of performing so that it was similar to that of high achievement-motivated people. The subjects who had been identified as high in achievement motivation exhibited the style of performance assumed to be typical for such people in both leader and follower roles. Although the latter finding may be considered supportive of the proposition that personality is more crucial than role, that conclusion should be approached with caution. One might wonder whether, if the high achievement-motivated people had participated in the same group as followers over an extended time, they, too, might have conformed to the role expectations. One exposure to the follower role in this kind of group may not have been enough to "teach them their place." In any case, it seems reasonable to conclude that those who exhibit what appears to be a low achievement motivation pattern can reverse themselves dramatically given the appropriate situational/contextual conditions.

The finding that a switch in social roles within a group can change an individual's style of pursuing a task is hardly trivial. Similarly, the possibility that achievement motivation is associated with social status in a group, as suggested by Klinger and McNelley (1969), has profound implications. Briefly, it further supports the notion that motivational patterns are by no means irrevocably set in early childhood. Motivation can be subject to modification as the person joins new groups, changes positions, and attempts new tasks.

Individualized Expectations. Not all social expectations can be readily classed as normative or role-related. Some seem to be associated with the individual, exclusive of role and group membership. Although such expectations may be influenced by normative and role factors, there is some value in recognizing that individualistic expectations do exist and that they may be equally crucial in some instances. For example, consider an employer's assumption that an employee is lazy or cannot be trusted. Such an assumption, though not readily included within the two previous expectation categories, is probably very important in determining the behavior of the employer and, subsequently, the work patterns of the employee (see Steers, 1981).

Task Characteristics

An important part of a motivational situation or context is the task itself. Whether or not a person will demonstrate motivation toward achievement is critically dependent on the nature of the task and on what it means to him or her. It is clear that there is important variation from task to task (see Maehr, 1974b), but what characteristics of tasks are likely to make a difference in eliciting personal investment? Undoubtedly, a variety of task features could be important. For now, however, we will outline four general dimensions that seem to capture most of the variation in this regard: inherent attractiveness, sociocultural definition, interpersonal demands, and task-associated incentives. Later, we will amplify this brief sketch of situational causes (see particularly chapters 3 and 6).

Inherent Attractiveness. Features of the task itself may be significant determinants of motivation in the situation—quite apart from any personal or social meaning that performance on the task might have. For example, everyone knows of jobs or tasks that are tedious, boring, or downright uninteresting. We all have to do such tasks at times, and some people have to do them more than others. Some tasks, however, are in and of themselves more interesting, more fun, and more attractive than others. Why this is true is not altogether clear, but research on *intrinsic motivation* (Deci, 1975) has suggested that a task that possesses a certain optimum level of uncertainty and unpredictability tends to be generally attractive. Although social experiences can reduce the search for novelty, new information, and challenge, it appears that, from the start, human beings have a built-in attraction to these features in tasks.

Sociocultural Definition. A given task may have specific meaning within a given sociocultural context. One's social or cultural group may define the task as desirable, repulsive, or irrelevant. In this regard, Barkow (1976) noted that the prestige ranking of a task within a particular cultural group may, by itself, best explain the motivation exhibited by members of that group. Furthermore, it has been pointed out repeatedly (Maehr, 1974a; Raynor, 1982) that tasks may be viewed as more or less instrumental to valued ends—that success in the performance of them may, to varying degrees, confirm one's identity or enhance one's view of oneself. How the task is defined by one's significant others is clearly an important feature of the task, one that undoubtedly affects motivation significantly. This point was made implicitly in the discussion of group norms and expectations, but it bears repeating here.

Interpersonal Demands/Relationships. There are immediate interpersonal demands in performing a task: Does it involve cooperation with others? To what degree does it involve skill in relating to and communicating with others? Earlier, in discussing the personality trait approach to motivation, we pointed out that some individuals might simply be more attracted to jobs that encourage interpersonal relations. Similarly, some people are more bothered by certain social arrangements, such as competition and conflict. At this point, we wish to make the additional point that such social facets of the task may have effects that generalize across individuals. Thus, at a very simple level, when a task demands group cooperation, the existence of interpersonal conflict among any of the members may be critical. Similarly, different organizational arrangements are likely to produce different results—such as when group decision making or participatory leadership is encouraged (Yukl, 1981). Clearly, tasks vary in how interpersonal relationships are involved.

Incentives. Certain incentives are associated with performance of a task. When one thinks of work, one most often thinks of money as the primary incentive. Certainly, money is an important incentive for working, but as will become increasingly evident in this book, it is only one of several incentives for most people in most jobs (cf. Lawler, 1971, 1977; Patten, 1977). Moreover, when one thinks more broadly about why people invest themselves in any given area of activity—not just work—one must think of multiple incentives. Money certainly doesn't drive the retired executive to take on a second career, nor does it provide the reason for devoting one's every free moment to sailing.

Different incentives are likely to be associated with different tasks, and the manner in which these incentives are designed, presented, or made available is important. For example, when money is a primary incentive, performance appraisal is often an integral feature of the process, and *how* the performance appraisal is conducted may be almost as important as the results it yields. Thus, such matters as fairness, employee participation, and clarity of feedback are sometimes equal in importance to the pay that comes as the result of the appraisal.

Sociocultural Context

Specific note should be taken of the fact that any task is performed in a sociocultural context. Although this has been implicit throughout our discussion of situational causes, it deserves emphasis at this juncture as a preparation for extensive discussion in subsequent chapters. We would call special attention to two facets of the sociocultural context: the organizational culture in which the task is performed and the wider sociocultural context in which the actors in any situation participate.

Few would deny that people participate in different cultures and that this participation likely makes a difference in their motivation (Maehr, 1974a,

1974b; Triandis et al., 1972). Anyone who has supervised workers from a culture different from his or her own knows this all too well. As a world economy increasingly touches every work organization and every job, this point cannot be ignored. The nature of work, its meaning, and how it should be done takes on different meanings around the world (Fyans et al., 1983). This differential meaning continually intrudes in the work place—sometimes creating conflicts, sometimes enhancing productivity, sometimes reducing it.

Besides the wider sociocultural context that shapes the situation, a task is often performed in an organizational context that may be described as having its own culture. The nature of the organization, its operation, the benefits it offers, the requirements it sets, and the people who make it up all affect how a person chooses to invest his or her time and talent. Recently, considerable attention has been devoted to this general topic. In his popular book, *Theory Z*, Ouchi (1981) has outlined three basic organizational schemes that make a difference in regard to motivation and productivity. Following an earlier analysis by McGregor (1960), Ouchi first defines a Theory X and Theory Y of management. Briefly, Theory X represents a more or less authoritarian approach to work or motivation. For all practical purposes, it is assumed that the worker works only for pay and cannot be trusted to work on his or her own initiative. The emphasis is on worker control and efficient use of human capital. Very little attention is given to the worker as a person, and, more important, little attention is given to the possibility that by involving the worker in the design and planning of a work task, motivation might be enhanced. In contrast, Theory Y represents an approach that stresses human relations in the development of positive work climates that enhance worker morale and good employer–employee relationships.

Theory Z is Ouchi's integrated summary of the best of both theories, plus an additional feature or two derived from current observations of effective management—particularly observations of the management of successful Japanese companies. Basically, Theory Z especially involves a commitment to the development of human resources. Along with its family emphasis, there is also an emphasis on worker participation in defining jobs and determining the overall direction and course of the organization.

Aside from the nature of Theories X, Y, and Z, the overall idea we are trying to convey is twofold. First, it appears that organizations do, indeed, differ in nature and that their natures can be assessed. More generally, organizations are characterized by cultures (Deal & Kennedy, 1982; Schein, 1984, 1985; Wilkins, 1983). At a simple level, organizational cultures can be defined as "the way we do things around here" (Marvin Bower, as quoted in Deal & Kennedy, 1982, p. 7). At a more complex level, organizations may be described in terms of operative norms, prevailing expectations, and operative goals (Maehr, 1974a). But most important, it seems very likely that the culture of the organization, its nature and saliency, can and does affect motivation and productivity (Litwin & Stringer, 1968; Staw, 1983; see also chapter 6).

Situation and Motivation: Some Concluding Thoughts

Examining the causal possibilities in social expectations and task characteristics that vary with situations provides a counterbalancing perspective to a focus on personality as a cause of motivation. Perhaps more than we realize, we are what we are expected to be and we do what the task and our significant others allow and demand. This point is especially relevant in considering cross-cultural variation in motivational patterns. It is perhaps equally important in understanding gender differences in motivation. As we look at motivational change throughout the life span, however, we must look especially at the social context that impinges on a person. One can hardly understand professional burnout or career shifts apart from such contextual factors, and perhaps one cannot fully understand the motivational changes that accompany aging without examining contexts. A focus on the situation, including how the task or job is defined, suggests an approach to motivation that is quite different from a focus on the person. Instead of thinking, first, about selecting the right people or changing people who don't have the right motivation, one examines the situation and asks what there is about it that might be changed. There is some reason to believe that this is a more promising possibility in many cases. People don't change easily, and one might wonder whether they should. However, one can't always change expectations or tasks, either. Clearly, then, motivational enhancement must exploit both perspectives.

Cognition and Motivation

Recent research on motivation has focused especially on how certain thoughts, perceptions, and meanings of the situation to the person affect how or whether the person will invest time and talent. That is, the intent has not been so much to identify personal traits or situational characteristics that might be operative as to identify certain thought categories and processes that mediate the person's response to any situation (Ames, in press; Salancik & Pfeffer, 1978). Essentially, this theoretical perspective argues that it isn't really personality or situation that is important but the thoughts, perceptions, and feelings that an individual has at the moment of behaving. One must know these thoughts and feelings to predict behavior. Of course, these thoughts are in part a product of the situation as well as a product of the person's past experience. Thus, the emphasis on cognitive processes as the immediate antecedent of motivation necessarily involves taking account of both personality and situational determinants. Present thoughts about the situation are critical, but previous experiences are the precursors of present thoughts. Thus, before concluding our overview of factors that are critical to an understanding of motivation, we must consider recent work on cognition and motivation. This is particularly desirable as a background to the theory of personal investment that will be proposed and elaborated on in subsequent chapters. Again, there are many theories, and various hypotheses could be reviewed; we are selective by necessity in how we organize the available theoretical options.

Cognitive theories of motivation have concerned themselves with two kinds of cognitions: thoughts about self and thoughts about the situation. Of course, different theories have highlighted different features of self, and various thoughts about situations are thought to be crucial.

Thoughts About Self

Self-Consistency. There was a time when psychology seemed to have forgotten about the *psyche*. Behavior in its simplest form was the object of concern, and if behavior was thought to be motivated by some internal process, that process was not identified directly or specifically with anything like a concept of self. However, clinicians and social psychologists have always found it difficult to ignore the fact that people seem to hold a kind of picture in their mind of what they are, can be, and do.

Early on, clinicians such as Carl Rogers (1951) pressed for a consideration of the importance of concepts of self in organizing, determining, and directing behavior. One of the hypotheses in this regard suggested that as judgments about self were formed, an individual endeavored to behave in a manner consistent with them. Presumably, individuals developed certain specific and general notions about themselves through social interaction; once formed, the concepts then guided subsequent behavior. Many theories of cognitive consistency suggested how individuals changed their judgments about the situation, their behavior, and themselves in order to hold a consistent view of themselves (see, for example, Bem, 1972; Festinger, 1957).

An early series of studies, based on consistency notions, is particularly interesting in this regard, because it led to the development of our own notions of the nature and origins of personal investment. A first study (Videbeck, 1960) simply demonstrated a basic notion that the judgment of significant others played a critical role in defining the self, as social philosophers had speculated (see, for example, G.H. Mead, 1934) and as clinicians had apparently observed (see, for example, Rogers, 1951, 1961). Follow-up studies (Haas & Maehr, 1965; Maehr, Mensing, & Nafzger, 1962) confirmed the importance of the judgments of significant others. These studies also implied that judgments of significant others might be more crucial at certain times and in certain circumstances than others. For example, judgments of physical development experts relative to aspects of the physical selves of adolescents were found to be especially powerful. Indeed, it seemed that the uncertainty of the adolescents regarding an aspect of themselves made them especially susceptible to change. Of special interest, it was found that as judgments of their physical competence changed, so did their preferences for participation in physical events (Ludwig & Maehr, 1967). An enhanced sense of competence was followed by increased participation. At the time, this finding was interpreted as simply behaving in accord with a new image of self—knowing one *can* do something is congruent with doing it. In retrospect, however, this may be an unsatisfactory interpretation, even though one might tolerate the logic on which it was based.

More recently, notions of cognitive consistency have been applied in predicting continuing interests in performing tasks. Mark Lepper and his colleagues (Lepper & Greene, 1975, 1978; Lepper, Greene, & Nisbitt, 1973) initiated a series of studies on the effects of extrinsic rewards on intrinsic interests; the studies were initially based on an essentially cognitive consistency notion. Considering that adding extrinsic rewards when a task is inherently motivating tends to reduce the motivational value of the task, they suggested that the subjects were squaring their behavior with the reality presented: If I am being paid to do this, it really can't be fun or worth doing for its own sake. More generally, a body of literature stemming out of cognitive dissonance theory (Festinger, 1957) argues that one should only reward to the minimum degree necessary to maintain the desired behavior. By overrewarding, one gives the person extrinsic reasons for performing a task. After all, if the reward is overjustification for performance, the logical conclusion is that the task is not worth doing for its own sake.

Whether or not one accepts a cognitive consistency explanation for the findings in these studies on intrinsic motivation, it is impressive that, in this case and elsewhere, people do try to square their thoughts with what they see happening to them. Inconsistencies in thought are motivating. We can tolerate some inconsistency some of the time, but apparently we can only tolerate so much.

Self-Confidence. In many situations, self-confidence, not self-consistency, is the critical determinant. Early on in the study of achievement and work motivation, the person's expectations of success or failure at a task were designated critical (see, for example, Atkinson & Feather, 1966; Vroom, 1964). One can view this as a perception of task difficulty and, therefore, as a function of the situation, but it is clearly also a judgment that one makes about oneself. A sense that one *can* do something if one *tries* has been characteristically associated with motivational patterns. Indeed, one of the most important developments in motivational theory in recent years—attribution theory—has revolved around this basic idea.

Bernard Weiner (1979, 1983, 1984) proposed that achievement motivation in particular could be understood in terms of causal judgments made by the person. He had conducted a study in which he had found that people who scored high on a trait measure of achievement motivation were likely to view the causes of their own behavior quite differently than those who scored low on this measure. Specifically, those who scored high in achievement motivation were likely to attribute a successful performance to something they had done, rather than to luck, chance, or an easy task. Conversely, they tended to attribute failure to external causes. Those who were low in achievement motivation exhibited a contrasting pattern: failure was more likely to be attributed internally than success. Briefly, it was as if the high achievement-motivated people were quite willing to take credit for their successes and were inclined to believe that their failures were a matter of accident or not trying.

This early observation of the attributional patterns of people who are high or low in achievement motivation remains interesting for many reasons. First, it pointed out that certain beliefs about one's causal role in the situation were perhaps at the heart of motivation, particularly achievement motivation. More specifically, it suggested the importance of not only the locus of causation but the belief that one *can* be effective. Thus, attribution theory emphasized that a crucial facet of motivation is the belief that one *can* do something if one tries. Parallel with that, it encouraged a renewed and productive focus on sense of competence and motivation (Kukla, 1978; Nicholls, 1983).

Applications of attribution theory to the motivation realm are varied and significant, but for our purposes it is most important that it focuses on the ownership of one's behavior. A renewed focus on perceptions of self as a causal factor in motivation gives rise to the possibility that at the heart of achievement, at least, is the belief a person might have about his or her capacity to do what is required to gain success and avoid failure. Indeed, one might proceed to rewrite the McClelland research on achievement motivation in these terms—simply viewing a cognitive variable, sense of competence, as the prime motivational factor, rather than unconscious motives such as *n* Achievement.

Attributional processes have emerged in the last decade as perhaps the primary variables in identifying the causes of achieving behavior. These processes have also been considered in understanding other behavior. In particular, attribution theory has been widely applied in the study of organizations and work behavior (Ames, in press; Lord & Smith, 1983). Assigning causes is apparently a natural precursor to much of our behavior, and the cognitive process of attributing causes is a major factor in determining motivation.

Self-Determination. A third type of self-perception concerns the perceived origins of the act: Does the person believe that he or she has initiated it? Although self-confidence may imply a sense of determination, there is a subtle and perhaps important difference between the two. Research findings on locus of control (Lefourt, 1976), attributional processes, and competence motivation (Harter, 1980; Harter & Connell, 1984) have hinted at self-determination as a factor, and the early work of deCharms (1968, 1972, 1976) as well as the more recent work of Deci (1980) have pushed this facet to the fore. Both deCharms and Deci stressed that behavior may be modified by perceptions of oneself as initating or reacting to a situation. We will illustrate several possibilities in this regard. In one of the most comprehensive studies on motivation change, deCharms (1976, 1984) attempted to turn around the desparate situation that existed in an inner-city school. The students apparently had no interest in what was going on in the classroom, nor did the teachers. To change the situation, deCharms initiated a program in which he attempted to teach the students to think of themselves as determiners of their own behavior. The plan called for the students to have some degree of choice over what they were doing and some responsibility for the outcome. It was deCharm's reasoning that the students had to feel that they owned the situation to some degree if they were to invest themselves in that situation. Before the program could be initiated with the students, however, deCharms had to convince the teachers that they were not mere pawns of the system. To do this, he and his colleagues initiated an extensive program in which teachers examined themselves, their situation, and their resources. They had to believe that they had choices, options, and opportunities. Administrative changes facilitated such beliefs, but *believing* was the critical factor. Only as the teachers developed a sense that they could determine their fate were they able to transfer a similar belief to their students. How teachers organized work in the classes was important; the students had to be participants in the learning enterprise. Again, it was the belief in self-determination, coupled with a sense of ownership, that was important in ultimately enhancing student achievement and morale.

In a similar vein, Hackman and Oldham (1980) have pointed out that jobs in which the workers feel they have some control in deciding how a task should be done and some responsibility in creating an outcome of significance serve to elicit personal investment. Later in this book (chapters 3 and 9), we will discuss in some detail how people develop the sense of self-determination that can have such a significant effect on the degree to which they put themselves into the situation with all the skills and energies they have available. For now, the essential point is that the sense of self-determination must be factored into the motivational process.

Thoughts About the Situation

In any given situation, one has thoughts not only about self but also about the situation. These thoughts are often—even characteristically—intertwined, so our separation of them here is arbitrary at best.

Perceived Options. An aspect of choice and decision theory models that has not been so clearly spelled out and applied as it might is that one acts in terms of perceived options. One may view oneself as creating or accepting options, but it is the perceived availability and acceptability of options that is critical.

Available Options. Before we can ask why a person engages in one activity but not another, we have to make sure that both activities were in fact regarded as viable options. People will act in terms of what they perceive to be available to them in any given situation; that is, they will act in terms of what they perceive as possible. For example, it may be difficult—perhaps impossible—for a Detroit autoworker to see himself as doing anything but working on the line. Moreover, he may also perceive availing himself of educational opportunities to upgrade or revise his skills as impossible or not appropriate. This may seem obvious, yet it must be recognized as a critical facet of the motivational process. When we wonder why a person does or does not do something, we must consider, first, whether that something is a viable option in his or her world.

Opportunity is crucial, as is most evident in the motivational patterns exhibited by people who hold membership in different social and cultural groups. As noted earlier, in the discussion of social expectations, the possibility of becoming a physician or going to college is not a viable option for some people, given the social context in which they exist. A recent study of outstanding achievement is of special interest in this regard. As discussed in chapter 1, Bloom (1982a, 1982b) and his colleagues have been studying world-class performers in athletics, music, mathematics, art, and neuroscience. There are many facets to this most fascinating study, but the one that fits most appropriately with the points being made here is that these performers, in an important sense, were born into the "right families." The families valued the particular activity involved, promoted and rewarded it, and knew how to facilitate it. That alone was not sufficient, of course—since not all children in a family would develop their talent to the same degree as the one who actually becomes the elite performer—yet the opportunity had to be there.

Thus, before one begins to look for forces, energies, emotions, and the like, that drive a person to do something, one ought to ask, first, about the options available to the person. Choosing to go to college may be a real choice among alternatives for one person—and this represents motivation. For another person, however, it may represent no choice at all and thus would be of questionable value as an indicator of motivation.

Clearly, the set of alternatives available to the person is a crucial factor in the motivational choices that will be made. It is probably also true—though perhaps not so self-evident—that the *number* of choices perceived to be available may be important. Or, since number is usually relative, the crucial variable may be whether or not the available choices have been decreased or increased. Recently, considerable concern has been expressed about the morale of people who work in a declining field or in a dying organization (Maehr,

1984b). College professors and teachers provide examples close to our hearts. Whereas there may have been many choices within an academic career path a number of years ago, those choices are fewer now. Fifty-year-old professors don't get many job offers now—nor, for that matter, do their younger colleagues in many disciplines. Perhaps equally if not more important, the opportunities within the framework of their presently reasonably secure jobs have diminished—drastically in some cases. Thus, whereas professors of sociology formerly could realistically consider obtaining grants for overseas travel during a sabbatical year, they now must worry about whether there will even be a sabbatical year, let alone travel funds. In sum, the professorial role, once replete with options and freedom, has become more limited in many cases. Research on loss of freedom (Brehm, 1966) has indicated that this might lead to diminished motivation and morale. Informal observation of the campus scene indicates that this has, indeed, occurred in many notable instances. To repeat the essential point, however, what is crucial is not only that an absolute number of options are or are not available but also what is happening to this set of options. Moreover, it must be stressed that it is the person's *perception* of the situation that is critical. Of course, the perceived variation in options that may be a function of organizational or economic change is also likely to prove important.

Perceived options have not always been considered integral to the motivational picture; which is unfortunate. Certainly, the perception of options is partly a function of incentives, judgments about self, goals, and other factors; but such perceptions also stand by themselves as an integral part of the motivational process, and they are worthy of study in their own right. Whetten (1984), for example, has concluded that higher education administrators, who are able to find opportunities for change no matter how bleak the situation, can successfully resist the adverse psychological effects of decline.

Options are sometimes related to judgments about competence, but not always. Let's take an example. In the past several years, there has been much discussion of morale and burnout in various professional groups. The feeling is often expressed that certain individuals have simply seen their options foreclosed and thus have become disillusioned with their jobs. The algebra teacher perceives that there is little more to his life than teaching algebra, the M.D. has seen about all he wants to see about the human machine, and the manager doesn't thrill to the thought of the next sales push. One thing that often comes up in these discussions is that the individual may have options in or outside the job of which he or she simply was not aware. Sometimes a manager or supervisor can point them out; sometimes friends help. In any event, it seems that an important role for managers and supervisors in enhancing staff motivation and morale is to suggest options and possibilities. This is a creative task but surely an important one. The central point here is that the motivational process begins with the perception of options, and this perception is crucial to whatever ensues. As noted earlier, this point is implicit in choice and decision theories of motivation. We believe it is a basic point, and it plays a major role in our own formulation of motivation (see chapter 3).

Acceptable Options. Implicit in what has been said thus far is that options must be not only perceived but also acceptable. This ties in with judgments about what is right and proper—judgments that are based in large part on one's membership in particular sociocultural groups and on the roles one plays. Thus, for example, the possibility of pursuing professional careers was seldom an option for our mothers, even though they knew these options were available for others, such as their husbands and children, and doubtless had the ability to pursue them had they lived under different circumstances. This point may seem obvious, but it is hardly insignificant. Indeed, such social expectations perhaps control the largest share of the motivational variance for most people. Thus, when considering why a person moves in a certain direction, one must look at the expectations that impinge on the person as well as the opportunities that are available and acceptable (Braskamp, Fowler, & Ory, 1984).

Judgments of Worth. Implicit in most theories of motivation is the notion that judgments of value are important. For example, in discussing the role of *n* Achievement in determining achievement, McClelland (1961, 1985b) also emphasized the importance of valuing achievement. Whether people direct themselves to economic pursuits rather than to leisure activities probably depends to a significant degree on such judgments of worth. Similarly, value is given a specific role in the formulation of theories evolving from the choice and decision theory tradition (Atkinson, 1957; Atkinson & Feather, 1966; Atkinson & Raynor, 1974; Campbell, Dunnette, Lawler, & Weick, 1970; Vroom, 1964). Unfortunately, however, value is more often cited than studied; that is, little attention has been given to the nature, measurement, and causal effects of value judgments. Long ago, Gordon Allport (1961; Allport, Vernon, & Lindzey, 1960) attempted to define personality in terms of various value types, and he and his colleagues developed an assessment procedure of some utility (see, for example, Maehr & Stake, 1962). Cross-cultural research has regularly underscored the importance of value in directing choices; thus, when we discuss why people invest themselves in a certain course of action, we cannot skirt the value question. Indeed, when we boil down the antecedents of motivation and personal investment to their simplest form, we are inclined to suggest that people do what they believe they *can* do and what they believe is *worth* doing. Judgments of opportunity to perform and the value to the person in performing sum up most of what we need to consider in discussing motivation. The former involves not only the personal sense of competence but also perceptions of options. The latter involves not only the norms people live by as the result of the sociocultural groups in which they participate but the individualized goals they hold for themselves—what they are and what they hope to become.

Judgments of Justice. Somewhat related to and certainly overlapping with their various judgments of worth are the judgments people make about the organization, group, or situation they are considering as a focus for their personal investment. In recent years, considerable research regarding morale, motivation, and commitment in a work context (Adams, 1965; Mowday, 1975) has been concerned with questions of equity: Is the system fair? In work organizations, this question is often raised in regard to how employees are compensated or promoted and how performance appraisals are conducted. But the question is actually broader; it also relates to general issues of employee alienation, participation, and commitment.

The findings of a recent survey of U.S. workers (Yankelowich, 1982) underscore the importance of this cognition in mediating motivation. As noted earlier, recent evidence does not indicate that the work ethic has somehow been lost by the American worker, resulting in the industrial malaise that many segments of U.S. industry have recently experienced. Rather, Yankelowich has argued that the primary problem is that the worker does not see that extra effort returns an acceptable level of reward. Compensation is not considered commensurate with effort. This kind of equity question apparently relates directly to industrial productivity. Moreover, the cause seems to rest more in the hands of management than in the hearts and minds of the laborer.

The issue of equity is important, and the sources of equity perception must be considered in the attempt to sum up and integrate the reasons why people do or do not invest themselves in any particular course of action.

What Causes Motivation: An Interpretive Summary

This review of various perspectives on motivation suggests a variety of factors that may affect motivation and personal investment. Although this review may reflect the challenge of the problem as well as the variety and richness of the available data, it may also present a less than coherent picture of motivational causes. To counteract that possibility, we provide an interpretive summary of what we may have learned from the research and theory reviewed in this chapter.

Individuals Differ in Motivation

It is difficult to ignore the continuing effect of past experiences on the way people approach achievement situations and particularly on their beliefs.

Each person has his or her own personal history, and this history is reflected in the person's motivational patterns. In particular, people's beliefs about their adequacy to perform tasks is critical, especially in terms of achievement. Various acquired beliefs about what is valuable are likewise important. These basic individual motivational orientations are sometimes formed early in life and endure over time. They may generalize across a wide variety of situations, and they are sometimes difficult to change.

Situations Affect Motivation

A number of features of situations are also likely to affect motivation and personal investment. Among these, the nature of the job is paramount. Also important is the social group in which the task is performed, the success or failure experienced, and the role the person plays in performing the task. People are not just products of the past; they are also creatures of the present.

Social and Cultural Factors Are Important

Broad social and cultural factors also affect motivational orientations in at least two ways. First, an individual's personality is formed in sociocultural contexts. The motivational predispositions, orientations, and biases people bring to each new situation are a product of their experiences in past social and cultural contexts. Second, sociocultural norms and attendant expectations are significant factors in defining options and directing choices. A person acts as a product of, as well as a continuing member of, sociocultural groups.

Cognitions Mediate Motivation

Recent research has suggested that one can best understand the collective and interactive effects of personality, situation, and context by focusing on the person's present thoughts. These thoughts are arguably the immediate antecedents of motivation and personal investment. One cannot always recover the experiential histories people bring to a specific situation, but there is reason to believe that these experiential histories are adequately reflected in how people value a present situation as well as in how they perceive their own capacity and opportunity to perform in that situation. Moreover, the recent emphasis on cognition in understanding motivation underscores the possibility that previous history and present experience interact to give present meaning to a given situation. Simply put, it is the meaning of the situation to the person that is critical. The importance of that general conclusion will become increasingly evident in subsequent chapters.

3
Toward a Theory of Personal Investment

W hy *does* a Thomas Edison regularly work around the clock—or a Harold Geneen (former head of ITT) but in a 50-hour-plus work-week? Just as intriguing and certainly equal in importance, why does a 40-year-old workaholic attorney suddenly chuck it all and retire to a 160-acre farm in Arkansas? Why does a 30-year-old mother of three put her comfortable ways aside and return to school with the hope of attaining an MBA? Why does an ever-faithful secretary suddenly make a habit of coming to work late, dawdle on the job, and show a decided drop in productivity? Chapter 2 presented an array of possibilities to consider in answering such questions. Is there any way to integrate these possibilities into a coherent whole? We think so, and it is our intention in this chapter to outline a theory of personal investment that can provide a conceptual framework for understanding motivation.

Basic Elements of a Theory of Personal Investment

The theory of personal investment to be presented here is based on a 25-year program of research on motivation (Braskamp, Fowler, & Ory, 1984; Maehr, 1974a, 1974b, 1976, 1978, 1983, 1984a; Maehr & Kleiber, 1981; Maehr & Nicholls, 1980). The theory draws heavily on a variety of theoretical perspectives. In many respects, it represents an integration of theoretical options such as those set forth in chapter 2, but the use of the term *personal investment* is meant to imply a particular perspective on motivation. Briefly, the perspective is reflected in five propositions:

1. The study of motivation begins and ends with the study of *behavior*. The behavioral patterns associated with motivation are collectively referred to as personal investment.
2. The *direction* of behavior is of primary significance; thus, the focus is on the apparent choices and decisions made by people.

3. It is the *meaning* of the situation to the person that determines personal investment.

4. The meaning of a situation can be assessed, and its origins can be determined.

5. Motivation is a *process* that is embedded in the ongoing stream of behavior.

Motivation and Behavior

The basic rationale for focusing on behavior in the study of motivation was set forth in chapter 1; our purpose now is to reinforce that point. One cannot *see* motivation; rather, motivation is *inferred* from behavior that is observed. That notion must be well established before one can proceed further.

Motivation as Investment

Given the first proposition, the question that immediately follows concerns *what* behavior is being studied. In the first chapter, we outlined several behavioral patterns that prompt motivational inferences. All of these are fitting objects of study under the label *motivation*. We suggest, however, that in studying human social motivation, the problem of predicting, understanding, and influencing the *direction* of behavior is of primary significance. For the most part, people tend to be active; the question regarding motivation, then, concerns why they are active in one way or another. Why do they invest themselves in a particular activity?

Meaning and Motivation

The third proposition introduces an element that is only implicit in what has been stated thus far: The critical antecedent of motivation is the meaning of the situation to the person. Perhaps that basic notion is already suggested by using the term *personal* investment, but it must be made explicit at the outset. Thus, the theory we shall propose is essentially a cognitive theory of motivation. It assumes that the primary antecedents of choice—as well as persistence, variation in activity level, or performance—reside in the thoughts, perceptions, and beliefs of the person. We use the term *meaning* to indicate that a certain collection of thoughts is of primary importance. We will have a good deal more to say about this central issue later in the chapter.

Assessing and Predicting Meaning

The fourth proposition may seem gratuitous, but it is necessary to reinforce an awareness that observation and assessment of meanings and their origin are essential. We intend to present a theory that is operational. As we define terms, we will specify measurement procedures. For the most part, three types of measurement procedures are called for: (1) observations of behavioral patterns, (2) assessment of contextual factors, and (3) indices of the cognitions collectively called *meaning*. Because we stress the role of cognition in determining personal investment, we are not inclined to limit ourselves to fantasy measures of motivation, such as those employed by David McClelland and his colleagues (Atkinson, 1958; McClelland, 1985a, 1985b).

Motivation as Process

Finally, we view motivation as a process that is embedded in the ongoing stream of behavior. People continually follow certain preprogrammed patterns or scripts (Schank & Abelson, 1977), habits, and more complex routines—such as going to work, picking up children from work or school, watching TV—that make up an important share of a day's activities (Langer, 1978; Staw, 1977; Taylor & Fiske, 1978). People also exhibit more all-encompassing patterns, such as preparing to be a physician, pursuing a career in drama, or taking up a new hobby. At certain junctures, decisions or choices must be made—whether to continue the pattern, start a new activity, revise the patterns, and so on. The study of motivation focuses on these critical junctures, and the motivational process culminates in the observation that action is taken or a course is pursued. We refer to this culmination of the motivational process as personal investment. The study of motivation thus involves the definition of critical junctures and the identification of factors that determine which plans are followed.

The Central Role of Meaning

We must return to that burning and abiding question: Why does a person invest himself or herself in any given course of action? On the surface, at least, our solution is simple: It is the *meaning* of the situation to the person that determines personal investment. That is, whether or how people will invest themselves in particular activities or courses of action depends on what the activities or courses of action mean to them.

Although one could identify a variety of factors external to the person that affect personal investment, all such factors are filtered through the perceptions of the person. They are mediated by the meanings these events hold for the individual involved. Consider the example of three individuals who are each offered $500 to paint a house. One is a 16-year-old boy who has previously asked for the chance to do odd jobs to earn extra income. He accepts the opportunity immediately and gets to work in earnest as soon as possible. The second person is a professional house painter who weighs other alternatives, considers his status in the profession, and rejects the offer. A third person is a friend who would have been willing to contribute his time and talent for free if asked but is offended by the offer of money. He declines, giving the excuse that he is really too busy. Clearly, the job and the money meant very different things to these different people, and their inclination to perform was controlled significantly by this meaning. In no sense would the objective factors, such as the amount offered or the effort demanded, emerge as the critical factors determining the choice to invest themselves in this endeavor.

People exhibit different patterns of personal investment because they understand the investment situation differently. They invest in or avoid tasks because of these understood meanings, and even when they engage in the same tasks, they often do so for different reasons and with noticeably different results. People hold meanings in reference to certain courses of action, and these meanings have effects on how or whether the people invest themselves in any given situation. Although it is also likely that the situation itself may create or modify the meanings that are held, such meanings are the immediate antecedents of personal investment. Whether or not people will invest time, talent, and energy in a particular area or activity is a very individual, subjective, *personal* undertaking.

On the Meaning of Meaning

Although it may be relatively easy to accept the simple assertion that meaning determines personal investment, unless and until we specify the meaning of *meaning*, the assertion has little value. More precisely, what do we mean by *meaning*? In general, meaning refers to thoughts and perceptions and to purposes and goals. For our purposes, meaning is composed of three interrelated facets: (1) *personal incentives* associated with performing in a situation, (2) thoughts about *self*, and (3) *options* perceived to be available in a situation. A brief word about the general definition of meaning and the interrelationships among these facets is in order before each facet is considered in detail.

First, it should be noted that the three meaning components are commonly featured in theories of motivation, under one guise or another. However, the special way we define these facets is important and deserves fuller elaboration. Moreover, in considering these facets, it is important to keep firmly in mind that they operate collectively and interactively.

Second, each of these facets is cognitive in nature; they are all categories of thoughts and perceptions. It is also assumed that they are available to a person's consciousness so that a person can report them on questionnaires and in interviews.

Third, it is assumed that the thoughts and perceptions present at the moment of acting are critical. Therefore, it is also assumed that although a person may have relatively enduring thoughts and may bring perceptual biases into any given situation, thoughts and perceptions are often subject to change with the situation.

The diagram presented in figure 3–1 summarizes the overall pattern of relationships envisioned by the theory. Briefly, it is assumed that information from the present as well as experiences from the past form meanings of the moment. These meanings of the moment are the immediate antecedents of the behavioral patterns from which we infer that a person is or is not motivated. Clearly, access to the meanings held is critical in understanding how people will invest themselves in a particular situation. This requires assessment of the kinds of meanings individuals are likely to bring to any given situation. It also requires assessment of the effects of certain situations on meanings and personal investment. All of this is implicit in the diagram presented in figure 3–1.

The Nature, Function, and Variety of Personal Incentives

The term *personal incentives* refers to the motivational focus of the activity: What does the person expect to get out of performing? What is the value of

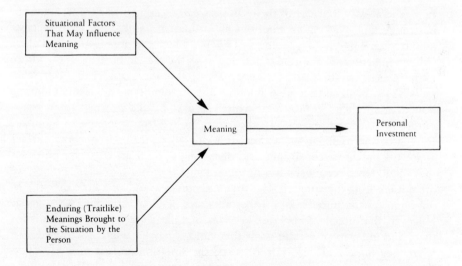

Figure 3–1. An Outline of the Factors Leading to Personal Investment

the activity? How does the person define success and failure in the situation? Or, simply, what incentives are salient for the person?

The term *incentives* has been used to describe a host of situational factors, presumably external to the individual, that affect behavior. A distinction is made between *needs*, which are inherent in the individual—that is, internal—and *incentives*, which are external (Chuny, 1977). Although such distinctions may be useful in some instances, they also pose problems; for example, it is often difficult to differentiate needs and incentives in practice. More important, for our purposes, the designation of incentives as external does not accord well with a cognitive theory of motivation, which stresses the *perception* of the external as critical. Our use of the term *personal incentives*, which owes much to Veroff and Veroff (1980), stresses what the person perceives to be attractive or unattractive in his or her environment. The use of the word *incentives* calls attention to the importance of situational variations that may occasion motivational change; the use of the qualifier *personal* stresses our view that it is the person's apprehension of the situation that is critical. At an earlier point in our work (Maehr, 1983; Maehr & Nicholls, 1980), we used the term *personal goals*. The word *goals*, however, is all too readily identified with level of performance and less readily associated with direction of activity. So *personal incentives* it is, representing, we hope, an interest in the subjective definition of what is attractive or to be avoided.

The Nature of Personal Incentives

In a general way, our use of the term *personal incentives* as a critical concept implies certain working assumptions about human nature. The term suggests an intentional psychology (Klinger, 1977) in which the organism makes plans (Miller, Galanter, & Pribram, 1960) and lives the present in terms of the future as much as in light of the past (Allport, 1955). It is not necessary to assume that individuals spend considerable amounts of time identifying goals and planning how to attain them. In fact, people often seem to be unconcerned about goals, purposes, or incentives; that is, they seem to live from moment to moment, from situation to situation, without thinking about the consequences of their actions. Contextual constraints and demands, aside from whatever purposes they might have, seem primary. By employing the term *personal incentives*, we are not ignoring the apparent fact that individuals spend very little time thinking about goals, purposes, and the outcomes of their activities. We suggest, however, that people do operate in terms of what a given situation yields for them and in terms of certain goals they hold. They have latent knowledge of what they hope and expect from a specific situation and, if properly questioned, can state what these expectations are. Moreover, these beliefs about the situation should and will affect their behavior in specifiable ways. In short, we can ask people what they hope to accomplish in a given situation, and they can provide answers (see chapter 4).

The Variety of Personal Incentives

Anyone who is reasonably acquainted with the vagaries of human behavior must be aware of the likelihood that a number of incentives may be operative in guiding how people invest themselves or whether or not they become involved in a specific activity. Theories of human motivation suggest a broad range of incentive possibilities. The particular needs selected for special attention by McClelland and his colleagues suggest possible goals that guide what we call personal investment (see chapter 2). The need for achievement, the need for affiliation, and the need for power, in particular, might be considered examples of personal incentives.

Certainly, there are also many other personal incentives that one could logically identify. Recognizing such variety, there is also value in organizing these diverse personal incentive possibilities into a limited set of categories. Our initial efforts (Maehr, 1983, 1984a) eventuated in the designation of four broad personal incentive categories associated particularly with achievement. These categories are listed and briefly defined in table 3–1.

Task Personal Incentives. There has been a long and enduring interest in how individuals behave when the only apparent reward is something inherent in the task itself. Usually, research along this line has contrasted performance under obvious external reward conditions and under conditions in which such external rewards seem to be minimally present or nonexistent. The external reward conditions may vary from direct and explicit payment for a job to the somewhat more subtle and complex condition in which external standards and expectations are merely emphasized. In any case, the attempt is made to vary the degree to which the task itself elicits motivation. Thus, a conception has emerged that sometimes, something about the task itself is motivating, and when this is the case, behavior takes a different form than when the individual performs the task for reasons external to the task.

In general, then, something about the task in, of, and by itself may be the goal of the effort. The question that is immediately forthcoming concerns what it is about a task that can be the goal of behavior. Two types of task-

Table 3–1
Personal Incentive Categories

Intrinsic		Extrinsic	
Task	*Ego*	*Social Solidarity*	*Extrinsic Rewards*
Understanding something	Doing better than others	Pleasing others	Earning a prize
Experiencing adventure/ novelty	Winning	Making others happy	Making money

related personal incentives are often distinguished in theory but are sometimes difficult to distinguish in practice: (1) what might be termed *pure task absorption*, and (2) the goal of *demonstrating competence*.

Virtually total task absorption is often reflected by both children and adults in play. Indeed, play might be defined as the state in which such absorption in a task occurs. However, on occasion—often to the surprise of employers—such total task absorption is seen in work settings. Perhaps no one has studied this at greater length and in greater depth than Csikszentmihalyi (1975, 1978, in press), and several findings deserve mention at this point. First, a total kind of absorption in the task without apparent thought about surrounding conditions and events is a significant human phenomenon. It is not limited to children. It may occur in playing a game or in solving a problem. Csikszentmihalyi reported instances of this occurring in a significant way in surgeons engaging in a complex operation and in mountaineers in the process of scaling a cliff. Although one may see very little similarity in these events on the surface, they apparently all can elicit the total absorption in a task, the loss of self in the process of doing, and the reduction of awareness of an external world that may set standards, evaluate, and provide rewards or punishments.

The most common term that has been used to describe this condition is *intrinsic motivation*. We all have known it to occur in our own lives as well as that of others, and in that sense it is not an unknown quantity. Yet it is one of the more difficult entities, processes, events, or whatever, to define, describe, and explain. For now, we simply call attention to the existence of such a personal incentive possibility.

Often associated with yet conceptually distinguishable from pure task absorption is what the Harvard psychologist Robert White (1959, 1960) called "competence motivation." The observations on which he based his theorizing were not very different from those described by Csikszentmihalyi; that is, he focused particularly on children and animals at play, seeking out challenge and by no means solely controlled by simple notions of rewards and sanctions. White pointed out that a certain amount of failure, pain, or punishment could be rewarding or could at least serve to attract further effort. Conversely, success was not sought at all costs. A moderate amount of risk taking and challenge seeking was seen as a regular feature of human behavior. White proposed that there was a competence motive that in many ways was as important as such primary drives as hunger, thirst, and sex.

By suggesting a competence motive, White introduced a goal that can be seen as different from the one identified with Csikszentmihalyi's analysis. Compared to the "flow experience" described by Csikszentmihalyi, the competence situation may be seen as less intrinsically tied to the task. Certainly, there is some implication that the self is somewhat separable from the situation. It is also implied that the *person* is becoming competent at *something*.

The person is not just doing something because it is interesting or exciting; the goal is to grow, to learn from experience, to become more skilled and knowledgeable. For example, there are occasions when we actually enjoy just hitting a tennnis ball against a wall for an hour or so. Although there is simple pleasure in muscle movement, we suspect that the primary joy is derived largely from a sense that we are somehow improving our strokes and footwork.

The designation of a competence personal incentive implies that, at some point, the activity is subject to standards and, as such, is liable to external defintions of success and failure. One can therefore perceive a slight and subtle difference between the research focus implied by Csikszentmihalyi and the White conception of task-related motivation (see also Harter, 1982; Harter & Connell, 1984).

Ego Personal Incentives. Whereas task incentives might involve competition with self, ego incentives refer directly to social competition (Maehr & Sjogren, 1971). The goal is to "beat" someone, to do better than another, to win, to be the best. As we have confessed, we like to beat a tennis ball against the wall on occasion. We will confess, further, that these occasions often occur after a humiliation in a match. Somehow, we lost to an opponent when we wanted and expected to win. Thus, our practice was prompted not by sheer delight in improving our competence but by the anticipation of beating so-and-so the next time around. It is this goal of beating so-and-so that we refer to when we use the term *ego incentives*. Broadly, success is measured in terms of others; the goal is not only to improve one's own performance but to do better than others (Maehr & Sjogren, 1971).

In considering competitiveness, one cannot ignore the role that general conceptions of the self play. Although we will discuss this matter further later, several points can be appropriately made at this juncture. Generally, competitive conditions make the person's sense of competence especially salient. The individual is forced to think about whether he or she is good or bad at such tasks like this, and reflecting on one's ability in this way is likely to have important modifying effects on motivation.

Social Personal Incentives. Social incentives are often a critical facet of human behavior. They are important not only in leisure activities but also in school and work settings. Employees often state that they value the job because of the interpersonal relationships, and productivity may be enhanced or diminished because of the social context. Thus, interpersonal conflicts are often a major source of lowered productivity, and positive interpersonal relationships may not only improve morale but also enhance productivity.

Holding social personal incentives is likely to result in behavioral patterns that are different from those that follow when the person places considerable emphasis on task or ego incentives. The goal is affiliation and, perhaps, the support and approval of others. We suggest, further, that under social personal incentive conditions, *faithfulness* is more important than simply doing the task for its own sake (task incentive). Faithfulness is also more important than doing the task to show that one is better than someone else (ego incentive). Indeed, cooperation should prevail when social personal incentives are predominant.

Extrinsic Personal Incentives. Over the past decade or so, a heated debate has ensued over the role of extrinsic rewards. Moving from a cognitive frame of reference, many researchers (Deci, 1975, 1980; Lepper & Greene, 1978; Lepper et al., 1973) proceeded to demonstrate certain negative effects of extrinsic rewards on motivation to perform an activity. The most widely generalizable finding was that when a task was in itself interesting to the individual, adding extrinsic rewards decreased this interest. This finding had particular relevance to education and provided a basis for attacking the indiscriminant application of reinforcement theory (Lepper & Greene, 1975; Maehr, 1977). But this finding was also considered in terms of the adult world of work, where its applicability proved problematic.

Intrinsic or internal motivation is also an important characteristic in a work organization, and jobs are often designed to enhance such a motivational orientation (Hackman & Oldham, 1980). But one cannot imagine work without extrinsic rewards—or at least without pay. Indeed, research on work motivation clearly indicates that pay is positively associated with what can only be called intrinsic motivation—that is, a love for the job, commitment to it, a willingness to put forth extra effort and to take initiatives (Nadler, Hackman & Lawler, 1979; Staw, 1983; Staw, Hess, & Sandelands, 1980). The resolution of this apparent dilemma possibly resides in the definition of extrinsic incentives (Porac & Meindl, 1982). Clearly, significant problems exist in this regard.

When the term *extrinsic incentives* is used, most people immediately think of money, benefits, and perquisites. Certainly, money is readily seen as an extrinsic reward in an educational setting, and it is not surprising that studies within an educational context would show negative effects as a result of feedback so obviously extrinsic to the task. But compensation within a work organization is replete with a variety of meanings. It has symbolic value relating to social status, work productivity, and approval. In addition, it is often the only feedback the person receives regarding his or her competence. This leads us to suggest that in considering extrinsic incentives one cannot be content simply to associate them with money, perquisites, and benefits. Rather, we must make a special point of stressing that it is the *perception* of these factors that is important, not their objective presence in a situation. We suggest, further, that it is when the feedback is perceived as having very little *informative* value regarding the preceding three types of personal incentives that we may refer it to this category. Often, money, perquisites, and benefits have little or no important informative function for the person in a particular situation; they simply provide means to pursue his or her other interests. It is under such conditions that we can speak of compensation as an extrinsic personal incentive.

The Function of Personal Incentives

In defining personal incentives, we have indicated how they function to influence behavior. Moreover, we have suggested how different personal incentives will have different effects on personal investment. In concluding our discussion in this regard, we wish to bring the relationship of personal incentives to behavior into even stronger focus. Accordingly, we will concentrate specifically on how holding certain personal incentives leads to specific behavioral patterns.

Task Personal Incentives. When a task personal incentive is strongly held, individuals are likely to spontaneously select tasks that challenge their ability and competence. They will select activities that have a number of different characteristics: tasks for which the individual is responsible for the outcome, tasks for which performance can be evaluated as successful or unsuccessful (that is, where a standard of excellence is applicable), and tasks for which the outcome of the performance is uncertain. In other words, when task personal incentives are especially salient, individuals are likely to select and choose to perform in achievement tasks, as these were defined earlier (see chapter 1). Moreover, when task personal incentives guide the individual, he or she performs much along the lines suggested in the case of a person who is high in achievement motivation, as defined by McClelland (1961, 1985a, 1985b; see also Atkinson & Raynor, 1974, chap. 2).

Ego Personal Incentives. When ego personal incentives are salient to the person, mere performance on the task is not sufficient. Rather, the goal is to do better than someone else. Although a standard of excellence may be applicable for both task personal incentive and ego personal incentives, when ego personal incentives prevail, the standard of excellence is social—the goal is to do better than someone else, to outdo another, to beat someone.

Sense of competence plays an especially important role when ego personal incentives prevail. Under these conditions, people with low perceived competence are not likely to risk failure. They will either choose tasks on which they can most certainly succeed or they will opt for tasks on which they have virtually no chance of succeeding. In either case, their behavior may be interpreted as avoiding any direct confrontation with how competent they are, because they are fearful of the answer. In contrast, people with a high sense of competence are more likely to risk failure and confront challenge. In short, competition may be fine for motivating individuals who already think of themselves as highly competent at the task, but it may have distinct negative effects on those who are uncertain of their competence (Kukla, 1978; Maehr, 1983, 1984a; Nicholls, 1979, 1983, 1984b; Nicholls & Miller, 1984).

Social Personal Incentives. In contrast to both task and ego personal incentives, social personal incentives tend to minimize challenge-seeking behavior and prompt faithful conformity to the expectation of others. Holding social personal incentives encourages faithful effort. Thus, for a boring and tedious task—a task that requires much effort but little ability—social personal incentives may play an important facilitating role. When individuals or groups are guided by task or ego personal incentives they tend to avoid tasks that primarily require effort rather than ability. When social personal incentives are held, effort is encouraged even when ability is not challenged. People can demonstrate good intentions and often obtain social approval for faithfulness, whereas they cannot demonstrate competence or superior ability through faithfulness alone. Social personal incentives do not ordinarily prompt the pursuit of an unusual path or encourage challenge seeking, nor are they ordinarily associated with enhancing ability or competence. Rather, the goal is to enhance relationships with others.

Extrinsic Personal Incentives. Earlier, we alluded to the problems involved in defining the role of extrinsic incentives. We attempted to resolve these problems to some degree by stressing, first, that personal incentives represent a cognitive construction of events. In this regard, we focused particularly on the perceived informational value of certain job-related rewards. Assuming, then, that we can identify when extrinsic personal incentives are primary for a person, what types of behavior might we expect? We propose two hypotheses.

First, when a person engages in an activity for extrinsic reasons, he or she will continue to perform if and only if extrinsic rewards are forthcoming. Behavior must be tied to the rewards in a clear fashion in the person's mind. There is no reason to believe that this is not equally true for other personal incentives as well, but there is a special point in stressing this principle in connection with extrinsic personal incentives. Sometimes, it is assumed that paying someone to do something that he or she is not inclined to do for any other reason will naturally and inevitably lead to the development of intrinsic interests and thereby ultimately permit us to reduce the payment. We are seldom so naive as to try this in the world of work, but many of us have tried it in our child-rearing. How often have children been bribed to practice the piano, do their homework, or clean their room? There is strong reason to believe, however, that once the task is defined as something that is contracted and paid for, the performer comes to expect a payoff. If performance is to proceed on a different basis, a redefinition of the task must occur—and there is little evidence that this happens simply because merely doing the task for whatever reason will eventuate in intrinsic reasons for performing.

A second hypothesis is that if fulfilling extrinsic personal incentives is the goal of the behavior, then a positive correlation should exist between the amount of reward and the degree of personal investment. The higher the pay, the higher the motivation should be. Moreover, we propose a subhypothesis that people guided by extrinsic personal incentives will pursue those courses of action that they expect will be maximally efficient in bringing these extrinsic rewards. This pattern, too, is not alien to the pursuit of other personal incentives, but a significant contrast in behavior occurs when different personal incentives are perceived. The pursuit of a task personal incentive, for example, is likely to involve trying something new and risky. Novelty has its own apparent reward, and taking a risk is involved in meeting the kinds of challenges that lead to the attainment of competence. Thus, taking the easiest course is not compatible with pursuing a task personal incentive orientation. But there is really no reason to risk losing money if money is the only motivating force. Whereas a firm expectation of reward should be motivating when extrinsic rewards are salient, degree of uncertainty in outcome is a motivating force when task personal incentives predominate.

Personal Incentives and Challenge. The differential effects of incentives are most apparent in their effects on challenge-seeking behavior. Although discussions of motivation certainly cannot be limited to this particular situation, it is clear that challenge seeking is of important interest, particularly in the area of work and achievement. Thus, J.W. Atkinson's (1957; Atkinson & Feather, 1966; Atkinson & Raynor, 1974) extensive work on motivation and achievement revolves significantly around the challenge-seeking situation. One way of summing up the essential generalizations presented thus far is to consider how personal incentives modify the preference for various levels of challenge.

The four graphs in figure 3–2 illustrate hypotheses regarding how individuals respond to challenge when the four different personal incentive conditions are dominant. Graph 1 essentially suggests that all people are attracted to challenge when task personal incentives are salient for them. Graph 2 suggests that challenge is differentially attractive, depending on the person's sense of competence. Graph 3 suggests that challenge is unimportant when social incentives prevail. Finally, Graph 4 suggests that personal investment increases as rewards increase. By implication, it also suggests that the person does not experiment with means, manners, and ways of obtaining the reward but simply gets it in the simplest and most direct manner.

These hypotheses have varying degrees of support, but they help clarify the nature and implications of the four proposed personal incentives. They

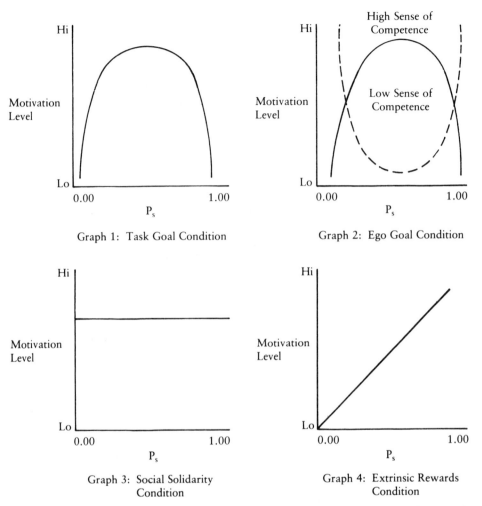

Graph 1: Task Goal Condition

Graph 2: Ego Goal Condition

Graph 3: Social Solidarity Condition

Graph 4: Extrinsic Rewards Condition

Figure 3–2. Hypotheses Associated with Risk-Taking and Challenge-Seeking under Personal Incentive Conditions

suggest, further, how variation in the salience of personal incentives might affect behavioral patterns of some importance in the realm of work and achievement.

The Nature of Selfhood

The second facet of meaning that is critical in the determination of personal investment is the judgments and beliefs that relate to one's definition of *self*. There are many ways to define selfhood, and many components can be considered more or less integral. The topic of selfhood is much discussed within psychology (Wylie, 1974, 1979); indeed, the term *psychology* seems to imply that selfhood is the proper focus for psychological research. Here, we wish to use the term *sense of self* in a rather general sense, defining it as the more or less organized collection of perceptions, beliefs, and feelings about who one is. We have identified four facets of self that seem not only all-encompassing but useful: (1) identity, (2) self-reliance, (3) goal-directedness, and (4) sense of competence. Each of these facets is defined briefly in table 3–2.

Identity

By *identity*, we mean that the individual perceives himself or herself as associated with certain groups and holds selected others to be significant (Maehr, 1974a, 1978). The person's reference groups affect a wide range of behavior (Homans, 1950). For example, the effects of social expectations, discussed earlier, depend significantly on whether or not the individual recognizes the expectations as appropriate to himself or herself. Moreover, self-identity affects knowledge about and acceptance of certain purposes and goals. But self-identity not only defines what is worth striving for, it also defines how striving should occur. Socially normative expectations thus derive from the person's identity; that is, they are a direct function of the person's definition of self as a member of a particular social or cultural group.

Self-Reliance

The second facet of selfhood involves the person's perceptions that he or she can chart new waters and confront challenges, difficulties, and uncertainties

Table 3–2
Components of Sense of Self

Identity

    The critical feature here is the perceived characteristics of individuals the person believes to be important in his or her life. It is presumed that what these significant others value will modify his or her behavior.

Self-Reliance

    "I don't need anyone to motivate me. I motivate myself."
    "I like to work on tasks for which I alone am responsible."

Goal-Directedness

    "Successful completion is the primary goal of any undertaking."
    "I aim my activities toward a future goal."

Sense of Competence

    "I succeed in whatever I do."
    "I can succeed at anything I want to do."

Note: Statements in quotes have been taken from the Inventory of Personal Investment (see chapter 4).

with confidence. Self-reliance is not the same as sense of competence; it is a special factor that is important in its own right. This facet of self encompasses the special dimension often thought to be associated with achievement-motivated people (McClelland, 1961) as well as innovators and pathfinders (Sheehy, 1981). That dimension concerns the individual's perception that he or she essentially controls his or her own destiny. The person is not a pawn but an origin, an initiator, a determiner of what will happen characteristically or in any given situation (deCharms, 1968, Deci, 1980).

Goal-Directedness

The goal-directedness facet of selfhood is often implicit in comparisons of people who vary in motivation to achieve. It refers very specifically to the self-ascribed tendency to set goals and organize one's behavior accordingly. In an important sense, it appears that the person who is high in goal-directedness has a sense that he or she is *becoming* something rather than just *being* something (Allport, 1955). Thus, the category encompasses such critical components of achievement over the long term as the ability to delay gratification (Mischel, 1966) and the tendency to consciously set performance goals, schedule oneself, and make plans for the future.

Sense of Competence

The fourth facet of selfhood encompasses the individual's beliefs about his or her ability. People who hold a high sense of competence express confidence in their abilities, recover quickly from defeat, and are optimistic about success. Generally, then, sense of competence refers to the person's judgments that he or she can or cannot do something. Such judgments vary in degree and extent; they may be limited to one area or generalized broadly across a variety of performance domains. People hold rather firm opinions about their ability to succeed at tasks if they try, and this component of self is often associated with achievement motivation (Kukla, 1978; Nicholls, 1983, 1984a; Nicholls & Miller, 1984; Roberts, 1984).

Early research indicated, quite simply, that individuals tend to do what they feel competent to do (Ludwig & Maehr, 1967). That conclusion has not been invalidated by subsequent research, but it has shown to be simplistic. In particular, recent research on motivation and achievement has indicated that the person's sense of competence will likely guide preferences and choices that have a major impact on the continuing development of talent and ability (Maehr & Willig, 1982). Those who have a high sense of competence in a performance area are not only more than likely to continue performing in that area, but they are also more than likely to initiate and maintain activities that enhance their ability. They will challenge their ability, test it, and thereby enhance it. Those who are less sure of their competence need special encouragement from others if they are to confront the kind of challenge that is likely to be self-enhancing. Thus, at an early stage of experience in an area of activity, people develop a sense of competence that serves as an inner guide toward the performance and practice of self-enhancing tasks. In one study involving performance on school-like tasks (Fyans & Maehr, 1979), this sense of competence was already powerfully evident in the fourth grade. We suspect that it may be a reality before that time in many areas of activity. Regardless of when it comes into being, however, it remains an important force throughout life.

Sense of competence is in itself a powerful determiner of whether or not individuals will invest themselves in any given area of activity. But, as we have already indicated, sense of competence is also important as it interacts with certain task conditions. Thus, when the task is socially competitive or fosters ego incentives, the person's sense of competence modifies personal investment. People who believe they are competent are attracted to the task as an opportunity for self-enhancement, whereas people who are uncertain of their competence do what they can to avoid a test of their ability.

Perceived Options

The third major facet of meaning is *perceived options*—the behavioral alternatives or action possibilities that a person perceives to be available to him or her in any given situation. The person acts in terms of those perceived available choices in the situation.

Chapter 2 discussed the nature and origin of perceived options and suggested the role they play in determining behavior. Briefly, we suggested that a distinction must be made between options that are perceived as *possible* and those that are perceived as *acceptable*. It is not very likely, for example, that an aboriginal living in the Northern Territory of Australia will take up the cello, especially if he or she has not seen a cello. Besides what is perceived as available in the person's world, however, there is also a parallel perception of the appropriate options in which to invest time, talents, and energies. What is appropriate, of course, is defined in terms of sociocultural norms that happen to exist for the individual in his or her particular culture or social group. Thus, interacting with a computer terminal is not a salient option for many young people growing up in the inner city, even though they may know quite a bit about computers and their properties. Knowing that people work and even play with computers—and that they themselves could learn to use one if they wished to—may still not rule out the fact that becoming a "computer jock" simply is not acceptable in the groups in which they hold membership. That is, if computer interests and skills are not encouraged and rewarded by the reference group—if they are categorized as something done only by others, in other groups and contexts—choosing to spend leisure and learning time interacting with these devices will not be an acceptable behavioral option. To entice such young people into becoming skilled in the use of computer technology, one would have to do much more than provide simple instruction relevant to the nature and use of computers.

In sum, the perception of the availability and the acceptability of options is crucial in the motivational process. People choose and direct their behavior in terms of what seem to be available and acceptable possibilities.

Antecedents of Meaning

Thus far in this chapter, we have outlined two basic propositions associated with personal investment theory:

1. People invest themselves in certain activities depending on the meaning these activities have for them.
2. Meaning involves three interrelated categories of cognition: personal incentives, sense of self, and perceived options.

A critical question that follows is what determines meaning? By way of anticipating the expanded discussion prompted by this question in subsequent chapters (see, particularly, chapter 5) we will outline here the basic factors that are likely to be important in this regard.

In general, we think of meaning and personal investment as having their source in the dual factors of *situation* and *person* and in a complex of Person × Situation interactions, as suggested in chapter 2 and portrayed in figure 3–1. Figure 3–3 expands this categorization by posing five antecedent categories: performance situation, personal experiences, information, sociocultural context, and age or life stage. A word or two about each of these should illustrate the conditions that might affect the meanings held by the person in a performance situation.

Personal Experiences, Personality, and Meaning

We assume that each individual comes to a situation with a "package" of meanings derived from past experiences. That is, individuals characteristically hold certain personal incentives and views of self and may be especially aware of or inclined toward selected behavioral options. Some individuals, for example, typically approach each task as if it were a competitive game in which some win and others lose. Similarly, people are likely to hold a general sense of their competence in given performance areas. They bring these meanings to each new situation.

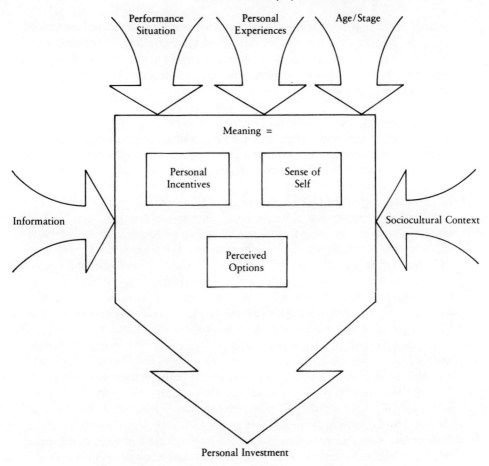

Figure 3–3. Antecedents of Meaning and Personal Investment

The Performance Situation

The character of the present situation also has effects. At least two aspects of the present situation may affect the meanings held: social expectation and task design.

Social Expectation. In any social group, a social organization tends to emerge; norms and roles come into being, and social status evolves. This social organization often develops apart from the formal organization and is frequently peer-initiated and peer-controlled. Associated with such organization is a set of expectations for the participants, both collectively and individually, regarding how they should perform, behave, and even feel. These expectations also affect people's perceptions and definitions of personal incentives, action possibilities, and sense of self. If the situation, the peers, or both are changed, meaning and personal investment will likely also change. The role of social expectations was discussed at length in the preceding chapter. Our purpose here is to remind the reader of what was said there and to stress that social expectations affect behavior by affecting the meaning of the situation to the person.

Task Design. Any consideration of why a person does or does not invest his or her time, talent, and energy in a particular situation must focus at some point on the task itself. There is strong evidence that various task variables determine which personal incentives are salient in a situation. A formidable body of research deals with how the structure and nature of the task might affect the meaning of the task to the person. This research is varied in theoretical orientation, method, and scope, but it suggests, collectively, that four interrelated and overlapping factors are of prime importance in determining which personal incentives will be salient in any given situation.

The first factor is what we will simply label *inherent attractiveness*—how interesting, meaningful, or intrinsically motivating the task is to the person. Certain tasks are simply more fun to do—at least for most people— and certain tasks are inevitably boring drudgery. Thus, tasks vary in the degree to which they enhance a task personal incentive orientation.

In their review of factors associated with internal motivation, Hackman and Oldham (1980) suggested a number of variables associated with the nature and definition of a task that are likely to be important in this regard. Two of these variables—task identity and skill variety—relate to the intrinsic motivational properties of a job. *Task identity* is the extent to which someone can begin and complete an identifiable piece of work by his or her own efforts. *Skill variety* is the extent to which someone needs to use a number of different skills and talents to complete the diverse aspects of a job or task. We would add a third factor that may be implicit in Hackman and Oldham's model but, in our estimation, should be made explicit. This third factor is *challenge*, by which we mean that the task is not too difficult or too easy for the person; that is, it should tax the person's ability—but not too much.

We hypothesize that only as these factors are strongly associated with a particular job or task will this task have the potential to elicit a strong task personal incentive orientation. However, not all tasks have the potential for creating a task orientation, simply because they cannot be defined in such a way that they have a strong identity or provide variety or challenge. In such cases, additional incentives must be present to elicit investment.

Feedback is a second factor that may affect the meaning of the task to the person. By *feedback*, we mean the evaluation of task performance: what is evaluated, how the evaluation is done, and what use is made of evaluation information. Few aspects of tasks and task performance have been studied more extensively, and it would be futile to attempt an exhaustive review of the literature at this point (see, for example, Henderson, 1980; Ivancevich & McMahon, 1982; Nadler, 1977, 1979). We suggest, however, that feedback essentially can serve three overlapping purposes, all of which affect meaning and personal investment.

First, feedback defines the task—what is expected of the performance and how performance on the task relates to other tasks and to overall goals of the organization and even of the wider society. If a task performance is not carefully evaluated, that may imply that it is unimportant—that it really makes no difference to others how or whether it is done.

Second, feedback defines the person's role in relationship to the task. In discussing feedback and evaluation, one first thinks of assessing a person's (or group's) productivity or effectiveness. Feedback also can communicate information about the person's competence and sense of worth and, related to this, the implied expectation that the person is or is not capable of playing a more or less independent role in performing the task. Communication of effectiveness might communicate such an expectation, but the style of the message, as well as its substance, might also be important. For example, regular and repeated external evaluation might suggest that the person cannot be trusted to work on his or her own (Chhokar & Wallin, 1984). Feedback that involves the person to the greatest degree is most likely to foster task personal incentives. For example, if it is possible to permit employees to set their own goals and then use performance appraisal as a means of helping them understand how and to what extent their selected goals are being reached, it is possible that the feedback will foster a task personal incentive orientation. However, if performance appraisal is conducted with little or no input from the people being appraised, it tends to serve a controlling function, and extrinsic incentives are likely to prevail. Also, if performance appraisal is designed in competitive terms, an ego personal incentive situation will be encouraged.

Third, feedback can serve as an important means for the work organization to define itself and to communicate this definition to *all* participants. Regular feedback to employees communicates values, and both the *what* and the *how* of the evaluations conducted are important. In terms of affecting the meaning a task has for a particular individual in an organization, the feedback can suggest what the person can expect to get out of working at a particular job for a particular company—what personal incentives can be effectively pursued. Thus, through the feedback process, the company can orient employees toward the pursuit of certain personal incentives in the work context.

It should be clear that the evaluation/feedback process in any task or within any organization may be a very powerful tool in determining the meaning of a job or task to the person. It can hardly be taken lightly if one is serious about positively affecting motivation and morale (see chapter 9).

Another variable identified by Hackman and Oldham (1980) as critical in determining the motivation a given job is likely to elicit is *autonomy*—the extent to which a person has freedom and independence in determining when and how to complete a job or task. Autonomy is important to people because it allows them to perceive success in completion of the job as a result of their own efforts and skills. With autonomy comes perceived ownership of the task and a willingness to accept responsibility for completing the task.

There is considerable evidence in the general motivational literature for the assumption that autonomy has important effects on motivation (e.g., Deci, 1975, 1980; Hackman & Oldham, 1980). More specifically, the evidence supports the hypothesis that increased autonomy leads to what we have called a task personal incentive orientation. However, reductions in autonomy are likely to make other incentives necessary and more effective. For example, in a tightly supervised situation, individuals are likely to respond to external control and clear, specific extrinsic rewards. More broadly, different styles of leadership (Yukl, 1981) will impart different meaning to the task. In particular, delegation of responsibility and sharing in decision making generally encourage development of a task personal incentive orientation, whereas autocratic leadership encourages an extrinsic rewards orientation.

Compensation, or pay, is often one of the first things people think of when considering motivational characteristics of a job. Of course, the rewards of a job are certainly broader and more diverse than financial remuneration. Indeed, that is a major point of our theory, and we suggest it directly in setting forth a variety of personal incentives that might be important. Compensation *is* important, however, and not just for certain individuals. There is every reason to believe that the type of compensation and the way it is administered is a most important factor in determining the meaning of a task to the person.

The whole matter of compensation is extremely complex and deserves the time and space of a whole book rather than just a brief notation in a chapter (see Lawler, 1971, 1977; Patten, 1977). Nevertheless, the point must be made that compensation is among the crucial variables to be considered in managing motivation. As we consider compensation, we have in mind not only wages but also benefits, so-called perks, bonuses, and the like—in effect, all factors that are *added to* the task for the more or less specific purpose of motivating people to do it. Moreover, it must be recognized that compensation has multiple functions in an organization. Therefore, we would caution against the simplistic assumption that extrinsic rewards merely serve as external controls—as a kind of bribery to get people to do what they ordinarily would not do. For example, extrinsic rewards often serve an important informational function. They can provide feedback on level of competence, social acceptance, personal achievement, in which case they might logically be assumed to encourage task and social personal incentive orientations.

In summary, we have suggested how various features of a task might affect the meanings that the task has for persons who are to perform it. Thus, we propose that the complementary factors of social expectation and task design are important elements in the situation which will affect personal investment. They do so by influencing the meaning of the task for the persons involved.

Information

The third factor of significance in determining the meaning of personal investment is *information*. Although information plays a role in all facets of meaning that lead to personal investment, its role is perhaps most relevant in regard to perceived options. For example, vocational information (or misinformation) likely plays an important role in determining the choices that are made in taking a path to achievement. Seemingly simple matters, such as setting forth the relationship between the skills needed to proceed along one or another career path, may change frustration to positive action. Individuals choose on the basis of perceived options, and these options are determined, in part, by the information available. Such information can be made available in a variety of ways: through formal or informal instruction, through literature, or through the visible examples of models.

The Sociocultural Context

Sociocultural factors also play a role in defining meaning and personal investment. Over the past several years, we have been especially interested in the cross-cultural variation in the meaning of work and achievement (see Maehr, 1974a, 1974b; Maehr & Nicholls, 1980). We have increasingly come to the conclusion that people in different cultures exhibit different work and achievement patterns simply because they understand work and achievement differently.

How cultures may create differential meanings for work and achievement is suggested in an analysis presented by Maehr and Nicholls (1980). Employing data gathered with the semantic differential (Osgood, Miron, & May, 1975), Maehr and Nicholls examined the concepts that were most closely associated with success and failure in four cultural groups: the United States, Iran, Japan and Thailand. Success and failure were found to have different meanings in the different countries. Moreover, these differences are such that they apparently relate in a significant way to the manner in which individuals are likely to pursue success and avoid failure. More broadly, they imply differences in achievement and work patterns. Thailand, for example, differs from the other groups in how success is associated with respect and tradition. There, success and, perhaps, work and achievement are situated in a traditional framework that is closely associated with recognition and the respect of others. Although courage is not associated with success in the United

States, it does relate to success in the other societies. The place of punishment is also interesting; although it is far from success and close to failure in Iran and Japan, it is not a salient feature in the definition of success and failure in the United States and Thailand. Possibly, this suggests that there is appreciable cross-cultural variation in the degree to which failure is associated with the overt negative evaluation of others. Of the four cultures, Iran most closely approximates the classical pattern of individualistic achievement. First, there was a tendency for the Iranian respondents to attribute success to themselves and to associate themselves with success but not with failure. Second, in Iran, *competition* is strongly identified with success, whereas in the United States and Japan, *cooperation* is associated with success. Curiously, all four cultures see both competition and cooperation as remote from failure, and a combination of the two as a possible contributor to success. It would be hazardous to interpret these results in a definitive fashion, but they do suggest how achievement meanings vary and how this variation might be significant in directing achievement patterns.

Complementary to this study are the results of a study reported by Triandis et al. (1972) that examined the perceived antecedents and consequences of success in four different cultures. Ability and effort were found to be important antecedents to success in the United States, Greece, and Japan, but not in India. The Indian perception of success seems to be constructed more along the lines of what is thought of as political success in the West, rather than in terms of the demonstration of excellence.

These interesting findings of cross-cultural variations in meanings regarding success and failure suggest, further, the importance of culture in determining meaning and, ultimately, personal investment. Such variations in meanings may lead to differential behavior patterns, and these behavior patterns may be differentially functional in terms of individual or societal goals. Thus, not all meanings are likely to be equally "good" in terms of achievement, progress, and growth. In a follow-up study to the Maehr and Nicholls (1980) analysis of the varied cultural meanings of success and failure, Fyans et al. (1983; see also chapter 8) launched an extensive cross-cultural analysis of the meaning of achievement in thirty different cultural groups. This more extensive research confirmed the earlier finding that considerable variability existed in the definition of success, failure, and achievement, but it also suggested a common measure that distinguished cultures in terms of their essential attitude toward achievement. This attitude was not unlike Weber's Protestant ethic. Those sociocultural groups that were strongly identified with this ethic stressed work, knowledge, and freedom and tended to play down family, tradition, and interpersonal concerns. Moreover, individuals in those societies seemed to be seeing *themselves* as an avenue toward success, rather than the family, the clan, or some other reference group. They seemed to be distancing themselves from traditional ways as well as from family and interpersonal ties.

Most obviously, sociocultural factors play a most important role in determining not only what is worthy of an individual's personal investment but also *how* the person should invest himself or herself by making certain behavioral options more salient and acceptable than others. To a significant extent, it is the person's social or cultural group that determines that a given area is an acceptable area in which to perform. Thus, a given sociocultural group may define a task as desirable, repulsive, or irrelevant. As implied earlier, the individual's culture thus appears to affect investment in achievement not only by defining what success or failure means but also by delineating *how* success should be pursued.

Age or Life Stage

Meaning and its various components are a product of cognitive development (Nicholls, 1984b). Although we are considering meaning and its components as they would likely be present in an adult, it should be obvious that such cognitive functioning is not present at birth. Indeed, during the early school years, a good deal of growth and differentiation occurs, ultimately resulting in the complex cognitive processes we assume to be operative in the adult we are describing. For example, a person's sense of competence is, first, a function of arriving at a perception of "self" that is different from "other." Moreover, whereas adults have rather clear conceptions of the nature of ability and competence, these ideas are not so clear in the mind of the child in the early elementary years (Nicholls, 1984b). In addition, the adolescent years involve increasing differentiation of personal incentive possibilities and an expanded potential for the definition of behavioral alternatives. We are choosing to pass over the growth in thinking that precedes the cognitive functioning associated with what we have labeled *meaning* in our theory of personal investment. Although such matters deserve scrutiny in their own right, the larger demands of this book require that we concentrate on another correlate of age that is likely important in affecting personal investment at different age levels. Focusing especially on the adult years, we call attention to the fact that, with age, adults are likely to experience or be participants in different situations or social contexts. More generally, the experiential world of adults changes over time in significant ways, and perceived options, sense of self, and personal incentives likely shift with these contextuual shifts. Therefore, changes in motivation and personal investment patterns are likely to vary with age.

Almost inevitably, in the course of growing older, people experience changes in status and roles (George, 1980; Kelly, 1982b). For example, a young woman may take on the role of mother, which may affect not only her job role but also that of her husband. Retirement also occasions a change in status and role that may affect a person's orientation toward work and career. Maehr and Kleiber (1981), for example, have suggested that older individuals not only are less likely to be concerned with success and failure in work and career but are more inclined toward personal goals of growth and self-actualization. In the early interviews that led to the more formal studies reported later in this volume, we asked individuals to define success and failure, to give us examples of success and failure in their lives, and to tell us about people they thought were or were not successful. It is perhaps not very surprising that their answers were as often associated with family (e.g., parenting) or community (e.g., serving as church organist) as with vocation or career. Of special interest at this juncture is that the definitions seemed to vary with age or with life stage. Apparently, meanings associated with various life contexts—including, particularly, those associated with work, home, and leisure—vary as people pass through various life stages. More generally, as an individual's life circumstances shift, so do meaning and personal investment.

Conclusion

This chapter has set forth the essential features of a theory of personal investment. Besides providing a synthesis and integration of the variety of proposed causes viewed in chapter 2, we have presented a certain perspective on issues of motivation. We hope that the usefulness of that perspective in examining the worlds of adults will become clear in subsequent chapters. We do not wish to limit the theory of personal investment to any particular age, stage, status, or culture; rather, the primary intent of this book is to consider adults and their personal investments, and to report research that amplifies, elaborates, and tests the validity of the structure reported here. Subsequent chapters will put this framework or perspective to the test in the real world by suggesting applications and interpretations.

4

Assessing Meaning and Personal Investment and Their Causes

A number of years ago, we concluded that very little was known about motivation in adulthood. We were only partially correct. Numerous studies employing adult subjects have been conducted, but a majority of these studies have involved college students in decidedly artificial situations. When these studies reached beyond the Halls of Ivy for subjects, they often dealt with adults in other kinds of controlled settings. Thus, there was no large body of research on "normal" adults across a variety of settings and throughout the life span. Currently, as the issue of industrial productivity has become salient, there has been increased concern with the study of motivation of adults in work settings (see, for example, Hackman & Suttle, 1977; Locke & Latham, 1984; Staw & Salancik, 1977; Steers & Porter, 1983). Yet our knowledge of adults and their personal investments is by no means complete. Previous research has provided only a partial picture of how motivational patterns may change with age, career stages, and significant life circumstances.

Because of such perceived limitations in available knowledge, we initiated a program of research concerned with motivation in adulthood. More specifically, we assumed that motivation must be studied in relationship to role and life station changes that are characteristically experienced by people as they move through the adult years.

As the first stage in this research, we adopted a theoretical viewpoint that would serve as an acceptable guide in beginning our search. The theoretical viewpoint with which we began was outlined in chapter 3, but several additional observations are appropriate at this point.

We initially tended to interpret adult behavior in terms of achievement theory. Achievement had been the dominating interest in much of our own previous research, and it has provided a lively and productive focus over the past several decades for researchers who were interested in motivational questions. It soon became clear, however, that this perspective was much too narrow. Achievement is not the only concern of adults; other concerns are of equal or greater concern both on and off the job. Indeed, leisure activities may rival involvement in work for most persons. Task and ego personal incentives do not predominate in people's lives; rather, a broad range of social incentives and values seem to be of greater importance (Kelly, 1982b; Kleiber, in press; Steinkamp & Kelly, 1985a, 1985b). Studying adults thus demands an openness to the broader realm of human motivation and to a wide array of incentives, goals, purposes, and motives.

Our initial work also indicated that we needed not only to broaden our focus but also to employ constructs that could take account of change in context and role. Motivation is not set for life; life circumstances appear to affect it in important and interesting ways. More specifically, it seemed that success, failure, joy, and happiness are defined differently at different stages within a person's life.

Finally, we examined the utility of current methods of studying motivation in adulthood (Maehr & Kleiber, 1981). We are often not able to study older adults in the same way that we have become accustomed to studying younger people in educational institutions. Coercing people to submit to testing and queries of various types and to formal observations with traditional psychological instruments is often inappropriate in assessing behavior in less controlled settings. Although standard testing procedures have an acceptable place in analyzing work motivation, they also have limitations.

Thus, our first thoughts in launching a study of adult motivation and development tended to focus on measurement, but not just on measurement as an isolated entity, divorced from theory. Throughout our work, the implications of theory for measurement, and vice versa, were always in the forefront. We had to become specific about the measurement procedures implied by our theory and about how the development of measurement procedures could not only specify but also enhance the theory. As we tried to assess personal incentives, for example, we essentially defined and redefined what personal incentives are. As we analyzed what we measured, we enlarged our conception of the nature of the phenomena we were measuring. In these chapters, we will report the results of an extensive study of motivation and personal investment. It is not our final word on the topic, however, because at this point, we can report only the first fruits of a continuing program of research. Two types of results are reported. In this chapter, we report our work devoted to developing acceptable methods for assessing motivation. In succeeding chapters, we report results obtained by using these instruments and relate these results to other work in the area of adult development and motivation.

Assessing Motivation in Adulthood

The Role of Assessment

There is a long history and considerable experience in assessing motivation in children in controlled settings such as schools. The history is not so long nor the experience so great in assessing motivation in adults in the world at large. The older the person, the less likely it is that appropriate assessment procedures are available for assessing motivational orientations. Thus, the first step in our research had to be the development of assessment procedures.

The motivational perspective outlined in chapter 3 opens up a host of new problems and possibilities. For the most part, the problems cannot be pursued nor the possibilities realized until procedures have been developed for assessing the critical facets inherent in our perspective. Theory and measurement should go hand in glove—and it is not always self-evident which is hand and which is glove in this otherwise appropriate metaphor. Throughout our development of the personal investment theory, our concern with questions of measurement has gone beyond the requirement that concepts be carefully defined to a requirement that they be defined *operationally*. That is, we have endeavored to define the critical constructs of the theory in such a way that they can be readily translated into measurement procedures. We considered it especially important to spell out procedures for dealing with complex, cognitive variables, such as meaning.

An Outline of the Measures Needed

In developing our theory of personal investment, we specified a number of measurement and assessment procedures. In broad outline, we assessed three classes of *variables:* (1) the behaviors that are specifically indicative of personal investment, (2) the meanings that are directly antecedent to these behaviors, and (3) the factors that create or influence these meanings. Before describing the specific procedures we have constructed, a summary word about the general assessment demands of the theory is in order.

Assessment of Personal Investment. First, we needed to assess variation in those behavioral patterns that are indicative of personal investment: choice, persistence, continuing motivation, intensity, and performance (see chapter 1). Various procedures have been employed in assessing these behavioral variables in research settings; the variations are almost as numerous as the motivational settings that might be designated. (See Ames & Ames, 1984; Feather, 1982; Kleiber & Maehr, in press; and Nicholls, 1984a, for a potpourri of examples). To illustrate, we can identify behaviors that can be assessed in a particular setting: secretarial staff performance. Table 4–1 presents a number of measures that can and often are made in such a setting and relates them to the more general and abstract categories of personal investment designated in chapter 1. Of course, the measures that are employed in a specific setting may embrace features of several categories, as is implied in table 4–1. When we refer to personal investment, we are referring to behaviors that not only are measurable but are, in fact, regularly measured—or at least observed and noted.

Table 4–1
Secretarial Behaviors that Illustrate the Nature and Level of Personal Investment

General Categories	Illustrative Examples
Choice	Absenteeism
Persistence	Length of Service
Continuing motivation	Voluntary participation in skill upgrading programs
	Taking work home on occasion
Activity level	Pages typed
Performance	Overall performance rating by superior

Assessment of Contexts. Besides assessing the behaviors that constitute personal investment and the meanings that mediate these behaviors, it is also crucial to assess qualities of contexts that may influence personal investment. Personal investment is influenced by certain meanings that people hold, and these meanings, in turn, are partially determined by the nature of the situations in which people find themselves. The measurement problem is twofold: (1) to determine whether a given context is likely to encourage the participants to hold certain meanings, and (2) to determine whether the environment is compatible with the enduring meanings held by the participants. These problems are certainly interrelated, and it may be that an environment that fosters certain meanings is also one that is compatible with people who characteristically hold such meanings. However, these related assessment problems may suggest slightly different assessment approaches.

In chapter 3, we outlined a set of contextual factors that lead individuals working in particular environments to hold certain personal incentives. In a controlled setting, one can conveniently establish the relevant variables in such a way that these personal incentives are likely to emerge. For certain purposes, however, it may be of interest to assess whether or not conditions conducive to the emergence of one or another personal incentive exist. For example, suppose that a supervisor finds out that in one department, the absentee rate is clearly higher than in all others, productivity is low, and interest in upgrading skills is nonexistent. The first and most natural consideration in this regard is the work climate—what it is like in this department and how it is different from other departments. Although the supervisor might generally sense that something is wrong, this usually does not suffice; it is necessary to confirm and specify such general impressions. This requires procedures that enable one to analyze the existing work climate. Is the work organized and supervised to discourage a task orientation? Do the incentives available on the job simply not match the personal incentives brought to the job by the people who are hired? Does the situation foster conflict?

Clearly, it is necessary to identify and assess features of the setting that may affect meaning and personal investment in such situations. From what has already been indicated, at least two different but complementary perspectives can guide the assessment of contexts. First, we can assess the degree to which any given contextual variable is present and draw conclusions about the likely impact on personal incentives. The Job Diagnosis Survey developed by Hackman and Oldham (1980) is a procedure that can be used to determine whether the task as designed is likely to be motivating in and of itself—that is, in our terms, to examine the performance context in terms of whether it encourages the emergence or maintenance of task incentives. This procedure can be built upon to identify contextual factors associated with personal incentives.

A second strategy in considering the effects of context on personal investment concerns the question of the match between the person and the context. Thus, if competition is a salient feature of a given context, people who come to the situation with a competitive orientation are likely to be more productive and, generally, more positively disposed to the situation. The assumption, of course, is that it is the interaction of the person with the situation that is critical. This perspective goes beyond the assessment of contexts *per se* to the complementary and simultaneous assessment of person and situation.

Later, we will describe a procedure that employs both of these perspectives in providing an assessment of the likelihood that people will be personally invested in their work. For now, we are simply illustrating the type of measurement that is anticipated in the theory of personal investment.

Assessment of Personal Incentives. As indicated earlier, individuals hold certain personal incentives, have a certain sense of self, and perceive certain options as available to them in a given situation. How might these be assessed?

At least two kinds of assessment problems were posed by our theory: (1) the problem of assessing current meanings that arise in specific situations, and (2) the problem of assessing relatively enduring meanings that a person may bring to a situation—meanings that exist more or less as personality traits. In our theory, meanings held by individuals operate as both state and trait variables: although people may characteristically hold a certain set of personal incentives, situational factors may change the precise meanings held at any given moment. Thus, research instruments sensitive to meaning variations in both instances are needed. But what kind of procedures might be applicable here?

The variety of available approaches break down into two overlapping types. One type of approach is geared to reflecting the reality as the person conceives, construes, and constructs it; that is, it is more or less phenomenological. Parallel to this approach are various format possibilities, ranging from unstructured interviews (Braskamp, Fowler, & Ory, 1984; Duda, 1980, 1981) through innovative structured queries via an interview or a questionnaire (Steinkamp & Kelly, 1985a, 1985b) to the more psychometric inventory (Farmer, Maehr, & Rooney, 1980). There are, as yet, no clear guidelines that any single procedure is best; a multimethod approach is advised. Moreover, it is not clear that any one method is better in the analysis of states rather than traits. It does appear, however, that in the development of trait measures for general usage, standard psychometric formats and procedures serve quite well.

All the approaches to measurement briefly reviewed here were pursued to develop a complete understanding of why individuals invest their time and talent in one but not another way. In the remainder of this chapter, we focus on the development of two specific instruments: (1) the Inventory of Personal Investment (IPI), a trait measure of meanings associated with personal investment; and (2) the Inventory of Work Investment (IWI), an ominbus measure of situational factors, meanings, and personal investment in work settings. These instruments reflect our primary measurement interests of the moment. More to the point, the results presented in the subsequent chapters are based largely on these two instruments. Finally, it may be noted that, collectively, these measures illustrate how many of the assessment problems created by the theory can be solved.

The Inventory of Personal Investment

Background and Purpose

The Inventory of Personal Investment (IPI) is designed to assess meanings individuals might bring to any given situation that could affect personal investment. More specifically, it is designed to assess two categories of meaning: personal incentives and sense of self. In chapter 3, we discussed the hypothesis that an individual brings certain meanings to each situation and that these meanings are likely to affect the initial choice to participate in the situation and the early reactions to what is confronted in the situation. Moreover, since we hypothesized that personal investment is significantly determined by the *match* between what a person brings to or looks for in the situation and what the situation provides, it is clearly important to assess such personal meaning biases.

The IPI represents a first attempt at assessing two meaning systems that may play a major role in predicting personal investment in a range of activities. It is a measure of personality, in that it assesses individual differences in meanings held by people and relates them to behavior across a broad range of situations. Of the three meaning components defined in chapter 3, it is assumed that the perception of options (e.g., job opportunities) is most situationally based. Personal incentives and sense of self were assumed to have a more trans-situational quality. Accordingly, these are the facets of meaning that are included in the IPI. Because the IPI grew out of the theoretical framework outlined in chapter 3, the nature and definition of meaning set forth there formed the approach to defining content areas to be covered and procedures to be employed.

Format and Structure

In format and structure, the IPI is not an unusual instrument. It employs formats similar to those commonly employed by attitude, interest, preference, and personality tests. Although earlier work on the assessment of meaning associated with behavioral patterns involved considerable experimentation with item format and structure, most items in the IPI are reduced to a Likert-type format. The reasons for this are varied, but the result has been enhancement of the utility of the instrument and improvement of the psychometric properties.

Item Development

The initial item set was based on extensive interviews with a wide variety of adults working in a broad range of settings. Over the course of several years, we interviewed several hundred individuals about situations in which they had experienced failure or success, had felt good about themselves, and had felt proud about and satisfied with something they had experienced. In these interviews, we made a point of homing in on what had led to these experiences, feelings, and thoughts. After organizing, categorizing, and reflecting on the responses we received in these interviews, we proceeded to construct a series of standardized questions that could be easily administered and tabulated. In addition, we dug into our files and considered items that had proved useful in our research and that of others, adapting as seemed appropriate. In other words, the initial set of items was the product of extensive observation of the nature and nurture of motivation and personal investment. The preliminary item set contained well over 500 items; we disposed of 300 items through ratings and analyses by our staff.

Initial Item Administration

Once we had developed a comprehensive set of items, we administered them to a heterogeneous sample of adults, as described in table 4–2. This was not a random sample of adults residing in the United States. Rather, we made a specific effort to select individuals who would be representative of a broad assortment of vocational and professional types. As can be seen in table 4–2, the sample was reasonably broad and heterogeneous, consisting of over 700 adults, largely middle-class and middle-aged, who were engaged primarily in white-collar and professional occupations.

Table 4–2
Classification of Individuals Taking the IPI

Occupational Category	Number	Percentage
Academics		
College/university professors	210	28.2
College/university administrators	30	4.0
Educators		
Elementary and secondary teachers	83	11.2
Mercantilists		
Attorneys, physicians, clergy, etc.	21	2.8
Middle management	117	15.7
Sales	7	0.9
Executives	11	1.5
Owners of small firms	8	1.1
Bureaucrats	84	11.3
Clerks	80	10.8
Other		
College/university students	79	10.6
Homemakers	13	1.7
Retired	1	0.1
Total	744	99.9[a]

[a]Percentages total less than 100% because of rounding.

Following the administration, we conducted a series of item and factor analyses. The results of these analyses yielded a factor structure somewhat more elaborate than the one we outlined in chapter 3. Eight of these factors may be appropriately labeled personal incentives and three are sense-of-self factors. Table 4–3 contains brief descriptions of the factors, and table 4–4 contains a more technical description of the statistical results.

The eight factors associated with personal incentives are relatively independent. The average mean score is above 3 (the middle point of the 5-point scale used in the IPI) for all scales except Financial. The variability of the responses for each scale is also quite similar (standard deviations range from .46 to .70), and the internal consistency (reliability of the scales as measured by the coefficient alpha) is acceptable for scales of this type.

The eight personal incentive factors are essentially derivable from the four broad categories originally proposed in chapter 3, as suggested in the classification scheme presented in table 4–5. If we use correlations among scales to indicate associations among scales, we can conclude that the correlations are highest between the two scales classified into each of the four classes identified in table 4–5. That is, although the scales are relatively independent, they are most closely related if they are part of the dyad classified within one of the four major areas. This is most readily defensible in the case of Task (TA) and Excellence (EX) incentives.

Table 4–3
Description of Inventory of Personal Investment Factors

Personal Incentives

Task Involvement (TA)
People are totally involved in what they are doing. They regard the work as exciting and fun, and they enjoy adventure and novelty. To them, successful people like challenges and like to solve problems. They feel satisfied and positive about themselves when they accomplish something others could not do, when they understand something for the first time, and when they are responsible for their accomplishments.

Striving for Excellence (EX)
People continually think of ways to improve themselves, spend long hours of work to do a good job, like to compete against themselves, do not mind working when others are having fun, and enjoy trying to solve problems others consider impossible. They value work and take pride in their work.

Competition (CO)
People gain satisfaction and feel positive about themselves when they win. They consider that successful people are competitive, work hard for promotions and money, and like to win. They do not feel bad when they beat someone in competition, and they are not afraid of competition even if it is strong. They do not have the need to be popular, and they are able to look out for their own interests.

Power (PW)
People seek out and enjoy positions of leadership and authority. They view themselves as alert and are confident in working with others. They trust their intuitions in making judgments and are sought out for advice. They do not like to be bound by other people, things, or events but strive, instead, for positions in which they can be in control.

Affiliation (AF)
People like to be in the company of friends and enjoy helping others even if it means sacrificing personal gains. They are friendly, trusting of others, and able to show warm affection to their friends.

Social Concern (SC)
People gain satisfaction by sacrificing personal gains for others, committing themselves to social and civic causes, and demonstrating religious commitment.

Financial Rewards (FN)
People value money, watch their financial status carefully, and seek out positions that allow them to receive bonuses and additional income from their work. They regard financial status as an indicator of success and state that monetary rewards motivate them to do their best and to work harder.

Recognition for Accomplishment (RC)
People want recognition for what they do and work harder when they receive recognition. They work hard so that they can receive respect from their co-workers, and they do their best work when others encourage them and tell them they did well.

Sense of Self

Goal-Directedness (GD)
People are ambitious self-starters, with definite and difficult goals in mind. They delay immediate rewards for future payoffs and strive for new goals once previously set goals are met.

Self-Reliance (SR)
People enjoy working on tasks that are open-ended, difficult, and challenging. They can work by themselves on difficult projects and do not become anxious if they do not know how well they are doing.

Competence (COMP)
People have considerable self-confidence and recover quickly from failures and defeat. They feel that they can succeed and view themselves as self-made people.

Table 4–4
Intercorrelations and Reliabilities of IPI Scales

	Task	Excellence	Competition	Power	Affiliation	Social Concern	Recognition	Financial	Goal-Directedness	Self-Reliance	Competence
Task		.39	.40	.25	.16	.20	.37	.12	.22	.11	.22
Excellence			.30	.41	.17	.13	.22	.12	.52	.24	.39
Competition				.37	.20	.03	.33	.28	.46	.22	.45
Power					.05	.05	.36	.44	.32	.07	.22
Affiliation						.35	.31	−.02	.18	−.05	.17
Social Concern							.13	−.03	.21	−.05	.14
Recognition								.41	.13	−.19	.08
Financial									.19	.04	.17
Goal-Directedness										.34	.44
Self-Reliance											.28
Competence											
Reliability	.82	.68	.75	.80	.65	.68	.78	.81	.72	.79	.62

Table 4–5
Theoretical Classification of IPI Factors

Personal incentive categories, original designation	Task	Ego	Social	Extrinsic
IPI personal incentive factors	Task Excellence	Competition Power	Affiliation Social Concern	Financial Recognition
Relationship to possible intrinsic/extrinsic reward continuum	Intrinsic Rewards			Extrinsic Rewards

In chapter 3, we suggested that task personal incentives are of two types, much along the lines that have emerged in this analysis. More generally, we can conclude that the factor analysis primarily yields a specification and further definition and delineation of the more general scheme set forth in chapter 3. This is partly attributable to a possible bias in selecting an initial item set, even though a concerted attempt was made to include a broad range of items. In general, the factor analysis results in an interpretable set of factors to be associated with personal investment. It is a good start at identifying a reliable and valid set of scales capable of predicting personal investment in a diverse range of settings.

Three factors emerge in relationship to self. These factors were essentially anticipated in chapter 3, and we have labeled them in accord with the categories designated there. Note, however, that no group identity factor was obtained. Reference group is probably too idiosyncratic to be assessed readily in general terms, as was necessitated by the format chosen for this instrument.

Conclusion

Our efforts in developing a measure of personal incentives and sense of self have not gone unrewarded. The utility of this measure will become increasingly evident in subsequent chapters. However, in concluding the story of the development of this instrument, it is well to remind ourselves of several issues that are critical to the development of a theory of personal investment.

First, it should be stressed again that meanings can and do vary with situations. However, they also can and do remain constant as situations remain similar. Thus, the IPI's predictive value rests largely on the fact that it focuses on work or achievement settings. In this regard, the preliminary IPI findings relative to salient goal structures are of special interest. Previous research had indicated the utility of four general categories (cf. chapter 3). Results obtained in developing the IPI indicate that it is by no means appropriate to limit our thinking to those four goals.

The Inventory of Work Investment

Background and Purpose

The Inventory of Work Investment (IWI) is an omnibus measure designed to assess not only personal incentives and sense of self but also options that the person may perceive to be available in work contexts. Thus, the IWI attempts to assess all components of meanings that may be associated with personal investment. The IWI also obtains information on employee views of the work climate, satisfaction with the job, and commitment to the work organization. With qualification, satisfaction and commitment may be taken as indicative of personal investment in the work context.

The IWI is designed to provide a comprehensive analysis of personal investment, but in a very specific context—the context of one's particular job. The 32 dimensions assessed by the IWI are outlined in table 4–6 and organized there in terms of the major components of the theory. The sample on which the analyses of the IWI were based is described in tables 4–7 and 4–8. Generally, the sample represents a wide range of work organizations; within each organization, a broadly representative sample of employees completed the questionnaire. Thus, we can have some confidence in the reliability and generalizability of these preliminary results with the IWI.

Meanings Associated with Personal Investment

Personal Incentives and Self-Judgment. As noted earlier, the IWI assesses the three major components of meaning associated with personal investment. Personal incentives and sense of self are assessed with items selected from the IPI. In effect, the IWI is a shortened and more refined version of the IPI, incorporating the items that are most representative of the eight IPI factors. Items included in each of the eight scales measuring personal incentives are presented in table 4–9, and items of the three sense-of-self scales are presented in table 4–10.

Perceived Options. Two scales were designed to elicit judgments regarding the options a person perceives in his or her job, career, and work organization. One scale, marketability, deals primarily with a sense of general career options; the other scale, organizational advancement, deals with the sense that the person has options within his or her current organization. Examples of items employed in the IWI to assess marketability and organizational advancement are presented in table 4–11.

Contexts Associated with Personal Investment

Job Opportunities. The IWI assesses the organizational context through the perceptions of the participants. When the sum of the perceptions of employees

Table 4–6
Dimensions Measured by the Inventory of Work Investment (IWI)

IWI Scale	Meanings			Contexts		Personal Investment	
	Personal Incentives	*Sense of Self*	*Perceived Options*	*Job Opportunities*	*Organizational Culture*	*Job Satisfaction*	*Organizational Commitment*
Task							
Involvement	X			X	X	X	
Excellence	X			X			
Ego							
Power	X			X	X	X	
Compete	X			X			
Social							
Concern	X			X	X	X	
Affiliation	X			X			
External Rewards							
Financial	X			X	X	X	
Recognition	X			X			
Goal-Directedness		X					
Self-Reliance		X					
Sense of Competence		X					
Marketability			X				
Organizational Advancement			X				
Saliency					X		
General							X

Table 4–7
Organizations in the IWI Sample

Type of Organization	Location of Corporate Headquarters	Number
Regional airline	West, small city	77
Professional trade association	Midwest, large city	35
Health care center	Midwest, small city	79
Manufacturing plant	Midwest, small city	25
Fast-food chain	East, large city	42
Consulting company	Midwest, large city	52
Other	Mostly Midwest	38

relative to a particular job or work situation is computed, it may be assumed that this provides a global but realistic view of a particular job category or work situation in an organization. We hypothesize that these *perceptions* of the contexts are the immediate determinants of behavior. External features of the situation doubtless affect perceptions, but in the final analysis, the perceptions individuals hold is that which leads to specific behavioral responses.

Table 4–8
IWI Respondents Classified by Organizational Unit in Six Organizations

Organizational Unit	Number
Manufacturing	
Executives	10
Middle management	15
Airline	
Executives	9
Pilots	25
Mechanics	13
Service	30
Health care center	
Executives	7
Middle management	11
Department heads	17
Supervisors	20
Nursing coordinators	24
Professional trade association	
Executives	8
Middle management	27
Consulting company	
Executives	9
Program development, marketing research	19
Domestic sales	24
Fast-food chain	
Executives	3
Middle management	32

Table 4–9
Examples of IWI Items Used to Assess Each of the Eight Personal Incentives

Personal Incentives	Examples
Task	Were totally involved in what you were doing. Like a challenge.
Excellence	I am always thinking of ways to improve how I do things. I put in long hours of work just to do a good job.
Competition	Winning is important to me. I need to be number one.
Power	I seek out positions of authority. People seek me out for advice.
Affiliation	I try to be in the company of friends as much as possible. I work harder as part of a team.
Social Concern	I enjoy helping others even if I have to make some sacrifices. Showed acts of charity toward others.
Recognition	Having other people tell me that I did well is important to me. Received recognition/prestige.
Financial Rewards	I am happiest when I am making money. One of the best indicators of success is acquiring wealth and possessions.

Table 4–10
Examples of IWI Items Used to Assess the Three Sense-of-Self Factors

Factors	Examples
Goal-Directedness	I have my long-range goals clearly in mind. When I reach an important goal, I immediately strive for higher goals.
Self-Reliance	Tasks that I must do by myself are frightening to me. I get anxious when I don't know how well I'm doing.
Sense of Competence	I can succeed at anything I want to do. I bounce back quickly from defeat.

Table 4–11
Descriptions of Marketability and Organizational Advancement Scales and Sample Items

Descriptions	Sample Items
Marketability: Extent to which employees perceive that they can find good alternative jobs or career opportunities and feel positive about their future	I have said "no" to other job opportunities in recent months. It would take very little for me to move to another organization. I feel that I could get another job if I wanted to.
Organizational Advancement: Extent to which employees feel that they can advance in the organization and are not stuck in their current jobs	I feel that I am in a "dead-end" position in this organization. This organization provides me with opportunities for advancement. If one doesn't know the right people in this organization, one does not advance.

In the IWI, we developed a method of assessing context in terms of the four broad personal investment categories identified in our earlier research with the IPI. With the job opportunities scales we can assess whether the work or job itself contains features that are likely to make possible the pursuit of certain personal incentives. This allows us to ask an interesting set of questions. We can determine that certain incentives are an inherent part of certain jobs, and we can consider how people who focus on one or another personal incentive respond to these jobs. Thus, we can identify person–job incentive matches and mismatches and observe their effects. In other words, we can consider how the opportunity to pursue valued personal incentives affects personal investment.

Table 4–12 presents descriptions and sample items for each of the eight job opportunities scales, and table 4–13 presents the correlations among these scales. The scales are not highly correlated; that is, people were able to differentiate their jobs in terms of the extent to which the jobs give them a chance to pursue certain ends. Table 4–13 also contains the reliability coefficients. Note that the scales have acceptable levels of internal consistency.

Table 4–12
Descriptions of Job Opportunities Scales and Sample Items

Descriptions	Sample Items
Task: Can work on challenging and interesting tasks and projects and do meaningful work	To work on new tasks, projects, or activities. To solve work-related problems.
Excellence: Can improve their own skills and talents and be proud of their work	To feel responsible for a finished task or assignment. To redo a task to make it better.
Competition: Can compete for extra benefits and get ahead of others	To compete for bonuses, prizes, or cash. To feel good because I beat my competition.
Power: Can have leadership responsibility and receive status and respect from work assignments	To be given leadership responsibility for a task or project. To increase my influence over others.
Affiliation: Can feel needed, receive encouragement from others, and establish a loyalty to others	To feel wanted and needed by others at work. To work closely with one or more co-workers.
Social Concern: Can contribute to welfare of society from work and help others develop and grow	To watch others grow and develop. To see others benefit from my assistance.
Recognition: Can receive public and private recognition of good work	To get public recognition for a job well done. To earn respect from my friends because of my work.
Financial: Can earn promotions, good wages, and extra benefits by doing good work	To receive very good wages. To work on a commission basis.

Table 4–13
Reliabilities and Correlations among the Eight Job Opportunities Scales

	Task	Excellence	Competition	Power	Affiliation	Social Concern	Recognition	Financial
Task		.76	.52	.55	.58	.64	.60	.42
Excellence			.56	.50	.68	.66	.62	.41
Competition				.67	.50	.50	.59	.63
Power					.55	.61	.53	.49
Affiliation						.71	.58	.42
Social Concern							.59	.41
Recognition								.58
Financial								
Reliability	.82	.78	.70	.82	.74	.75	.76	.62

Organizational Culture. Closely related to the assessment of job opportunities is the assessment of the organizational culture or climate. Indeed, these two facets seem almost inseparable. In describing the assessment of work contexts, we refer specifically to the task a person performs and to his or her perception of the job as a means to pursuing certain desired ends. Organizational culture refers to the wider context in which that job is performed. Organizational culture is likewise assessed in terms of the four major personal incentive categories, in conformity with the conceptual framework of personal investment theory.

We also developed a scale to determine the degree to which the organizational culture is salient to the employee. Peters and Waterman (1982), for example, called attention to the importance of the clarity and saliency of the culture of the organization to the employee. Presumably, "excellent" companies are characterized by the fact that their employees not only know what the company stands for but also sense that there is an appropriate modus operandi. Examples employed in the assessment of the content and saliency of organizational culture are presented in tables 4–14 and 4–15.

The reliabilities and correlations among the four organizational culture and saliency of culture scales are shown in table 4–16. Three of the four organizational culture scales cluster together, but the ego scale is quite independent of the other three. Thus, people who perceived the organization as emphasizing task involvement also perceived the work environment as high in social solidarity and external rewards. In addition, these three scales as a group seem to emerge as the key determinants of the saliency of the culture.

Personal Investment in Work

Finally, the IWI provides an indication of the degree to which the person is invested in the work setting by assessing job satisfaction and commitment to

Table 4-14
Descriptions of the Four Organizational Culture Scales and Sample Items

Descriptions	*Sample Items*
Task: Emphasis on excellence, doing the job right, trying new things, improving productivity	Around here we are encouraged to try new things. Management expects us to be good, productive workers.
Ego: Emphasis on competition, contests among organizational units encouraged, conflict not to be avoided, overt recognition that there are powerful people in the organization	This organization establishes contests in which we compete for extra benefits. People spend a lot of time trying to know those who are in power.
Social: Emphasis on a family feeling among the members, caring for and respecting each person as an adult, participation of all workers in decision making	People have little trust in each other in this organization. In this organization, they really care about me as a person.
External Rewards: Emphasis on giving each person attention, reinforcement, recognition, salary bonuses, and feedback about work	People here are always getting awards and extra benefits by doing good work. There are many incentives here to work hard.

the work organization. Given our behavioral definition of personal investment, these two dimensions are not primary indicators of personal investment in a vocation or profession; in a work setting productivity, absenteeism, and dropout rates would probably better reflect personal investment. However, these two scales not only are of interest to the researcher but also are currently considered important to the manager and executive. They are used not to replace productivity measures but to complement them.

Table 4-15
Description of the Organizational Saliency of Culture Scale and Sample Items

Description	*Sample Items*
Saliency of Culture: Extent to which members of the organizational unit view the organization as having a clear direction and a set of expectations, policies, and values that are clearly communicated to the members of the organization	This organization is clear about what it expects from me as an employee. I know what this organization stresses. I know what really counts around here. Everyone in this organization knows what we value the most.

Table 4–16
Reliabilities and Correlations among the Four Organizational Culture Scales and the Saliency of Culture Scale

	Task	Ego	Social	External Rewards	Saliency
Task		0	.82	.76	.65
Ego			− .07	.07	− .12
Social				.81	.67
External Rewards					.62
Saliency					
Reliability	.80	.51	.85	.87	.82

Table 4–17 presents definitions and examples of items employed to assess job satisfaction, and table 4–18 presents examples of items used to assess organizational commitment. The internal reliability of each of the four job satisfaction scales and the correlations among them are presented in table 4–19. The correlations among the four scales are all positive but not high. The lowest correlation is between worker satisfaction associated with the task and the external rewards received from their efforts on the job. This pattern of relationships is similar to those obtained for the job incentive scales; that is, workers can readily distinguish the tangible external rewards, such as money, from the social and interpersonal aspects of the job.

Table 4–17
Descriptions of the Four Job Satisfaction Scales and Sample Items

Descriptions	Sample Items
Task: Worker does what he or she likes to do, enjoys the work itself	I am tired of my work. I like what I am doing so I don't think of anything else.
Ego: Worker enjoys directing others and is able to advance by working hard	There is little chance to compete with others to get ahead. I have good opportunities to direct others.
Social Solidarity: Worker enjoys working for supervisor and with co-workers	My co-workers and I work well together. I enjoy working for my supervisor.
External Rewards: Worker thinks he or she is receiving fair pay for work performed	I get rewarded in a fair way for the work I do. I feel I should be paid more for the work I do.

Table 4–18
Description of the Organizational Commitment Scale and Sample Items

Description	Sample Items
Organizational Commitment: Extent to which employees have a loyalty to, identify with, and feel a part of the organization and work to make it a successful organization	I have a sense of loyalty to the organization.
	I identify with this organization.
	It would take very little for me to move to another organization.
	I feel a sense of ownership in this organization.

Conclusion

The construction and preliminary testing of the IWI represents an important stage in our efforts to develop scales and instruments that operationally define and assess the critical components of our theory. The practical value of all this may be even more telling. The IWI is an instrument that can be conveniently employed in the organizational setting as a diagnostic tool. More specifically, as we will illustrate at length in subsequent chapters, the IWI can be employed to provide a variety of data on both the nature and the causes of employees' personal investment in their work. Essentially, it provides a comprehensive assessment of how the participants see themselves in relationship to their jobs and their work organization. It also indicates their level of commitment and job satisfaction and the general perception of the company for which they work.

An Interpretive Summary

Throughout the previous chapters, it has been at least implicit that the theoretical constructs to be employed in this analysis of motivation must be operationalized. One must assess what one believes to be crucial in defining

Table 4–19
Reliabilities and Correlations among the Four Job Satisfaction Scales

	Task	Ego	Social Solidarity	External Rewards	Total
Task		.32	.36	.25	.71
Ego			.36	.42	.74
Social Solidarity				.29	.67
External Rewards					.71
Reliability	.64	.65	.66	.61	.80

and explaining human behavior. In this chapter, we have described how we have followed that principle in practice. Our primary research goal in this regard was to demonstrate very specifically what we mean by each of the concepts that are basic to the theory of personal investment. In the course of doing this, we were forced to reconstruct our definitions slightly. Perhaps it is more accurate to say that only as we developed assessment procedures did we begin to understand what we were trying to say.

In this chapter, we have described the first fruits of our efforts, making more evident what we had in mind in chapter 3 as we set forth the first outlines of a theory of personal investment. But we think we have done more than that. We think that we have also set ourselves on a path that will present interesting new data for the analysis of workers and work organizations. Although the first fruits of our efforts relate, first, to the world of work, we wish to stress that we see these efforts as contributing to an understanding of personal investment in life generally. The world of work is, indeed, our focus in this book, but we admit to an ultimate goal of constructing a theory that is broadly relevant to the understanding of human motivation.

5
Meaning and Personal Investment: An Exploration of Relationships in Field Settings

H aving identified a set of concepts that appear to have some value in the specification and analysis of personal investment is no small achievement—or so we would immodestly suggest. In chapters 3 and 4, we discussed a set of tools for describing the nature and origins of personal investment. A next step is logical enough: to describe people under varying conditions and contexts with a specific view to testing the utility of the theory. Our question, first, is whether or not the conceptual and methodological tools we have developed are useful in understanding the behavior of adults in everyday circumstances. We will concern ourselves especially with the world of work: Why do some people invest themselves in their work and why do others not do so? Can the understandings and procedures we have outlined thus far provide a basis for understanding the motivation of people at work?

In chapter 3, we established a basic model for understanding the nature and causes of personal investment. In brief, that model implied a two-stage causal process: (1) certain factors external to the individual affect the meaning of a particular situation to the person, and (2) this meaning, in turn, leads to a certain pattern of personal investment. That general causal flow of events was outlined in figure 3–3. In chapter 4, we provided additional specification of the variables that are critical to this flow of events, and we outlined procedures for assessing important facets of meaning and procedures for identifying variation in personal investment. We also explored ways in which one might assess the varying presence or importance of certain external factors that affect meaning, particularly in job settings.

The focus of this chapter is how the cognitions we have labeled *meaning* are associated with personal investment, as suggested in figure 5–1. In the course of establishing the reliability, validity, and general usefulness of such measures as the IPI and the IWI, we also gathered extensive data on the nature and causes of meaning and personal investment. We already had a fairly firm idea of such causes and effects on the basis of previous research (chapter 3), but the research reported in chapter 4 expanded our thoughts and made us

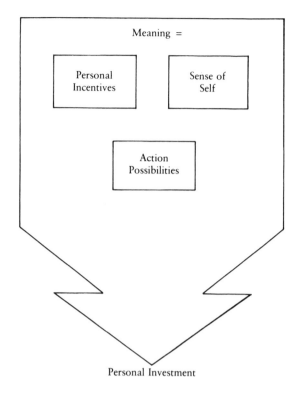

Figure 5–1. Pictorial Representation of the Focal Hypothesis of Chapter 5

aware of their wider applicability. In experimenting with the assessment of meaning, for example, we not only came to understand more about the incentives that guide people's lives but also found relationships with behavior that were obviously important; that is, we found that people who hold different personal incentives in fact lead different kinds of lives. To be sure, the theory predicted that finding in general ways. But in examining, more specifically, how meanings were associated with different patterns of living, something special was added. Not only could we now make predictions that might be useful to those who hire (or fire), but somehow the theory was becoming a theory of people in everyday life settings.

In this chapter, we limit ourselves to examining the relationship of meaning to various behavioral patterns indicative of personal investment. We will begin by reporting our study of high achievers. There are many reasons for considering people who excel—including the fact that such individuals fascinate most of us. By comparing people who excel with people in general, we are contrasting differing levels of personal investment. If meaning is, in fact, a major cause of personal investment, we should find that high and average achievers hold different achievement-related meanings regarding work. Moreover, the nature of these differences should prove interesting in their own right.

We will focus, second, on how people who hold different jobs or pursue different careers hold different meanings. Again, such an analysis has general interest value as well as utility. It also provides a further test of our theory and extends its applicability.

Finally, we will examine extensively how employees in a diverse array of work organizations invest themselves in their work as a possible function of the meanings they hold. In this case, the indicators of personal investment are measures of job satisfaction and commitment to the work organization.

Characteristics of People Who Excel

Few topics are of greater interest than "what it takes to make it to the top." Industrial and personnel psychologists regularly consider this issue, and such notable publications as the *Wall Street Journal* regularly publish their findings or opinions. Of course, there is interest not only in who excels in the world of business but also in excellence generally: What kinds of people become world-class musicians, athletes, and scientists? Probably, most people believe that there is something motivationally special about those who make it to the top, and it is often assumed that this special motivational quality is the prerequisite to excellence in all areas of human endeavor. This led us rather naturally to ask not only how certain personal meanings may be associated with career choices, job satisfaction, and commitments but also whether those who excel are characterized by a certain meaning profile. Is it possible that those who excel have a special, perhaps unique, personal incentive profile? Do they possess a different sense of self? Do they perceive their options differently? The immediately following line of questioning concerns whether these characteristic meanings held by the person are, in fact, necessary antecedents to excelling, regardless of vocational area.

Previous research has suggested that certain motivational characteristics are, indeed, critical components of outstanding achievement. Making it to the top in almost any area of endeavor possibly does require certain motivational characteristics. In an early study of outstanding scientists, Ann Roe (1953) emphasized precisely this point, and follow-up work (Maehr, 1983) has also stressed this possibility. Moreover, in Terman's (1954) study of gifted people, it became clear early on that outstanding achievement was associated not only with ability but also with certain motivational characteristics.

This general conclusion was again reached in Benjamin Bloom's (1982a, 1982b) recent research on world-class performers in a wide range of areas. In all cases, it was generally something called "motivation" that distinguished those who managed to excel. Ability and opportunity were certainly necessary components, but they were not sufficient. There was something motivationally special about world-class athletes, pianists, and outstanding artists, scientists, and mathematicians. To our knowledge, Bloom has not yet specified the special motivational component, nor has anyone else. One might have hoped that people who excel were all found to be high in achievement motivation, but—at least as it is defined by McClelland (1961, 1985a; see also chapter 2)—achievement motivation is not the exclusive nor the primary motivational orientation of high achievers in all areas. Rather, it best describes entrepreneurs.

Is there really something motivationally special about people who excel? If so, what is it? Does it perhaps take different kinds of motivation to excel in different areas? In terms of the theoretical framework of this book: Are high achievers characterized by unique meaning profiles? Do they have a characteristic personal incentive profile? Do they view themselves in special ways? Do they possibly also perceive their options differently? And, finally, is it possible that these meanings are antecedents or causes of different personal investment patterns of high achievers?

Preliminary Interviews with High Achievers

Before we attempted to develop our psychometric procedures for assessing meanings, we spent considerable time and effort interviewing individuals about their goals, incentives, feelings about themselves, and attitudes toward life and work. We wanted to get a "hands-on" idea of how people thought before we imposed our thoughts on them in the form of a standardized query. For these interviews, we systematically sought out individuals whom our staff had identified as high achievers in a broad range of career areas. Although we conducted these interviews to learn of the experiences of high achievers rather directly before doing more controlled research, we also learned some things that seem now, in retrospect, to have lasting validity.

One conclusion that could be reached through these interviews was that high achievers were very goal-oriented and highly confident of their own ability, regardless of the area in which they happened to excel. And it was interesting that high-achieving businesspersons, scientists, and professionals had more in common than we would have guessed. They talked about themselves and their careers in ways that were not dissimilar.

A member of the prestigious Life-Insurance Round Table made selling life insurance seem like a way of life—he was so absorbed in it. But just as interesting was the way he stressed the importance of believing in oneself. He was convinced—and he convinced us as well—that only those who had a high degree of confidence could possibly manage to excel as he had. A senior vice-president in one of the largest and most successful companies in the United

States stressed similar themes and offered a telling piece of advice: To be successful in business, one has to have self-confidence that "borders on arrogance."

These two people and virtually all the high achievers in our sample, by their own admission, had "large egos." Not that they were necessarily braggarts; indeed, they often expressed a quiet kind of self-confidence. They did not need to boast to assure others—or themselves—that they were good. They simply expressed the strong belief that they were people who could do what had to be done and would do it right. In almost every way, they saw themselves in an elite class, excelling over their peers in almost every way. They also saw themselves as setting standards that were uniquely their own. As one of them put it, "I have to satisfy myself." Scientists, professionals, and others in our sample all spoke similarly. For all practical purposes, our high-achieving interviewees were all concerned with excellence in their own performance, and all felt that their own personal standards transcended the norm. Most expressed confidence that they could live up to this transcendent standard.

After our interviews, we chanced upon the March 18, 1985, issue of *Time* magazine (Callahan, 1985). The title of that issue sums up our characterization of the self-perceptions of these high achievers: "Simply the Best." And our interviewees sounded very much like the Boston Celtics' Larry Bird when they indicated that when they're at their best they can do almost anything they want.

The importance of holding their own standards and considerable self-confidence does not fully characterize these exceptional individuals. Perhaps because they were so confident of their abilities (Kukla, 1978; Nicholls, 1985b; Nicholls & Miller, 1984), they expressed a predilection for challenge, for experiencing new events, and described themselves as "risk-takers" (cf. McClelland, 1961). Thus, they appeared to be oriented toward the future, to new possibilities and opportunities, and they seemed to relish the potential risks that might be associated therewith. Moreover, as we listened to them, we were struck by the boundless energy they seemed to exude. The dialogue in the interviews went rapidly, with the interviewees carrying on the conversation at a pace that sometimes outdistanced the interviewers. They were quick in speech as well as in wit. All in all, the interviews were never dull.

Finally, particularly striking were the personal similarities among these high achievers from diverse backgrounds and areas. Their responses were so homogeneous that we could only conclude that exceptional performers, regardless of area, were more alike than different. Similar incentives seem to guide them, and they were remarkably similar in the way they described themselves.

Although we came away from these interviews with many thoughts about motivation in general and the motivation of high achievers in particular, the overriding impression was twofold. These high achievers were dominated by an absorption in the task and were concerned with demonstrating, mostly to themselves, that they could achieve to their own high standards. Just as evident, however, was that these were supremely self-confident people.

Although all of the high achievers, regardless of vocational area, seemed to exude a special air of confidence, we did note that people in business were much more forthright in expressing this than academics were. Not that the academics seemed particularly humble or self-critical—they simply seemed a bit more guarded and less blatant in expressing confidence in themselves and their abilities.

Although listening to these high achievers talk was most intriguing and instructive, the interviews were only preliminary to a next step in our research: to compare the meaning systems of high and low achievers systematically in terms of our theory.

IPI Profiles of High Achievers

Once we had developed the measurement procedures described in chapter 4, we were in a position to begin confirming hunches derived from our interviews more systematically in terms of our theory. We proceeded as follows: First, we identified a group of individuals who, in our opinion, had excelled in their careers. Next, we examined how they might compare with the general sample. It is presumed that the meanings held by individuals who excel are associated with their success, but one cannot rule out the equally plausible possibility that the meanings are the result of the success.

Sample and Procedure. Before presenting data, a word or two about procedure is in order. First, we can argue only that the high achievers are more successful in their careers, on the average, than those who compose the sample as a whole. The high-achieving group was not selected on the basis of judgments by experts in the areas involved. They were selected by considering nominations from our staff, which inevitably means that they were known, at least by reputation, by someone in our research group, and therein may lie a bias. Nonetheless, we are comfortable in asserting that this group is certainly an elite group and would be so judged by any knowledgeable observer. The group includes internationally known scholars and scientists, chief executive officers of several major corporations, and individuals who have excelled in athletics. But we stress that they are successful in a special and limited sense. If we placed all the people in our sample on a continuum from high-achieving to low-achieving, the individuals in our higher-achieving group would inevitably be distributed toward the success end to a greater degree than our sample as a whole. Equally important, achievement is equated here with success in a vocation or career. Colleagues and peers of the members of our elite group would judge them successful; people outside their areas might or might not so judge them.

Such reservations aside, it is reasonable to conclude that we have, indeed, identified a group of people who are highly successful in their chosen careers, and we can also assume that they are more successful in their careers than our sample as a whole. It must be kept in mind, however, that in comparing the especially selected group to the sample as a whole, we are not comparing "succeeders" with "failures." Rather, we are comparing a highly successful group with a group that, though not exceptional, certainly can boast of a degree of success in life. The sample comprises middle- to upper-middle-class adults, typically holding white-collar positions. They did not come to our attention because they had problems. Thus, they are not so different from our elite group; therefore, large differences are not expected.

Results. The meaning profile of the "successful" group is presented in figure 5–2, along with a similar profile for the remainder of the sample. Some interesting differences are evident. Briefly, the high-achieving group definitely exhibits a different meaning profile from the group as a whole. This is reflected

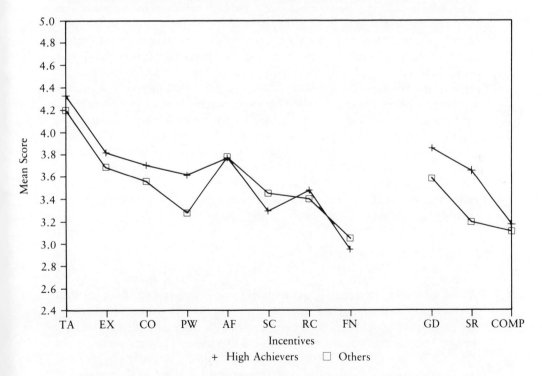

Figure 5–2. Profiles of High Achievers and Others in the Sample

in figure 5–2, and it is confirmed by various statistical comparisons, including discriminant analysis. The high-achiever group is consistently higher in terms of the task, excellence, and power personal incentives and the goal-directedness and self-reliance scales. The self-reliance and goal-directedness scales are the most important factors in differentiating the two groups.

Certainly, it is interesting that the high achievers are distinguished by self-reliance and goal-directedness. Everything we heard in our preliminary interviews, and most of what we know from everyday experience, is in accord with that essential finding. High achievers know what they want to do, and they believe they can rely heavily on themselves to accomplish what they set out to do. Similarly, those who were at the top of their professional or career groups indicated that they were more guided by the power personal incentive than others were.

Possibly surprising to some is that the high achievers do not exceed the rest on competition and apparently are not distinguished by socially oriented competition. We have wondered, from time to time, whether or not truly outstanding high achievers would worry less about beating others and would be more concerned with simply doing their jobs well (Braskamp, Fowler & Ory, 1984; Maehr, 1983). The very fact that these high achievers have done well in their careers might suggest that they should be above average in competitiveness. In our early interviews with outstanding individuals, we observed that high achievers occasionally used social comparisons when defining their own performance, especially in the early years of their career. Therefore, in the early stages of our work, we were inclined to think that they were a socially competitive group. After reviewing the psychometric results, as well as those reported by Spence and Helmreich (1978), we reexamined our interviews, probed more deeply into the protocols, and began to realize that although competition with a standard was important, the standard ultimately is not externally based; rather, it is more internalized. The benchmark becomes themselves. Just beating others is no longer primary; instead, consistency with their self-image is the standard to be reached. This general picture is possibly also reflected in the profile presented in figure 5–2.

Culture and Achievement

It appears that a special and unique configuration of meanings may be associated with outstanding achievement—at least in our sample. And there's the rub. Our subjects were all from one society—the United States. Are patterns of high achievers similar in other societies as well? Does it take the same personal profile to succeed with Mitsubishi as it takes with Central Soya or General Motors? More generally, the issue is whether the personal profiles requisite to excelling in one's career are the same or similar only if status is accorded in similar ways in the organization or society. The present success-related profile was derived from individuals who had made it to the top in organizations and in a society where status is presumably based largely on individual achievement. In a society or organization where ascribed status plays a more important role, one might find quite a different situation. Similarly, in societies where cooperation and group achievement are stressed, high achievement might take a different form (Schein, 1981).

This is an interesting and important line of questioning, for which there are as yet no definitive answers. In *The Achieving Society*, David McClelland (1961) argued that there is a core motivational component that is universally important to achieving success, regardless of culture. This point of view was subsequently criticized by Maehr (1974a). Building on this criticism, Maehr and Nicholls (1980) illustrated in considerable detail how the meanings of success (failure and achievement) and the perceptions of the routes to success vary cross-culturally. The essential hypothesis that emerged from their analysis was that cultures are likely to vary dramatically in the meanings that might be antecedent to achievement. The clear implication is that it would require a different motivational set to make it to the top in differing cultural contexts. In a more recent analysis (Fyans et al., 1983), this conclusion was modified to some degree. Briefly, Fyans et al. found that there was a core set of meanings that appeared to have cross-cultural validity and that these meanings were likely to be associated with modernization and basic economic and industrial growth, regardless of culture. The cross-culturally generalizable factor uncovered in their analyses suggested that the differential value placed on work, knowledge, and freedom was associated with modernization and a deemphasis on the importance of the family, tradition, and interpersonal concerns (see chapter 8). One cannot help but add that this core set of meanings resembles what was earlier termed the Protestant ethic (see McClelland, 1961; Weber, 1904/1930).

Where does all this leave us? Basically, it leaves us with the necessity to do further cross-cultural research. In chapter 8, we report a beginning effort in this regard. At that point, we will return to these questions regarding how culture modifies the conditions for achievement and status attainment.

Meaning and Vocation

When we discuss our theory with various groups, we invariably find it convenient to move quickly from the concepts to the use of these concepts in describing highly successful people—as we have done here. Most people are interested in the "high and mighty." Besides describing the distinguishing characteristics of high achievers, we suggest how they might have come to be that way; we possibly uncover the origins of high performance. Yet there is an equal need to understand the behavior of ordinary people. The meanings that people hold should be related to a wide range of choice and performance patterns. Personal incentives, for example, should distinguish people of different vocational and career orientations. The logic runs something like this: People who pursue one rather than another life path are probably investing their time and talent differently. If the meanings identified earlier are at all valid, they should be related to these differential investment patterns. Of course, there are many ways in which one may define or categorize a life path. The term may refer to leisure styles, moral predilections, family activities, careers, or a host of other possibilities. We will concentrate on differences in life path as indicated by career or vocation. Thus, the logic goes, individuals who are pursuing a specific career role or vocation should exhibit a unique meaning pattern; that is, they should differ in personal incentives and sense of self and also in the options they perceive to be available in their world.

How do people in different careers differ in the meanings they hold? To answer this question, we examined the personal incentives and sense of self of a number of career groups included in the samples we employed in developing and validating the IPI (chapter 4). In table 4–2, these groups were identified, somewhat flippantly, as academics, educators, mercantilists, and clerks. Although we conducted a broad variety of statistical analyses, we will concentrate here on three major comparisons that we consider to be of greatest theoretical significance.

Academe Versus the Marketplace

One of our nonuniversity friends likes to ask new acquaintances: "Are you a professor or do you work?" Another friend is fond of the phrase, "the leisure of the theory class"—by which, we surmise, he refers to the preferred lifestyle or vocational freedom available to academics. As professors, we are not entirely comfortable with the implications of these phrases, and we bristle a bit when we hear them. As with many stereotypes, however, they probably contain a germ of truth. Both seem to suggest the commonly held belief that there is something different about professors and people in business. In the present terms, this should mean that the two groups hold different meanings; that is, they are guided by different incentives, have different views of themselves, and hold different perceptions of options.

Do academics differ from businesspersons in terms of personal investment meanings? Indeed they do—or so our data would suggest. (Results of a series of analyses describing the differences in these and other groups in greater technical detail are presented in appendix A.) For purposes of general discussion, it may be most helpful to refer to figure 5–3, which presents profiles of mercantilists and academics. Several points of difference are of special interest. In comparison to those in academe, those in business define success and

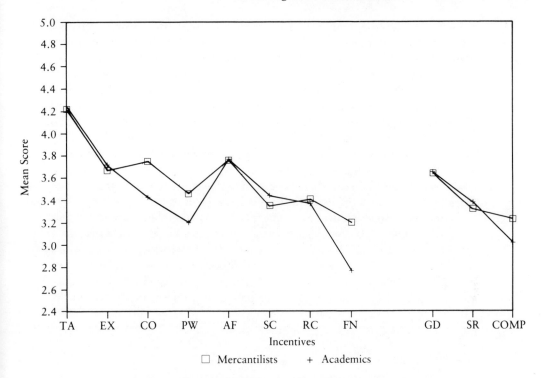

Figure 5–3. Profiles of Mercantilists and Academics

personal satisfaction more in terms of competition, power, and financial re-wards. It is interesting that people in business also express a higher sense of self-esteem or self-worth than academics do. Perhaps this stems, in part, from a "power of positive thinking" ethic that people accept as they participate in the world of business. Perhaps the demands of the business world are such that the self-critical person could not survive. In any case, this finding is in accord with our earlier observations of the greater hesitancy of faculty members to express confidence in themselves.

The main point we wish to stress is that the results are generally in accord with what we mght expect from what we know about the different career lines associated with the world of business and the academic world. The aca-demics in this sample are professors at four colleges that emphasize teaching and at one research university. The faculty members at the colleges do not have to be highly competitive and seek out power. Instead, teaching (their major function) stresses cooperation and service to others. In short, these pro-files suggest a general match between incentives and the work responsibilities in these two professions. Possibly, these differences are due to self-selection—that is, people selecting jobs to satisfy their personal incentives. Or perhaps these findings are the result of personal adaptations—that is, people adjusting their personal incentives to make them more consistent with the nature of their work. We cannot say for sure. Both processes tend to occur, and it is probably safe to assume that both are operative in the present case.

Because the academics represented scholars from two types of institutions—small teaching colleges and a large research university—we examined differences among these two groups. They differed in interesting and, to some extent, predictable ways, as shown in figure 5–4. University faculty members were higher in excellence personal incentives but lower in affiliation and social concern personal incentives. University professors were also more goal-directed and self-reliant. This pattern is also consistent with the types of work performed and the expectations of these institutions.

Now we wish to reinforce a point that has been implied throughout this discussion. The people who participated in our studies do not represent a random sample of academics or mercantilists; therefore, the two profiles should not be taken as representative of those two groups in the strictest sense. What we have found is that two groups that differ in personal investment, as judged by their life or career paths, do, indeed, differ also in the

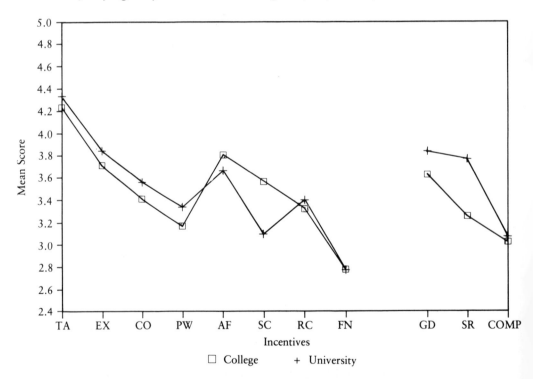

Figure 5–4. Profiles of College and University Faculty Members

meanings they hold. *How* they differ is interesting and suggests a number of hypotheses about the separate worlds of academe and the marketplace and about the meanings that may be antecedent to a personal investment in these two worlds. Thus, in view of our earlier observations, it is not altogether surprising that academics are lower on the sense of competence scale. Similarly, given their separate roles, the higher stress on competition, power, and financial personal incentives is in accord with expectations. One might have expected greater differences on the task and excellence personal incentive scales, and it is intriguing that we did not find them. After all, the greater freedom that academics presumably have and their presumed dedication to excellence for its own sake might logically have led to such an expectation. Why this expectation was not met is something we cannot fully explain. But the majority of the academics were teachers, not just scholars and scientists. Moreover, the people who composed our mercantilist sample were not a random sample from the business world. Possibly, too, we are prone to dealing in stereotypes when considering these two groups—stereotypes that have some value but not total validity.

"Indians" Versus "Chiefs"

Besides the broad comparisons of the world of academe and the world of the marketplace, another interesting comparison can be made. Again rather flippantly, we refer to this comparison as "Indians" versus "Chiefs." By these terms we refer to the possibly different vocational categories of office support staff (broadly, secretarial and technical) and the people they are likely to be supporting (private and public managers and faculty).

Figure 5–5 presents the profiles of these two groups. It can be seen that the "Chiefs" place more importance on striving for excellence, on competition with others, and on power. Compared to the "Indians," they are also more goal-directed and have a higher view of themselves as persons. Again, these differences are intuitively plausible in that they seem to accord well with the usual role demands of supervisor and subordinate. Also, leadership studies (Yukl, 1981) have suggested that effective leaders are generally distinguished by such factors as self-confidence, a predilection for seeking and enjoying authority positions, a tendency toward independence and self-reliance, aggressiveness, and an ability to take the initiative.

Conclusion

Certainly, comparing academe with the marketplace and comparing "Indians" with "Chiefs" does not exhaust the comparisons that could be made to better understand the complex of meanings exhibited by the individuals who composed our samples. Other comparisons were made, and the

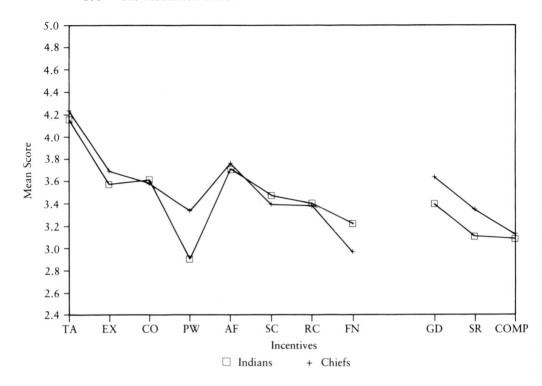

Figure 5–5. Profiles of "Indians" and "Chiefs"

results of some of them are reported in appendix A. Suffice it to say, however, that our core hypothesis has empirical support: Differential vocational invest- ment is associated with holding a different complex of personal investment meanings. Personal incentives and sense of self do differ for various voca- tional groups. These meanings also relate to behavioral patterns of some con- cern; they also relate to vocational choice and perhaps to other significant life patterns. Thus, the present differentiation encourages us to believe that the theory is not just a theory for the laboratory; it has applications in real-life settings.

Meaning and Work Investment

We have concluded that people who pursue different career lines or fill dif- ferent job roles apparently hold different personal incentives and views of themselves. It is not altogether unlikely that personal meanings play some role in determining vocational choice or retaining a given career pattern, although the reverse could also be true. Although the correlational nature of these data does not allow us to say for sure that the meanings held initially led to the vocational patterns exhibited, that remains a strong possibility, particularly when these data are considered in accord with theory and research reviewed earlier (see, for example, chapter 3). In any event, these relationships are interesting and useful in their own right, and they contribute to a growing conceptualization that meanings held by people are significantly associated with personal investment.

We turn now to a complementary and equally interesting set of data that further reinforces the Meaning → Personal Investment hypothesis. In this case, personal investment is indicated by measures of job satisfaction and organizational commitment.

Theoretically, at least, measures of job satisfaction and organizational commitment may be construed as real-life indicators of personal investment. The conclusion that people are truly committed to the job usually involves global observations of time and energy commitment. One can perhaps imperfectly approximate such behavioral indicators of commitment by eliciting the employees' free responses to questions about the degree to which they feel committed to their place of work. That is the approach employed with the IWI. And as we shall soon see, consideration of such measures of organizational commitment can prove most interesting and helpful in understanding motivation and personal investment in a work organization.

Job satisfaction is a time-honored, oft-used indicator of employee motivation and morale (see, for example, Feldman & Arnold, 1983). Satisfaction with one's job can be justifiably construed as a measure of personal investment in that the person is more or less attracted to the job. However, it must also be noted that the apparent degree of attractiveness indicated by a measure of job satisfaction is not necessarily a good indicator of the level of productivity a person will exhibit on the job (see Iaffaldano & Muchinsky, 1985; Vroom, 1964). In particular, one should be cautious in asserting that job satisfaction leads to productivity in a direct way. As Lawler and Porter (1967) pointed out a number of years ago, there is good reason to believe that productivity leads to job satisfaction, rather than the reverse, in many important instances (see also Iaffaldano & Muchinsky, 1985). Yet it may be noted that job satisfaction does lead to certain specifiable behavioral patterns that should have important effects on work behavior and the work organization in the long run. As Feldman and Arnold (1983) pointed out, job satisfaction has been found to be related to such employee behaviors as job turnover and absenteeism and to physical and mental health. Certainly, one might expect that these apparent outcomes of job dissatisfaction would not only affect the productivity of workers at some point but eventually would also take their toll on the organization. In addition, Feldman and Arnold's review of the literature reveals what common sense might have suggested—namely, that job dissatisfaction is strongly related to union activity. The more workers are dissatisfied, the more likely they are to organize and perhaps enter into an adversarial relationship with the company. In sum, although it cannot definitely be concluded that job satisfaction is a direct and simple indicator of motivation or personal investment, it clearly relates to behavioral patterns that are broadly associated with a positive orientation toward the job and possibly with the kinds of contributions the employee will make to the organization. Regardless of the status of the job satisfaction construct as an indicator of motivation and personal investment, measures of employee satisfaction and morale remain important indicators of the quality of work life and relate to important worker behavioral patterns directly and indirectly. Thus, there is some logic in incorporating a measure of job satisfaction into our analysis and treating this measure as one valid indicator of personal investment in work or in a particular job. Again, the IWI provides us with indicators of job satisfaction on the basis of employees' responses to verbal statements about their jobs.

It is readily granted that the IWI measures of job satisfaction and organizational commitment serve as fitting surrogates for at least some facet of the wider conception of personal investment. It seems almost impossible to ignore such measures in any analysis of work motivation. Thus, we will proceed to ask how meaning or the various components of meaning are associated with the degree to which an individual is likely to invest in any particular activity. How are personal incentives, perceived options, and sense of self related to how the person invests time and energy? In this section, we will examine these questions in the context of the work situation.

Procedures

Soon after developing the IPI, we began to experiment with parallel assessments of organizational climate or culture with perceptions of the job and with how these perceptions, in turn, are related to worker morale and commitment to the work organization. After some preliminary work, we combined measures of job attitudes and the work context with the IPI to create an omnibus measure, which we termed the Inventory of Work Investment (IWI). (The specific and technical properties of this instrument are described in detail in chapter 4.) The IWI provides an index of each of the three components of personal meaning (personal incentives, perceived options, and sense of self) as well as indices of personal investment (job satisfaction and organizational commitment). With the aid of the IWI data, we were able to consider relationships of personal meanings and personal investment in a rather comprehensive fashion. Figure 5–6 identifies the hypothesized causal framework that guided our analyses and specifies the set of variables involved. Procedurally, we determined the relationships of each of the meaning variables with each of the indicators of personal investment. The results of a variety of analyses are systematically summarized here.

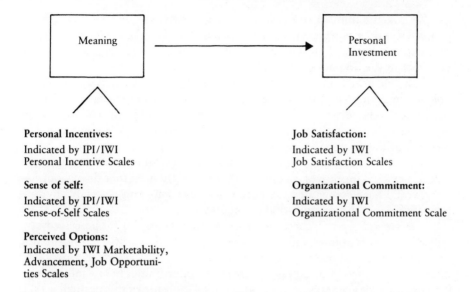

Personal Incentives:
Indicated by IPI/IWI
Personal Incentive Scales

Job Satisfaction:
Indicated by IWI
Job Satisfaction Scales

Sense of Self:
Indicated by IPI/IWI
Sense-of-Self Scales

Organizational Commitment:
Indicated by IWI
Organizational Commitment Scale

Perceived Options:
Indicated by IWI Marketability,
Advancement, Job Opportuni-
ties Scales

Figure 5–6. Pictorial Summary of Causal Relationships and Indices

Perceived Options → *Personal Investment*

Perceived options are a critical component of the meaning system that is considered antecedent to personal investment. The person makes choices between perceived possibilities, and action depends on the person's knowledge that certain courses of action are possible or acceptable. When we stress this point to various workshop groups, the usual response is a wide yawn—*everyone* knows that; tell us something new. It is true that everyone knows this in a general way. But perhaps precisely because we are all generally aware of such a self-evident point, we have tended to ignore the importance of the point. As pointed out in earlier chapters, behavior—and personal investment, in particular—must be understood in terms of the options that are psychologically available to the person. In our focus on the degree to which individuals are likely to invest themselves in a work situation, we begin by examining the matter of perceived options.

We argue that one can and should properly distinguish between external and internal (perceived) options. There is reason to believe that there is a correlation between the two; there must be if one is to behave effectively in the world. Elsewhere (see chapters 3 and 9), we stress how one can manipulate external events to create the perception of options, but our interest here is in *perceived* options. What does the person *believe* is available to him or her? How does the person view opportunities in the environment? What are likely events and happenings? What are likely courses of action?

We asked a number of questions that are useful for understanding how people view their work environment. Specifically, we asked three basic types of questions that relate to important kinds of options regarding personal investment in the domain of work.

First, we asked questions about the opportunities workers see as available on their jobs for pursuing the eight measured personal incentives. Thus, we considered the personal incentives individuals hold and the degree to which they consider them to be available in their jobs. We constructed a measure of the discrepancy or congruency of personal incentives and job opportunities. If individuals simply do not see opportunities to pursue their valued personal incentives on their jobs, we hypothesized that this incongruency would have some effect on personal investment—more specifically, on job satisfaction and organizational commitment.

The second type of question concerns the relationship of perceived advancement opportunities within the organization and job satisfaction and organizational commitment. Perceptions of the possibility of advancement are likely to be important instances of perceived opportunities in any job setting. Thus, it is of some interest to determine the relationship of this particular IWI measure with job satisfaction and organizational commitment.

A third index of perceived options or opportunities is embedded in the IWI marketability scale. Whereas the advancement scale relates to perceived opportunities *within* the organization, the marketability scale relates to perceived options *outside* the organization. Again, it is of practical and theoretical interest to relate this measure of perceived opportunity to both job satisfaction and organizational commitment.

All in all, we were able to examine three major possible antecedents of work investment in an organizational context. Moreover, our data can be interpreted in reference to the theory of personal investment which we are elaborating. We will discuss analyses directed to each of these questions in turn.

Perceived Job Opportunities → Satisfaction and Commitment. How do perceived job opportunities relate to job satisfaction and organizational commitment? This question involves a number of subissues. First, there is a methodological issue: Do the adults in our sample exhibit discrepancies between the personal incentives they hold and the perceptions they have regarding job opportunities to pursue these incentives in the work context? If job or organizational opportunities completely match personal incentives, there is no point in pursuing the matter of person–job matches further.

Table 5–1 presents the correlations between personal incentives and job opportunities on comparable or matching dimensions (e.g., task personal incentives and task job opportunities). Although the correlations are positive, they do not indicate a strong relationship between the importance a worker places on a personal incentive and the perceived opportunities available to

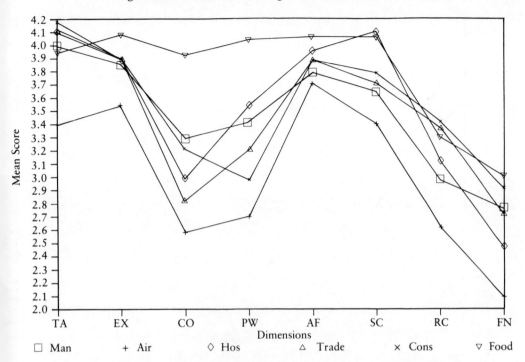

Figure 6–3. Average Scores of Employees in Six Organizations on Job Opportunities Scales

After considering the relationship of job opportunities and perceptions of the organizational culture, we proceeded to examine a related issue: How does the person's role in the organization affect the perception of organizational culture? Two questions were asked in this regard: (1) Do people with different levels of leadership in an organization view the organizational culture differently, and (2) do members of different units within the same company view the organizational culture differently?

The first question related especially to how positions at different levels of the organizational hierarchy might affect the perception of organizational culture. We found that although the perceptions at different levels in the organization were not altogether different, they were sufficiently different to suggest that people at different levels in the organization are likely to have different views of the organizational culture. As shown in figure 6–4, workers who hold executive or higher-level management positions or own their own companies do not regard the organizational culture in the same way middle managers do. The executives view their organization as stressing the task, social solidarity, and external rewards dimensions to a greater degree than the middle managers. It is interesting that the executives did not view the values stressed by the organization to be any more competitive than the managers did. In fact, they generally regarded their own organizations to

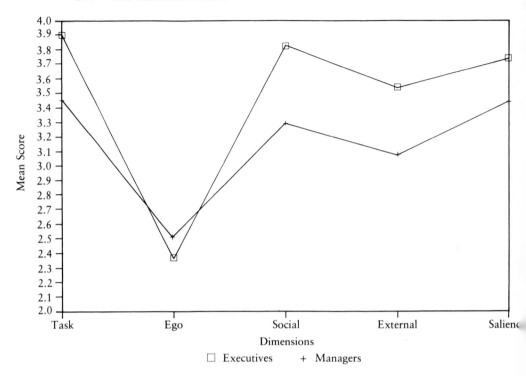

Figure 6–4. Average Scores of Executives and Managers on Organizational Culture and Saliency Scales

be relatively free of interpersonal competition and individual ambition to beat out others to get ahead. Also, the organizational culture is more salient to the executives than it is to the people in middle management positions. More generally, our results suggest that the lower a person is in the organizational hierarchy, the less salient the organizational culture is. These findings are not particularly surprising. After all, those in leadership roles often see themselves as defining what the organization is about, and it is predictable that they would say that they know what the company is trying to do. In addition, they are likely to consider advancement to be based on such factors as competence, rather than on politics. It is probably also true that as people move up and down an organizational hierarchy, the purposes of the company are likely to be understood to varying degrees.

These views of the culture by the two levels of employees can be contrasted with the views executives and managers have of opportunities in their jobs. Figure 6–5 shows the profiles of the job opportunities of these two groups. All differences are statistically significant ($p < .005$), with executives expressing more opportunities to pursue each of the incentives successfully than managers

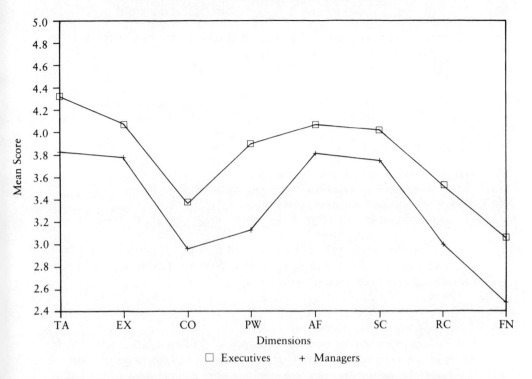

Figure 6–5. Average Scores of Executives and Managers on Job Opportunities Scales

do. Given this finding, jobs at the upper levels of management can be described as more enriched than those at the lower levels.

Even though the executives did not view the culture as stressing competition and conflicts, they viewed their own positions as providing them with greater opportunity to compete with others for rewards, to get ahead of others, and to exercise influence over others.

The second question relates more broadly to the similarity of perceptions of organizational culture across a wide variety of units within the different companies. Do cultural themes pervade an organization—and to what degree? Employee perceptions in three of the firms (airline, health care, and consulting) were analyzed by their group membership. Table 6–5 summarizes the statistical tests conducted for this analysis. In two of the organizations (airline and health care), group membership made a difference in how the employees viewed their work environment on three dimensions. In the airline company, the executives perceived the company's emphasis on task, social solidarity, and external rewards as greater than the other three groups of employees did. However, those in the three units in the consulting company were similar in their views on how each of their units stressed excellence, supportive working relationships,

Table 6–5
Differences in Perceptions of Organizational Culture among Groups in Three Organizations

Culture	Probability Levels[a]		
	Airline[b]	Health Center[c]	Consulting Firm[d]
Task	.001	.02	
Ego			.01
Social	.0029	.01	
External	.0035	.0007	

[a]Only probability levels of observed differences less than .02 are reported.
[b]Groups were executives, mechanics, customer service personnel, and flight crew.
[c]Groups were executives and nursing coordinators.
[d]Groups were executives, sales personnel, and research and development personnel.

and rewards for their work. They differed in their perception of the degree of competitiveness within the firm, with the executives viewing their culture as less competitive than the others did.

Conclusions

Several important conclusions can be reached on the basis of these results in the study of organizational culture. First, the concept of an organizational culture appears to be viable. Previous research of a more ethnographic nature has indicated that companies may differ in shared assumptions, expectations, role relationships, and norms. A most important facet of organizational culture is the shared meanings that exist relative to purposes and goals— what is worth striving for. In our research presented thus far, we have shown that it is possible to assess this aspect of organizational culture reliably. Moreover, companies are distinguishable in a credible fashion along these dimensions.

The Influence of Organizational Culture on Personal Investment

If an organization has a distinctive organizational culture, does it have an influence on the worker? Specifically, how is organizational culture related to personal investment? How is our measure of organizational culture related to worker commitment and to job satisfaction? In this regard, we consider first the *saliency* of the culture and its relationship to personal investment. Next, we examine the content of the organizational culture—that is, the relative stress placed on task, ego, social, and external rewards. How do the manifest values of the company relate to and possibly determine the degree of workers' personal investment in the company?

The Saliency of the Organizational Culture

The bottom line in our discussion of organizational culture has to be the effects on personal investment. There may be other reasons for defining and assessing organizational culture, but the ultimate question necessarily concerns whether variation in organizational culture eventuates in variation in personal investment.

It is logical to assume that an organizational culture affects individual performance only as that culture is salient to the individual. In our investigation, we studied the relationship of employee awareness of an organized set of shared values and goals within the overall organization to the personal investment of the employees.

As shown earlier, in table 6–3, workers' perceptions of the saliency of the organizational culture, regardless of which shared values and norms are stressed, are highly and positively related to both organizational commitment and job satisfaction. Given the correlational nature of this field study, we cannot definitely attribute causality to saliency as it relates to organizational commitment and job satisfaction. We can only suggest that a strong organizational culture, regardless of what it is and how it is manifested, influences personal investment.

This finding accords well with the ethnographic and more informal analyses of organizational culture discussed earlier. Others (Deal & Kennedy, 1982; Hackman, 1985; Peters & Waterman, 1982) have argued for the effects of making a company's values and mission salient to all who are involved in the corporate enterprise. Presumably, the good companies *know* what they are about. This knowledge is present at all levels—not only at the CEO or senior management levels. Rather, a major function of the senior executives is to communicate the values and purposes to the other members of the work community. We have found that employees are likely to be more personally invested in the organization when the company's values are very obvious to them. In other words, clear beliefs about the mission as well as the style of a company are associated with job satisfaction and organizational commitment.

The high correlations among the task, social, external rewards, and saliency organizational culture dimensions are also important. Companies that are viewed by their employees as emphasizing challenge in work, concerned with the social dimension of employee relationships, and recognizing and rewarding performance seemingly convey a sense of purpose and meaning to the employees. Perhaps it is through a special stress on these facets of the organizational culture that the mission of the organization becomes especially visible to the employee. And, as we shall soon see, it is to some extent through the stress on these aspects of company life that organizational commitment is engendered and job satisfaction enhanced.

A series of multiple regression analyses was conducted in which the organizational culture scales served as predictor variables along with the job opportunities and personal incentive scales to examine the relative influence of each set of predictors, classified by level—person, job, and organization. As shown in table 6–6, organizational culture scales emerge as critical variables in predicting both job satisfaction and organizational commitment. It is interesting that whereas both the task and external rewards dimensions are important in predicting both job satisfaction and organizational commitment, the power and social dimensions figure differently in predicting these two indicators of personal investment. Also, whereas the social dimension is important in predicting organizational commitment, the ego dimension is relatively more important in predicting job satisfaction. Looking at these results more closely, a strong and positive stress on supportive social relationships in the work place apparently is important in eliciting workers' commitment to the organization. Somewhat inexplicably, when the ego incentives are stressed within the organizational culture, there is a tendency for job satisfaction to be enhanced.

Reflecting on these results, we can see, first, that each of the four organizational culture scales is associated with the prediction of personal investment. This finding may indicate that as organizations make it clear that they are concerned with the work done, with the outcomes that eventuate, and with the meaning of the work to employees, they are likely to affect

Table 6–6
Personal Incentives, Job Opportunities, and Organizational Culture Scales that Are Significant Predictors of Job Satisfaction and Organizational Commitment

	Job Satisfaction	*Organizational Commitment*
Personal Incentives	9 Excellence 10 Task	3 Excellence 4 Power 6 Social Concern
Job Opportunities	2 Affiliation 3 Task 4 Financial 5 Recognition 6 Competition	1 Affiliation 9 Financial 10 Recognition
Organizational Culture	1 External 7 Social 8 Task	2 External 5 Social 7 Task 8 Ego
	$R^2 = .61$	$R^2 = .60$

Note: The number preceding each predictor represents the relative order in which the predictor contributed to the squared multiple correlation.

motivation positively. Note that it is not just that there is concern in some quarters with the work done; that is natural and inevitable if the organization is to survive. The point is that this concern must be specified and communicated. It is the *saliency* of this concern of the organization that is important in eliciting the personal investment of employees. This interpretation seems to support the previously discussed findings regarding the importance of the saliency of the culture in determining personal investment.

But why do certain organizational scales predict these measures of personal investment as they do? It is not particularly surprising that the task and external rewards scales appear to be important components in predicting both job satisfaction and organizational commitment. It is also understandable that when companies are concerned with social relationships in the work place, they encourage organizational commitment. But why would the ego dimension contribute to job satisfaction rather than the social dimension? It may be because the surveyed members of the six organizations are predominantly white-collar employees in middle-level managerial positions and above. Generally, such employees can be viewed as upwardly mobile, desirous of advancement. They may value the chance to compete and get ahead more highly than the chance to form relationships when they consider their jobs and what they offer.

As we reflected on the relationships between the organizational culture scales and personal investment, we were especially drawn to the findings on the task, social, and external rewards scales. Regardless of the analysis conducted, these three scales emerged as important components of organizational culture in regard to personal investment. Considering this, we decided to scrutinize the items of these scales to determine which items might be associated with personal investment. We wished to observe, in a more focused manner, the content of these items. What we found was most interesting and possibly also very instructive for understanding what it is about organizational culture that might be important in regard to motivation and personal investment.

Table 6–7 presents a summary of organizational culture item correlations that are especially interesting in this regard. By examining the general pattern of results, we can see that as the organization exhibits a special concern for the individual and a recognition of the worker's worth in the larger enterprise, the organization will tend to encourage commitment and job satisfaction. That may well be the most important message underlying the finding that task, social, and external reward scales have perhaps the most pervasive effects on personal investment. Certainly, this general interpretation of the pattern of results is supportive of Peters and Waterman's (1982) conclusions regarding the importance of treating every employee with dignity and as a "winner." It also underscores the importance of advocating innovation and assessing performance within a supportive environment. Moreover,

Table 6–7
Correlations of Organizational Culture Items with Organizational Commitment, Job Satisfaction, and Saliency[a]

Scale and Items	Commitment	Satisfaction	Saliency
Task			
I am encouraged to make suggestions about how we can be more effective.	.50	.46	.51
Excellence and doing it right are stressed at almost any cost in this organization.			.45
Around here we are encouraged to try new things.		.48	
In this organization, we are given a lot of freedom to carry out our work.		.45	
If someone has a good idea, invention, or project, management will listen and support it.	.48	.45	
Social			
In this organization, there is a family feeling.			.47
In this organization, they really care about me as a person.	.62	.55	.52
We are treated as adults in this organization.	.46	.57	.57
In this organization, there is respect for each individual worker.	.50	.52	.57
People at all levels of this organization share information about how well our company is doing.			.46
I am involved in decisions that directly affect my work in this organization.		.50	
External			
Employees in this organization receive a lot of attention.	.49	.45	.56
In this organization, they make me feel like I am a winner.	.59	.59	.54
This organization makes me feel like I am an important, productive person.	.61	.61	.50
This organization allows me to do those things that I find personally satisfying.	.45	.54	
There are many incentives here to work hard.	.47	.51	.45
I receive information about the quality of my work.	.46	.47	
In this organization, we hear more about what people do right than the mistakes they make.	.45		

[a]Only correlations of .45 or above are reported.

this interpretation speaks rather directly to what executives can do to encourage personal investment in the work place (see chapter 9).

The Individual in the Organization

Finally, we return to the problem of the match between person and environment, an issue that has surfaced throughout this book. In this case, we wish to consider very specifically whether individuals whose personal incentives match the culture of the organization tend to be more invested in the organization than those whose personal incentives are not similar to the organizational culture. We will also compare organizational culture–personal incentive matches with job opportunities–personal incentive matches. A person's satisfaction in a specific job is probably related to compatability with the organization as a whole, but is it fully so? Can we note any special and separate influences of organizational culture? Does an employee whose personal incentives differ from the organizational culture have different degrees of job satisfaction and organizational commitment?

Our data set contains significant potential for confronting these questions effectively, and one of our students (Mayberry, 1985) made a special point of uncovering answers contained in these data. Through a series of sophisticated analyses, Mayberry compared and contrasted a congruency (person–environment match) model with a separate components model for predicting job satisfaction and organizational commitment. That is, he first considered the effectiveness of personal incentives–job opportunities congruencies and personal incentives–organizational culture congruencies in predicting both job satisfaction and organizational commitment. He next considered how organizational culture and job opportunities, irrespective of individual differences in personal orientation, might serve to predict the same measures of personal investment. He concluded that the congruency model was, if anything, slightly less effective in predicting personal investment than just using the scales that measured job opportunities and culture. Thus, one could do at least as well or better in predicting job satisfaction and organizational commitment by simply looking at the scales measuring job opportunities and organizational culture without considering the degree of congruency between the individual employee and his or her job and organization. Tables 5–8 and 5–9 (in chapter 5) summarized multiple regression analyses conducted by Mayberry (1985).

At first glance, the results are surprising. Matching models have held sway in a variety of different behavioral science research areas in recent years (see Miller, 1981) and have played an important role in analyses of organizational behavior (see Brousseau, 1983; Schein, 1978). Moreover, simple common sense would lead us to expect that congruency or matching models would ultimately prove most effective in predicting job satisfaction and organizational commitment. But these results suggest that the matching model is not always the most appropriate and useful one to employ. Nor are these findings readily attributable to the usual technical problems that beset congruency measures; Mayberry used sophisticated scaling and analysis procedures that should have minimized the typical problems of enhanced error in combining two scales to form a congruency scale. Yet it may well be that the components of the work setting assessed by the IWI, particularly the organizational culture scales, do have pervasive and widely generalizable effects on job satisfaction and organizational commitment. Based on these results alone, we can venture that the assessment of the work environment by the IWI provides useful information for predicting personal investment and person–environment matches.

If the present results are valid, then one is encouraged to focus on general facets of the work place that are found to make a difference on employee behavior; one can focus on organizational culture variables and be confident of predictable effects on a broad spectrum of individuals. This makes these results directly applicable to the problems confronting managers of large organizations.

Mayberry's findings, however, do not altogether rule out the possibility that job satisfaction and organizational commitment can be explained by a congruency model. As shown in tables 5–9 and 5–10, the congruency model did account for at least half of the variability on both satisfaction and commitment. By examining the relative importance of the specific congruencies—that is, the extent to which each contributed to the overall relationship between the congruency and satisfaction (or commitment)—we can conclude that the same congruencies do not equally predict job satisfaction and organizational commitment. In general, the congruencies involving the social dimensions are more influential in predicting commitment than job satisfaction.

The second generalization is that the ego dimension is a more important predictor of both satisfaction and commitment when it is part of a congruency measure than when it is used by itself to predict these two indicators of personal investment. Of the ten significant congruency measures that predicted job satisfaction, all four possibilities involving ego were included and ranked 2, 3, 4, and 6 in importance. The ranks for predicting commitment were 1, 2, 8, and 9. Furthermore, congruencies involving the organizational culture scales were included in the final regression equation for each outcome; in fact, five of the ten involved organizational culture. The most influential was external rewards for job satisfaction. Congruency of opportunities and organizational culture scores on the external rewards dimension is related to job satisfaction, which suggests that a perceived consistency in the external environment leads to higher job satisfaction. In short, the measures involving congruencies provide added insight into the associations among personal incentives, job opportunities, and organizational culture and two indicators of personal investment.

In the final analysis, however, it is perhaps most interesting that organizational culture dimensions appear to deserve attention as antecedents of job satisfaction and organizational commitment. This is an important finding. If congruency measures were more predictive, we would have been confronted with a serious problem in advising organizational leaders. What could they do except concern themselves with employee selection? However, those at the top can influence staffing only to a limited degree, and the effects of staffing are not likely to yield quick results unless one has the opportunity to force the complete changeover of a staff—which is seldom the case. In summary, it is more effective to focus on the components themselves, because they include such environmental conditions as job design and the work climate. Moreover, the results support the basic notion with which we began this chapter—namely, that a holistic entity like organizational culture has its own effects on personal investment.

Conclusion

The popular media would have us believe that "excellent" companies possess what might almost be called a special personality, that they are of a generally different character than "run of the mill" companies. More generally, there is a widely held perception that every company possesses a unique character. These hunches are essentially confirmed in the research reviewed in this chapter. Companies *are* different, and they seem to be different in terms of characteristics that might appropriately be labeled collectively as "culture." That general finding is interesting in itself and is supportive of further work in the general domain of organizational culture, using not only ethnographic and case history methods but also psychometric procedures.

The results also speak directly to the special needs of executives and managers at all levels in an important and very practical way. In this chapter, we have suggested that in today's world of management, there is a need to understand organizations in holistic terms and to identify pressure points for influencing overall motivation and productivity. Not only is the concept of an organizational culture viable for general purposes, it is also a specifiable phenomenon. We have concluded that there is a relationship between organizational culture and personal investment—that knowing something about the cultural facets of an organization allows us to predict employees' job satisfaction and organizational commitment. At the very least, that is an important early step in determining how to manipulate organizational culture not only to improve work life but also to enhance the overall productivity of the organization.

We conclude, then, with the bold assertion that we have given reason for optimism regarding the concept of organizational culture and its usefulness in the realm of organization theory and practice. Certainly, many specific issues have gone unresolved, and much research is still needed. But the evidence is such that we can begin realistically to construct items of advice and counsel for those who lead and manage.

7
Age and Personal Investment

Without question, one of the most significant occurrences on the U.S. social scene in recent years is the shift in the age of our population. Anyone involved with marketing is unavoidably aware of—and perhaps drastically affected by—the rather sudden and dramatic shift in the relative proportions of young and old in the general population. The rapid rise in the birth and fertility rates—the "baby boom"—produced an extreme increase in the number of children and youth during the years 1956–1976. This has been followed more recently by a very rapid decline in the youth population for the remainder of this century. With fewer children being born, with a limited number of immigrants, and with more people living longer, we have become an aging society. The so-called graying of America has begun and continues (Maehr & Kleiber, 1980). Embedded in the statistics of successive "baby boom" and "bust" is the ineluctable trend toward an even older America. The baby-boom cohorts of the 1940s and 1950s are moving through the life span. Currently, they are young adults moving toward middleage; in the twenty-first century, they will reach old age. As they caused us to build schools, expand youth resources, worry about juvenile delinquency, and generally create a young-oriented society, so they will also probably focus societal attention increasingly on the later years of life. Inevitably, we will have an older work force. Inevitably, also, we will have more people wanting to and actually managing to retire. But the cohort that follows them—the children born in the 1960s and 1970s who will be expected to provide the financial and other support to make such retirement possible—is significantly smaller. In short, one can foresee the eventuality of having too many who need to be supported by a group that is too small to do the job.

The social and personal problems created by the emergence of an increasingly aging society are gradually becoming evident. Social Security and pension policies may have to be rethought and new revenue resources uncovered. Housing, health, and welfare agencies will increasingly be forced to reallocate their efforts and search for new expertise. At the base of what we can do is the issue of how our economic productivity as a society will be affected by all this. At a very general level, one may wonder whether the work ethic will be equally strong with each new cohort and whether achievement will continue to be valued. At a more specific level is the immediate question of the potential of the older worker. It is likely that people will no longer seek or be able to retire at age 65. Industries and professions that have depended on the resources of youth will have to depend increasingly on the resources still retained by the old. And that brings us to a very important question relating to this book and this chapter: How is age related to personal investment? Occasionally, one hears about a 75-year-old who still goes to the office every day, never takes a vacation, and remains a presumably productive contributor to an enterprise of some sort. More often, perhaps, one hears of people who should retire but won't. Increasingly, these days, we are hearing about individuals who are already burned out at midlife. Just what is the relationship between age and personal investment?

Personal Investment and "The Seasons of a Man's Life"

In the past decade or so, the popular media have flooded us with ideas and anecdotes regarding changing motivational orientations in adulthood. One of the more popular studies has been *The Seasons of a Man's Life* by Daniel J. Levinson (1978; see also Levinson, Darrow, Klein, Levinson, & McKee, 1974). Broadly, it is a study that deals with significant motivational changes, particularly during early and middle adulthood.

The study itself consists of biographical studies of forty men ranging in age from 35 to 45 years when the study began. Occupationally, the men were of four different types: executives, academics (biologists), novelists, and hourly workers. Levinson also examined autobiographies of approximately a hundred other men. Each person included in the study was examined carefully and in depth. The conceptualizations that evolved from the study are provocative, especially for a discussion of adult behavior and development.

Levinson's conceptualization is one of a number of stage theories that have emerged over the past several years. Though not specifically proposing a stage theory, Havighurst (1952) defined the concept of *developmental task* and outlined the likely problems and challenges to be confronted by people as they proceed through life. For example, in early adulthood, an individual confronts such challenges as selecting a mate, learning to live with him or her, starting a family, and getting started in an occupation. In middle age, the person is presented with the tasks of achieving a measure of economic and social responsibility, assisting teenage children in moving into the adult world, and simultaneously dealing with the problems confronting older parents. In old age, people must deal with decreased strength, failing health, and sometimes reduced income as they also begin to experience changes in work options. In addition, there are such special problems as dealing with the death of a spouse and making adjustments to the loss of friends. In short, biological, sociological, economic, and psychological factors converge to present the individual with a sequence of problems to solve that, though not always inevitable, are quite typical for people of a certain age.

Although Freud and early psychoanalysts seemed to be more concerned with reconstructing the world of the child (albeit often from data gathered on adults!), contemporaries in this tradition have been less tied to childhood periods. Erik Erikson (1950, 1959, 1968) exhibited a definitely expanded horizon on development that defines the full course of the life span. Erikson organized each life stage around a critical problem that is likely to have a good or bad resolution. For example, people in the later stages of their work or career lives are likely to have to make a kind of life choice between "generativity," in which the individual invests in the future (perhaps by mentoring younger people), or "stagnation," in which the person settles for a routine work existence and perhaps a passive approach to life more generally.

It seems, then, that individuals tend to confront and experience a number of age-graded events as they live out their lives. Stage theories serve as categorical systems for identifying and organizing these events. Most of them do more than that, however. In fact, they suggest rather directly that individuals are likely to invest their energies in different ways and to varying degrees at different times in their lives. Although the theories are not too specific about the nature, direction, and causes of such motivational shifts, they certainly suggest that they can and will occur—or at least they identify stages when such things are most likely to occur. Thus, one might surmise that during the "mid-life transition" stage, as defined by Levinson, certain individuals are likely to reorient their lives. This is presumably a time for reexamining where they have been and where they might go in life. Such reexamination leads to new goals, which in turn lead to new patterns of personal investment.

Does the Motivation to Achieve Decrease with Age?

Focusing on the suggestions implicit in stage theory, it might be expected that the motivation to achieve or to do a job well may show an overall decline with age for most people. After all, by midcareer, individuals know fairly well what they will accomplish, and most know what they will not be or do. The reassessments that often occur at this point conceivably could lead to a lessened interest in achievement. Although individuals may exhibit different responses to the life transitions and role changes that occur across the life span, one might expect an overall trend toward reoriented achievement motivation with age.

Phrasing these expectations in the language of personal investment theory, one might expect that as adults grow older, they would become less concerned with ego personal incentives and would value competence concerns and external rewards less. As these concerns decrease, other less achievement-related personal incentives would likely become more salient, particularly social solidarity.

There is, indeed, some evidence of a decline in achievement-related concerns as people age. In an early nationwide study of motivational patterns, Veroff, Atkinson, Feld, and Gurin (1960) found an overall tendency for achievement motivation to increase to a peak in middle adulthood and to show a rapid decrease thereafter. Contrasted to this was the finding that so-called power and affiliation needs showed basically increasing trends in the adult years. Atkinson (1978) and Raynor (1982) have further noted that these trends roughly parallel and possibly also partially explain the differential patterns in productivity and leadership reported by Lehman (1953).

The Atkinson-Raynor hypothesis is most interesting, but there are questions that must be considered before it can be fully accepted. First, the results are based on men, and there is reason to believe that the results might not be the same for women. A special point of interest for our discussion is that the results are based on "projective" assessment procedures, which tend to give a rather global assessment of motivational orientation and may reflect culturally limited definitions of achievement and other motivational orientations (cf. Maehr, 1974a). Moreover, support for the Atkinson-Raynor hypothesis is based largely on cross-sectional comparisons. Nevertheless, the results do reflect what might be predicted as the result of some of the research we have reviewed. Overall, men are simply less concerned with matters of achievement after the middle years.

Besides such evidence of general trends in motivational orientation across the life span, there are also indications of a more specific nature that motivational predispositions vary with age. A number of studies have focused on specific patterns of achievement-related behavior and style that may reflect motivational predisposition. A willingness to take moderate risks, to compete, and to make social comparisons and a general orientation toward the future are regularly cited characteristics of highly achievement-oriented people (Maehr, 1974a; McClelland, 1961, 1985a). It is clear that these are characteristics that are likely to affect a person's work life. The willingness to take moderate risks, for example, is thought to be a prime characteristic of the successful entrepreneur (McClelland, 1961; McClelland & Winter, 1971). Thus, variation in how, whether, or when an individual demonstrates such characteristics is likely to be important to more general patterns in the world of work. How are older people characterized in this regard?

The answer appears to be simple and direct, and it reinforces the basic patterns identified by Veroff et al. (1960) and specified further by Atkinson (1978) and Raynor (1982). First, older people have been characterized as relatively more conservative and cautious (Chown, 1961). Maggie Kuhn, leader of the Gray Panthers, exhorts her cohorts with the assertion that, at their age, there is "nothing to lose." But the evidence suggests that her message would have to be very provocative and inspiring to counteract the prevailing pattern of conservativism and cautiousness that characterizes the behavioral attitudes of the aged. A steady increase in anxiety and insecurity may be responsible for this pattern (Kuhlen, 1964), but it is also true that perceived rewards are rarely sufficient to justify setting higher goals and taking greater risks to achieve them (Chown, 1977). Second, the aged have also been described as possessing a tendency toward affiliation rather than competition and social comparison (Edward & Wine, 1963; Klein, 1972). Third, it seems more or less self-evident that a concentration on the future may be qualitatively different for the aged. Certainly, a delay of gratification takes on a different kind of meaning for the old than it can have for the young (Pollack & Kastenbaum, 1964).

Finally, from her review of the literature on personality and aging, Neugarten (1977) concluded that among the very few changes that seem to be predictable and general is the trend toward *interiority*—that is, toward becoming more introverted with age. One consequence of this change would likely be a deflation of the perceived importance of social reinforcers (for example, recognition). Thus, many of the conditions that typically elicit and define achievement motivation in earlier years seem to change with age.

Neugarten (1977) has pointed out, further, that the trend away from active mastery for men occurs *before* the onset of the influences that generally isolate individuals with increasing age (e.g., loss of health and income). But perhaps, as Kuhlen (1964) has suggested, the need for accomplishment simply becomes a less significant factor in social transactions for the man whose success or lack of success was established in middle age. This shift in midlife from getting what one wants to protecting what one has—a shift from a change orientation to a maintenance orientation—has been discussed by others as a critical transition in adulthood (Brent, 1978; Brim, 1974; Neugarten & Datan, 1973).

Reflecting on these results, Maehr and Kleiber (1981) have suggested, first, that it is necessary to take a rather broad view of achievement when considering the wide range of goals that an individual might hold throughout the life span. They also have pointed out the necessity of observing the behavior of individuals in different contexts and situations, and they have suggested the possibility of bias in looking for achievement motivation in certain contexts but ignoring it in others. For example, at some point in life, an individual might exhibit achievement motivation in a leisure area rather than in work (Kelly, 1981, 1982a). Finally, as people age, they are likely to be more intrinsically oriented than extrinsically oriented (Kleiber, in press).

Age, Meaning, and Personal Investment

There seem to be several reasons for systematic and predictable changes in motivation and personal investment across the life span. Idiosyncracies in experienced life events aside, a seemingly ineluctable tide of events can eventuate in motivational redirection for most people at certain definable life stages. To examine that possibility more specifically in terms of personal investment theory, we proceeded to examine age-related patterns in meaning and personal investment patterns. From a variety of possible approaches to analyzing the data, we settled on two basic strategies.

First, we conducted a number of analyses in which we considered age as a continuous variable and related it, in turn, to other IPI/IWI variables. In the main, this approach provided a quick first impression of the possible importance of age as an antecedent to meaning and personal investment. However, this approach carried us only a short distance in exploring the effects of age. Essentially, such an approach involved conceptualizing age as a variable that has continuous and monotonic association with meaning and personal investment. However, it appeared quite likely that the relationship between age and both meaning and personal investment would not be linear; that is, there are likely to be changes in meaning and personal investment at different life stages (e.g., first job, midcareer, retirement). Therefore, we also considered age in terms of stage categories, following an approach employed in earlier analyses of these data by Wigfield and Braskamp (in press). We categorized 1,095 adults in terms of four career stages: a younger career group (age 20–35), a middle career group (36–44), a later career group (45–54), and a group over 55 years of age. Such a categorization may imply that we are accepting the existence of inevitable age-graded patterns that manifest themselves regardless of culture or context. To the contrary, we do not assume the necessary existence of stages in the course of adult development, and our categorization is not meant to suggest this. Rather, we assume that, characteristically, individuals experience different developmental tasks—different life problems and opportunities—at different age levels and that these experiences are likely to influence personal investment. Our designation of categories, then, is one way of suggesting that different age-graded or age-related contexts are likely to be extant at different ages. Given the possibility of differential contexts for different age groups, what effects might we surmise would exhibit themselves in meaning and personal investment?

Age and Personal Incentives

Table 7–1 summarizes a series of analyses that considered differences in the importance of the eight personal incentives at successive life stages. The general trends suggested in these analyses are presented pictorially in figures 7–1 and 7–2. First, it may be noted in the table that important differential patterns emerged in five incentive scales—task, power, social concern, financial, and recognition. (The figures illustrate these differences.) Several conclusions are suggested by these data.

Younger people are more concerned than older people with their status among others; that is, they value financial rewards and recognition more highly. Older people are somewhat more intrinsically oriented, concerning themselves more with the task itself, and they value social concerns and helping others grow and develop more highly. This pattern is in line with some of the theory and research reviewed earlier. For instance, Maehr and Kleiber (1981) argued that people should become more task-oriented and concerned with social aspects as they age, with risk-taking and delay of gratification becoming less important. Raynor (1982) argued similarly, that older workers should become more intrinsically motivated. Furthermore, work on career stages (Gould, 1979; Hall & Nougaim, 1968; Rhodes, 1983) has shown that relationships with others and concerns about the work organization become primary in the later career stages. The patterns of relationships presented here are largely in accord with this generalization. The kinds of personal incentives that characterize the older people in our sample seem to be compatible with a personal investment in institutions and organizations not just because this is the way to earn money or get ahead. Older people are perhaps more attracted by the social aspects of the job and its inherent attractiveness.

Since our data are cross-sectional, one might wonder whether these results represent a special cohort effect. For example, the younger group in

Table 7–1
Differences in Personal Incentives at Different Life Stages

Personal Incentive	Overall Significance	Differences[a]
Task	.002	
Excellence	.84	
Competition	.14	
Power	.01	2–4
Affiliation	.04	
Concern	.01	2–4
Recognition	.0009	1–4, 2–4
Financial	.0001	1–4, 2–4, 3–4

[a]The age groups are as follows: 1 = <36 years; 2 = 36–44; 3 = 45–54; 4 = >54 years.

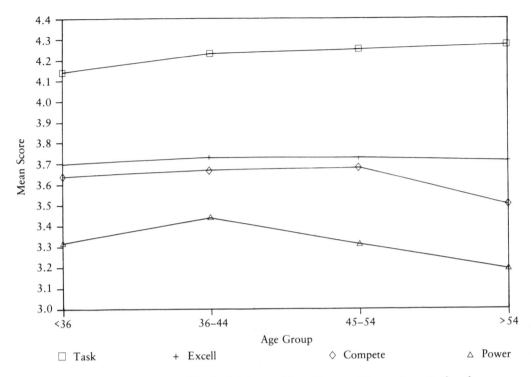

Figure 7–1. Average Scores of U.S. Adults on Four Personal Incentives Scales, by Age Group

this sample is roughly identified with the so-called baby boom generation. Although this group has been characterized in a variety of ways, the main point of relevance here is that they may be characterized as different in the ethic they follow and the incentives that guide their lives. Possibly, this is what is being captured in these results. Given the cross-sectional nature of the data, we cannot really answer such questions definitively. But there are at least two reasons why we might reasonably argue that we have uncovered a viable age-related trend.

First, our results are generally in accord with research results over a considerable period of time, in which different cohorts have shown essentially the same age tendencies. Second, the results accord well with what we know about the challenges confronting people at different age levels. Thus, it is not surprising that younger people are more concerned about money and getting ahead. They may, in fact, need more money, and they may be in positions where they need to view their job as largely instrumental to other goals. Nor is it likely that they will be captivated by the social aspects of the job. In all likelihood, the social relationships they have on the job are relatively new and

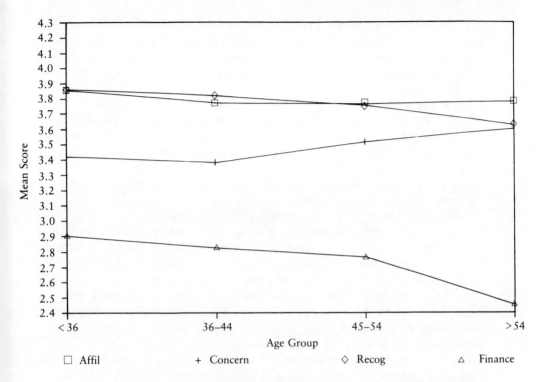

Figure 7–2. Average Scores of U.S. Adults on Four Personal Incentives Scales, by Age Group

are perceived as transient. In sum, it seems reasonable to conclude that the age trends uncovered in our results represent changes in personal incentives that reflect the typical challenges and opportunities confronting people in our society at successive age levels or career stages.

An interesting result is that people in the middle career stages (36–54) are found to be more concerned with power than those younger and older. They are also slightly but not significantly more competitively oriented. Certainly, the finding of greater stress on power in the middle group is readily interpreted as an orientation that is likely to be age- or stage-related, not idiosyncratic to the particular cohorts that composed our sample. Not only have other researchers observed increased stress on power orientations in what we have designated the middle career group (see, for example, Veroff et al., 1960; Veroff & Veroff, 1980), but this finding also accords with what we know about the kinds of work contexts in which people at these levels are likely to find themselves. People in the middle age groups are more likely to be in positions of formal authority or at a stage in their career where they are assuming more and more leadership roles. Thus, if one is willing to assume that personal incentives are likely to shift as roles, challenges, and opportunities change, these results seem to be quite plausible. We might note, further, that there was a suggestion in our results that this interest in power diminishes somewhat after the middle career ages, particularly as people approach retirement.

It is somewhat perplexing that the differences in competitive orientation at the different career stages were slight and were not statistically significant. On the basis of some previous research (Veroff et al., 1960; Veroff & Veroff, 1980), one might have expected an increase in competitive orientation during the middle career ages, followed by a decrease as people approach retirement. The present results reveal no real change in competitive orientation during the early and middle career stages.

All in all, though, our results are generally in accord with the findings of others in suggesting that age does bring about change in motivational orientations. Moreover, we suggest that these changes are largely compatible with the kinds of developmental tasks confronted by individuals at these age levels. As people confront different challenges or life options, personal incentives change in what can only be described as a reasonably compatible way. Thus, when people have the opportunity to play leadership roles, they are more likely to feel good about or express satisfaction in the exercise of authority. More broadly, this seems to suggest that personal incentives are not indelibly inscribed on the person. They are, as we argued in chapter 3, somewhat enduring but nevertheless subject to change with the situation. What we have added in looking at age and personal investment is that age likely establishes situational changes that change personal incentives. That interpretation of our results is certainly of some interest for further research on the aging process.

Age and Sense of Self

None of the three sense-of-self measures—self-reliance, goal-directedness, and sense of competence—were linearly associated with age. An analysis of the sense-of-self indices according to life stages indicated significant age-related patterns only in goal-directedness, as portrayed in figure 7–3. The major feature of this pattern is a marked increase at the 45–54-year stage, followed by a sharp decrease at the over-54 life stage. That general pattern may reflect a less focused job-controlled life-style, which is possible as people reach the end of their career.

In general, these findings do not support the notion that age brings about an overall loss of sense of competence or self-reliance. They do suggest that what we have labeled goal-directedness is less pronounced at older age levels—and that seems perfectly logical.

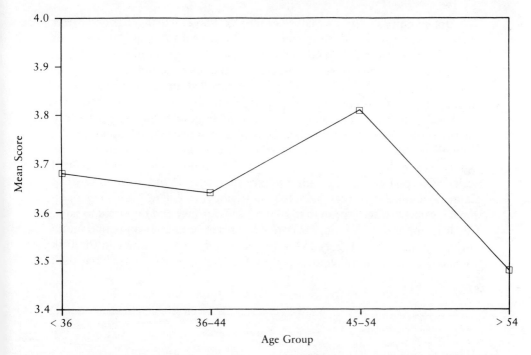

Figure 7–3. Average Scores of U.S. Adults on Goal-Directedness Scale, by Age Group

Age and Perceived Options

Although age does not have a pervasive effect on sense of self, it does appear to have a major influence on the personal incentives of U.S. adults. Moreover, we argue that the changes in personal incentives develop from the circumstances in which people find themselves. This leads us naturally to an examination of some of the perceived options associated with jobs and specifically to a consideration of how these options appear to change as people get older. It may be recalled that the IWI not only allows us to consider personal incentives and sense of self but also assesses perceived job options. Specifically, it assesses the perceived job opportunities for pursuing certain incentive possibilities on the job or in the work context. It also provides an assessment of the range of options that might be available to the person for job mobility—that is, perceived marketability (the ability to find job possibilities outside the current place of employment) and perceived advancement (ability to attain higher levels of employment within the organization). We now consider just how this third facet of meaning might be affected by age or career stage. Our examination is based on the subsample of people who responded to the IWI ($N = 303$).

Job Opportunities. First, we consider the question of whether age and career stage are associated with the perception of different job opportunities. For example, do older people tend to see more or greater possibilities for attaining task personal incentives? Of course, any such perceptions are likely to be a function of the jobs people hold, so we controlled for this factor as we examined the relationships between job opportunities and age/life stage.

Briefly summarized, people at different life stages did express a pattern of job opportunities that suggests that they do not have similar job opportunities throughout life. More specifically, the pattern of job opportunities was significantly different for the task, power, recognition, and financial reward scales. The patterns of job opportunities that were found are portrayed in figures 7–4 and 7–5. Generally, job opportunities to fulfill task and power personal incentives reach a peak in the 45–54 age category and then tend to taper off. It is interesting that opportunities for attaining recognition continue to rise in the last age category (54 years and over). The findings in the task category suggest that individuals in the 45–54 age group are more likely than

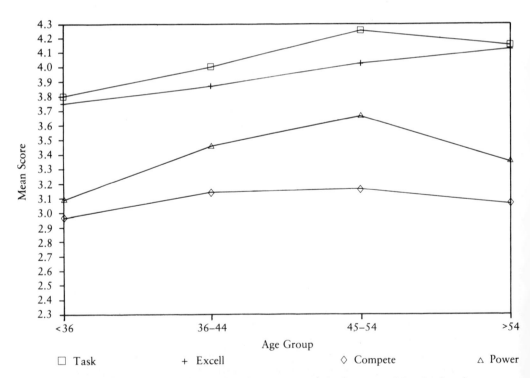

Figure 7–4. Average Scores of U.S. Adults on Four Job Opportunities Scales, by Age Group

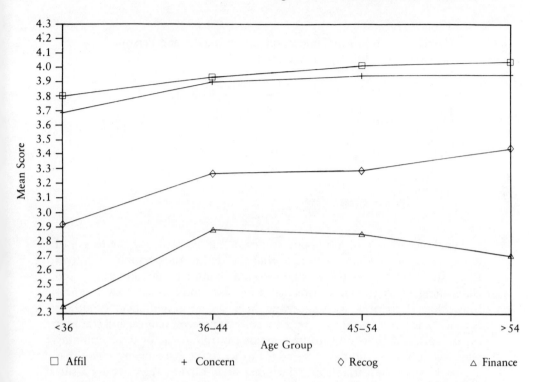

Figure 7–5. **Average Scores of U.S. Adults on Four Job Opportunities Scales, by Age Group**

those at earlier ages to have the most intriguing and challenging jobs, that other concerns (such as family and financial needs) are beginning to wane, and that they now have become fully absorbed in their work life as a kind of raison d'etre. Moreover, it is not surprising that at this stage of their work life they would express enhanced opportunities to pursue whatever power incentives that they have. They are most likely to have reached the highest levels of authority and leadership that they will reach in their work life. But recognition apparently comes later. Given the nature of our sample—people who are reasonably successful in largely white-collar jobs—this is a credible picture. We caution, however, that this may not reflect the patterns of those who have been less successful in the job market. It probably would not reflect the patterns of unskilled laborers or of those who have seldom experienced anything but marginal work roles.

Reflecting on these results, we should note, further, that these findings can be partially interpreted in terms of time in the organization. Table 7–2 presents the correlations between time in the organization and workers

Table 7–2

Correlations between Time in the Organization and Personal Incentives and Job Opportunities

Dimension	Personal Incentives	Job Opportunities
Task	.16	.35
Excellence	.04	.23
Competition	.09	.14
Power	.13	.38
Affiliation	.19	.30
Social	.13	.46
Recognition	.22	.16
Financial	−.14	.05

personal incentives and job opportunities. It can be seen that the length of tenure in an organization is not generally related to the personal incentives held but is related to perceived job opportunities to do interesting and challenging work (task), to exercise leadership and influence over others (power), and to offer assistance and help in the development of others (social). Thus, it is not age per se but a correlate of age, tenure, and status in the organization that seems to be a major controlling factor in determining perceived job opportunities. This adds further to the evolving argument that age itself is not the variable on which one should focus. Age is really a surrogate measure of the kinds of opportunities and challenges that are likely to be present for people, and it is these opportunities and challenges that are most critical in determining meanings and personal investment.

Advancement. The relationship of age to a second facet of perceived options—opportunities for advancement—was also considered. Figure 7–6 portrays the perceptions of advancement opportunities of the combined sample of people who responded to the IWI. Note, particularly, that separate results are not presented for managers and executives in this case. This is because these two groups showed a very similar pattern across age. In any event, the results shown in figure 7–6 are most interesting. It can be seen that the perception of advancement opportunities increases dramatically among those in the 36–44 age group. Again, these results are not altogether surprising; one would expect that this would be the stage of life when people could see opportunities for advancement. Moreover, the results mesh nicely with the previously discussed perceptions of job opportunities and perhaps also suggest reasons for changing personal incentives with age. The second life stage (36–44) is realistically the stage of anticipation in fulfilling certain desired goals. In the later stages, people have either reached what they have defined as goals or have had to adjust their striving accordingly. They thus perceive

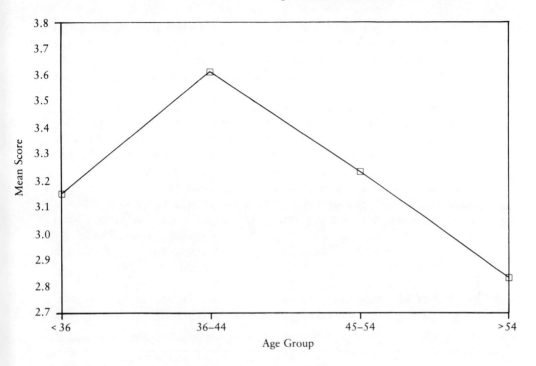

Figure 7–6. Average Scores of U.S. Adults on the Advancement Scale, by Age Group

that they have interesting jobs (task job opportunities), can exercise power, and are recognized and financially rewarded—or that they have done as well as they can expect to do in this regard.

Whether or not this broader interpretation is correct, the fact is that advancement opportunities are likely to diminish in the latter stages of a person's work life. That is clearly reflected in the results presented here. Although such an observation is neither surprising nor profound, its implications are not to be ignored in the fuller understanding of work behavior and human development. The developmental tasks at this stage of life are likely to involve coming to terms with where one is in one's job or career. If the individual initiates a career shift, it is likely to be horizontal—a shift into a different job—or an investment in different spheres of his or her life (e.g., leisure).

Marketability. The perceptions of both job opportunities and advancement relate specifically to perceived options within a particular work organization or context. The marketability scale relates to perceived options outside of the current work situation. One might realistically expect age to be associated with a decrease in perceived marketability, but one might also expect that this would depend somewhat on a number of other factors. Among these other factors would certainly be the type or level of job that a person holds. We were able to examine some of these interesting issues with our data set (see figure 7–7).

Generally, marketability follows the same pattern as advancement. Therefore, the results here tend to reinforce the larger picture that is emerging regarding the changing circumstances of work that accompany age. Not only are the range and number of opportunities likely to be fewer within the organization, the individual is likely to have fewer alternatives. He is where he is after the mid-career stages. (Whether *she* is where she is is a question that we will consider in chapter 8.) The point is that the data on marketability suggest a general pattern of plateauing in terms of job opportunities. This does not necessarily have a negative effect on motivation. Indeed, the findings regarding personal incentives and sense of self possibly indicate the opposite: the person simply digs into the job to a greater extent than ever and apparently finds fulfillment in this.

Job–Person Matches. In examining the meanings associated with personal investment in work, it has become clear that a critical factor is working out a

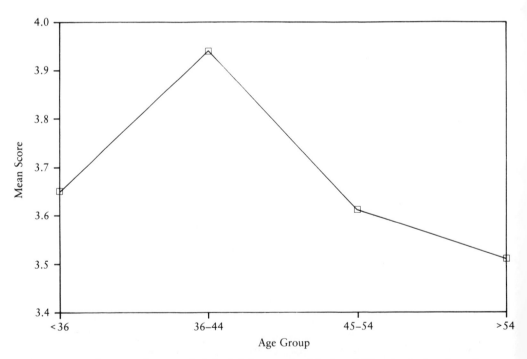

Figure 7–7. Average Scores of U.S. Adults on the Marketability Scale, by Age Group

match between worker and job. This takes time, and such factors as age or tenure are possibly related to achieving such a match. Therefore, it is logical that we should look, finally, at the relationship of age or life/career stage and the degree of matching between our sample of workers and their jobs.

There are many reasons for assuming that as people get older, they are likely to have positions and responsibilities (jobs) that more closely fit not only their skills but also their motivational orientations. On logical grounds alone, one can assume that a self-selection process has been operative longer in older people. Either they have already selected themselves out of situations in which they cannot pursue what is important to them—or someone else has removed them from these contexts. Then, too, there is the matter of socialization, in which people learn to adapt their personal predilections to the demands of their work. Thus, there are a variety of reasons why one might expect age to be related to person–job matches in a systematic fashion.

To confirm this expectation in our samples, we conducted a series of analyses. A measure of job opportunities–personal incentive congruency was correlated with age for each of the eight dimensions. Each of the eight correlations was negative, indicating that age is, indeed, associated with increased congruency between people's goals (i.e., personal incentives) and the opportunities for pursuing them in their jobs. That in itself is an important and interesting finding. But perhaps the most interesting findings in this regard are those displayed in figures 7–8 through 7–11. These graphs portray personal incentives and parallel job opportunities across the four stages of life designated earlier. It will be noted that personal incentives and job opportunities are portrayed such that one can readily view how personal incentives of individuals tend to converge or diverge at different life stages. Generally, it can be seen that personal incentives exceeded job opportunities for those aged 36 and younger. But note that—particularly in the areas of power and financial reward—people aged 54 and older had, on the average, opportunities that were perceived as greater than their personal incentives for power and financial rewards.

It appears that whereas incentives outdistance opportunities of younger people, opportunities do, in some cases, exceed aspirations for older people. This seems to accord well with what we sense regarding motivational change throughout the life span, although it has seldomly been demonstrated so clearly in empirical terms. However, the full meaning of this finding in regard to personal investment is by no means self-evident. One might surmise that having less of what one wants could serve to arouse and focus behavior toward reducing the discrepancy or striving toward congruency. Having more than one wants would arguably have an opposite or no effect in directing the course of personal investment. Given the evidence available, however, this is speculative, and no definitive conclusions are possible. Yet, at the very least, these findings of differential discrepancies between opportunities and

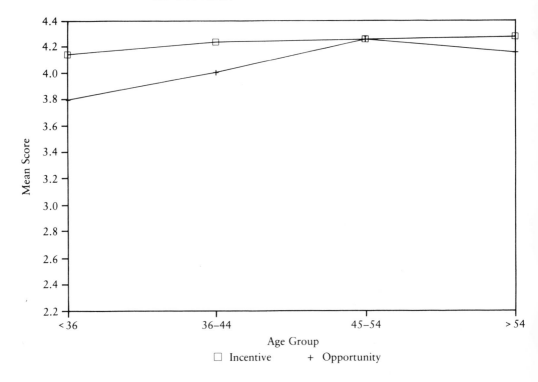

Figure 7–8. Average Scores of U.S. Adults on Task Incentive and Opportunities Scales, by Age Group

incentives at different age levels present some intriguing questions for further research.

Age and Personal Investment

In an important sense, the bottom line of our examination concerns, specifically, how age relates to personal investment. In this regard, we considered the relationship of age with job satisfaction and job commitment, the two measures of personal investment contained in the IWI. The results are most interesting in each case.

Job Satisfaction. Generally, age was found to be one of the significant predictors of job satisfaction, which is certainly not unexpected given previous research (see Doering, Rhodes, & Schuster, 1983, for an extensive review). Moreover, this generalization tends to hold fairly well across levels and types of jobs—a finding that is also compatible with job satisfaction research. Furthermore, the increase in job satisfaction appears to be continuous and, for the most part, linear across

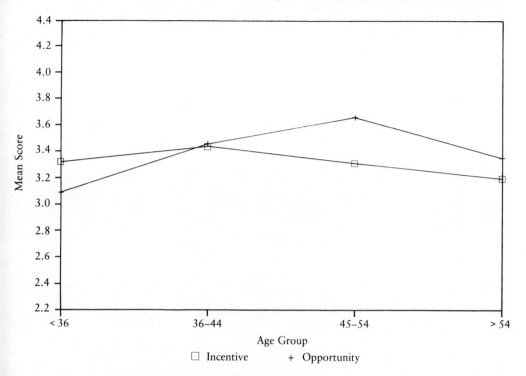

Figure 7–9. Average Scores of U.S. Adults on Power Incentive and Opportunities Scales, by Age Group

age, with no significant decrements or increments at different life stages. Perhaps a certain plateau of job satisfaction appears during the middle years, but job satisfaction continues to be higher even in the oldest age group. The general pattern is presented in figure 7–12.

Organizational Commitment. The pattern of relationships between age and organizational commitment is similar to that obtained for job satisfaction. That is, there is an overall trend for organizational commitment to increase with age, and this trend tends to hold across different types of positions. The results are portrayed in figure 7–13, which presents a picture of the increase in organizational commitment for all employees in the sample across the designated life stages. Before age 36, workers show relatively little organizational commitment, but this commitment increases and to some degree stabilizes during the middle years. During the latter decades of their careers, they show a significant but by no means abrupt increase in loyalty to their work organization.

Again, these results accord well with what might be expected on the basis of previous research. We may note, as we did before, that age is correlated

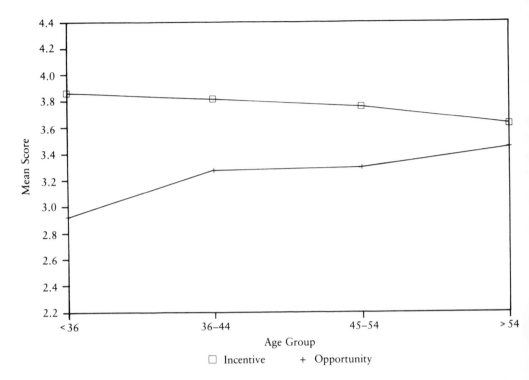

Figure 7–10. Average Scores of U.S. Adults on Recognition Incentive and Opportunity Scales, by Age Group

with job tenure. Thus, because older people have been with the organization longer, it is to be expected that they would exhibit greater commitment to it.

High Achievement and Age

Finally, we return to an interesting, recurring issue in this book. Do high achievers differ from the sample as a whole in exhibiting changes with age? The overall comparisons of high achievers were discussed in detail in chapter 5, but a brief summary discussion might be in order at this point. Generally, the results indicate that high achievers are higher than others in task involvement and in striving for excellence and power. They are also more goal-directed, but they are significantly lower than others in affiliation. High achievers focus more on the job itself and on getting ahead, rather than on social considerations, such as receiving support from others. The question at this juncture, however, is how such patterns may change with age. The results are intriguing. Briefly, the nonselected group showed more changes

Table 5–1
Correlations between Personal Incentives and Job Opportunities and
Organizational Culture on the Same Dimensions

Personal Incentives	Job Opportunities	Organizational Culture
Task	.28	.29
Excellence	.21	.10
Competition	.26	.04
Power	.29	.14
Affiliation	.27	.14
Social Concern	.24	.13
Recognition	.18	.11
Financial	.06	.00

satisfy the personal incentive in question. Thus, the first, basic methodological point is that the two scales do not measure the same things. Separately,
they yield different kinds of information. Similarly, the correlations between
the employees' personal incentives and the perceived opportunities in the
wider organization, as indicated by the organizational culture scales, are not
high. Apparently, there is no significant relationship between the importance
placed on personal incentives and perceptions of the emphasis on the pursuit
of certain incentives in the organizational context. The values stressed in the
organization are not mirror images of the personal incentives of the workers.
The culture of the organization is thus more than a summation of what the
employees believe is worth pursuing.

In sum, there seems to be a perception of what exists "out there" that is
not complementary to an individual's own desires or values. That perception
seems to be indexed by the job opportunities scale. To some extent, it may also
be assessed by the organizational culture scale, although this scale does not
directly endeavor to get at perceived options as we have defined the construct.

Having assessed perceptions of options available for pursuing personal
incentives in the job and possibly in the organization as well, we then studied
the relationships of these perceptions to job satisfaction and organizational
commitment. How do certain perceptions of opportunities available in a job
relate to job satisfaction and to organizational commitment? Are the opportunities to pursue certain incentives, such as task or excellence incentives,
especially related to job satisfaction or commitment? Conversely, when competition is stressed in a job context, is that likely to be associated with job
dissatisfaction or to lack of commitment to the organization?

Table 5–2 shows the correlation of perceived job opportunities with job
satisfaction. Perceived job opportunities in all the personal incentive categories are associated with satisfaction and commitment. There is only a suggestion that perceiving opportunities to pursue certain personal incentives
may be more important than others. Thus, the opportunity to pursue compe-

Table 5–2
Correlations between Job Opportunities and Job Satisfaction and Organizational Commitment

Job Opportunities	Satisfaction	Commitment
Task	.54	.53
Excellence	.50	.50
Competition	.39	.45
Power	.40	.42
Affiliation	.53	.58
Social Concern	.43	.50
Recognition	.49	.52
Financial	.53	.49

tition and power personal incentives does not seem to be as strongly associated with either job satisfaction or organizational commitment as the opportunity to have a pleasant social context in which workers can do well and be recognized for it.

Advancement → Job Satisfaction/Organizational Commitment. A second indicator of perceived options contained within the IWI is the organizational advancement scale. The relationship of perceptions of the possibility of organizational advancement to job satisfaction is indicated in table 5–3. The correlation between perceptions of organization advancement possibilities and job satisfaction is rather high ($r = .52$); that is, perceptions of greater possibilities of job advancement within the organization are generally associated with greater job satisfaction. Similarly, advancement and organizational commitment are related ($r = .51$). Thus, workers who view their futures in the organization in which they are currently employed as bright are more apt to express greater job satisfaction and commitment to the organization than those who do not see their futures so positively.

Marketability → Job Satisfaction/Organizational Commitment. The third index of perceived options is measured by the marketability scale. In this case, options are external to the organization and depend on the workers'

Table 5–3
Correlations between Job Satisfaction, Organizational Commitment, Marketability, and Organizational Advancement

	Commitment	Marketability	Advancement
Job Satisfaction	.64	.46	.52
Commitment		.52	.51
Marketability			.58

own skills and competencies. We predicted that workers who perceive more opportunities for themselves outside the organization might be happier in and more committed to the organization in which they found themselves; after all, they have chosen to stay in the organization in which they now work. In general, our data support this generalization. The correlation of marketability with job satisfaction is .46, and the correlation with commitment is .52. Thus, workers who view themselves as marketable are more satisfied with their current jobs than others are.

Personal Incentives → *Job Satisfaction/*
Organizational Commitment

It has often been assumed that certain people possess a kind of work ethic that drives them to involve themselves in their work. We discussed this possibility to some degree in chapters 2 and 3 when we considered the role of personality in determining motivation and achievement and the degree of personal investment in an activity such as work. The IWI does not contain a "work ethic" scale, but it seems appropriate to consider whether certain profiles of personal incentives might be more associated with personal investment in the job, apart from any idiosyncratic conditions of that job. Are people of a certain type simply more likely to be satisfied with their jobs or more committed to the work organization, regardless of the kind of job or organization? Certainly, many personnel managers believe this. As discussed earlier, many who are in charge of hiring and firing think in terms of "good people," rather than in terms of the "right person for the job."

We conducted two multiple regression analyses, one for job satisfaction and one for organizational commitment. In each case, the predictor variables were the personal incentives and sense of self dimensions assessed by the IWI. The results are presented in table 5–4, where it can be seen that there is little basis to assume that there is a pattern of personal incentives or sense-of-self

Table 5–4
Significant Personal Incentive and Sense-of-Self
Predictors of Job Satisfaction and
Organizational Commitment

Job Satisfaction	Organizational Commitment
Task	Task
Affiliation	Power
Financial	Affiliation
Goal-Directed	Concern
	Financial
	Goal-Directed
$R^2 = .09$	$R^2 = .18$

judgments that is associated with work investment as defined by satisfaction or commitment. Thus, the combination of sense of self and personal incentives generally does not reliably predict job satisfaction and organizational commitment. Thus, there is no basis for assuming that anything like a generalizable work ethic trait is operative in determining personal investment as indexed by general job satisfaction or organizational commitment.

The Interaction of Meanings in Determining Personal Investment

Thus far in this section, we have looked at each facet of meaning separately in terms of its relationships to personal investment in the job. It has been difficult to refrain from commenting on the possibility that these meanings operate in concert and interactively in affecting personal investment. One might logically expect that individuals not only hold certain meanings that are important regarding personal investment but also hold perceptions that there are opportunities in their work environment for successful pursuit of personal incentives. Similarly, it is important not only that people see that they have opportunities for advancement but also that they believe that the pursuit of advancement is worthwhile. Therefore, we considered how the meanings work collectively or interactively to affect personal investment.

Personality × Situation. In considering the interaction of facets of meaning in determining job satisfaction and organizational commitment, we conducted essentially two types of analyses. First, we considered whether certain characteristics of the individuals that may be construed as relatively enduring might interact with perceptions of the situation to influence personal investment. It will be readily recognized that in pursuing this question, we are following a well-trodden research path—one that has been a part of achievement theory for some time (Atkinson & Feather, 1966; Maehr, 1974b). In the present case, we assumed that sense-of-self and personal incentive profiles might represent somewhat enduring traits of the individual, much as measures of achievement motivation or power motivation represent relatively enduring traits within McClelland's need theory of motivation. We then asked whether or not these traits "cause" the person to relate to situational opportunities, such as advancement, in different ways. Operationally, we considered whether each of the personal incentive and sense-of-self indices interacted with marketability and advancement. Following McClelland (1985a), for example, one might expect that people who are high in achievement motivation or power motivation would react differently in situations where they perceive greater opportunities for advancement. The perception of marketability in a certain career context might also be related to or interact with enduring motivational orientation (possibly indexed by measures of personal incentives and sense of self). In any event, we systematically considered whether each of the personal incentive and sense-of-self factors interacted with marketability and advancement in determining job satisfaction and organizational commitment.

The results related to this first question are summarized in tables 5–5 and 5–6. Certain interactions emerge as important predictors of commitment and job satisfaction—though to a greater degree in organizational commitment than in job satisfaction. It is especially interesting that when individuals with excellence and power personal incentives perceive opportunities for advancement, they are most likely to be committed to the organization. Similarly, high sense of competence, complemented by advancement opportunities, is associated with organizational commitment. Equally interesting is that the perception of advancement opportunities for those high on the affiliation personal incentive dimension does not lead to organizational commitment. This finding is more or less in accord with what is expected, and it leads to the general conclusion that, as McClelland has argued over the years, certain individuals are likely to be differentially attracted by different opportunities for advancement. We have also reported results regarding marketability, but it is not so easy to interpret these results, as they cannot be readily set in terms of any theoretical or practical frame of reference.

Perception of Opportunities. A second question involved how the perception of the extent of opportunities available in the job or organizational situation for attaining valued incentives affects job satisfaction and organizational commitment. That is, we considered the discrepancy between personal orientation and job/organizational opportunities.

The degree to which people believe they can pursue valued personal incentives in any given context is likely an important factor in how they invest

Table 5–5
Significant Predictors of Satisfaction and Commitment Based on Personal Incentives, Sense of Self, and Advancement

Predictors	Satisfaction	Commitment
Personal Incentives		Task
		Affiliation
		Financial
Sense of Self		
Advancement		
Interactions	Task × Advancement	Excellence × Advancement
	Esteem* × Advancement	Power × Advancement
		Affiliation × Advancement
		Concern × Advancement
		Esteem × Advancement
	$R^2 = .34$	$R^2 = .39$

*Esteem = sense of competence

Table 5–6
Significant Predictors of Satisfaction and Commitment Based on Personal Incentives, Sense of Self, and Marketability

Predictors	Satisfaction	Commitment
Personal Incentives	Task	
Sense of Self	Goal-Directed	
Marketability		
Interactions	Task × Marketability	Task × Marketability
		Power × Marketability
		Affiliation × Marketability
		Concern × Marketability
	$R^2 = .26$	$R^2 = .34$

themselves in their jobs. The match between the individual's personal incentives and job opportunities and its potential effects on work investment must be an important consideration in the analysis of work motivation. For example, people who hold a high orientation toward excellence would be most likely to invest themselves in a job if that job not only requires competence but provides opportunities for assessing and evaluating competence. They would likely be most unhappy in a situation where competence is not recognized or valued. The notion of matches and mismatches between the individual and the organization is a common one both for managers and executives who hire and promote and for organizational psychologists (Wanous, 1980). The matching process between the individual and the organization involves two interrelated themes. First, a mismatch between the person's abilities and the abilities needed to perform the job results in lower job performance—a primary concern of management. Second, a mismatch between individual values and incentives and the reinforcements available through the organization leads to reduced job satisfaction and organizational commitment. Such mismatches likely also result in lower job performance. Obviously, both ability/skill and personal incentives/job opportunity mismatches are likely to be important in affecting the employees' personal investment in work, but we are especially concerned here with the latter type of mismatch.

The research evidence on the impact of a mismatch between the individual's desires and the organization's ability to satisfy them indicates that the consequence is low job satisfaction (Mobley, Griffeth, Hand, & Meglino, 1979; Porter & Steers, 1973). The research evidence on the consequences of a mismatch on organizational commitment is less definitive, but the matching model, as depicted by Wanous (1980) and others, suggests that lower organizational commitment is a consequence of the incapacity of the organization to provide opportunities for individual workers to pursue incentives they value.

Through the IWI, we assessed two components of reinforcements available through the job and through the wider organization. First, we assessed the organizational culture around the four incentive themes of task, ego, social concern, and external rewards. Second, we assessed workers' perceptions of the extent to which their jobs allow them opportunities to satisfy their personal incentives. Finally, we were able to relate these factors to two affective outcomes specified in Wanous's (1980) matching model—job satisfaction and organizational commitment.

We examined the relationship between the discrepancies (mismatches) in two ways. First, we obtained correlations of discrepancies between personal incentives/job opportunities and overall job satisfaction (the sum of satisfaction with task, ego, social, and external rewards incentives) and organizational commitment. The correlations are presented in table 5–7. All relationships are negative; thus, the extent to which the job provides opportunities to satisfy each of the personal incentives (resulting in a zero difference or discrepancy) is related to the degree of satisfaction and commitment. If we use a global measure of the congruency between incentives and opportunities to fulfill them on the job, we can conclude that congruency is related both to job satisfaction ($r = -.56$) and to commitment to the organization ($r = -.47$). More specifically, a match of incentive and opportunity seems to be most important in regard to external rewards, followed by task involvement and affiliation. Thus, in general, discrepancies, defined as the differences between incentives and opportunities, are important in their relationship to both job satisfaction and organizational commitment.

The second set of analyses was conducted by Mayberry (1985), who ran a series of regression analyses to determine the degree to which personal incentive and job opportunities/organizational culture congruencies were as-

Table 5–7
Correlations of Discrepancies Between Organizational Culture/ Personal Incentives and Job Satisfaction/ Organizational Commitment

Discrepancy Factors	Satisfaction	Commitment
Task	−.40	−.32
Excellence	−.42	−.34
Competition	−.29	−.27
Power	−.33	−.22
Affiliation	−.44	−.42
Social Concern	−.29	−.26
Recognition	−.44	−.38
Financial	−.48	−.42

sociated with job satisfaction and commitment to the organization. Mayberry conducted two multiple regression analyses to determine whether congruencies were more predictive of job satisfaction and organizational commitment than the person's scores on the actual scales. In other words, does knowledge of a person's congruency between incentives, opportunities, and culture provide additional information about job satisfaction and organizational commitment? The first analysis involved determining estimates of the differences between personal incentives and job opportunities by multiple regression—a sophisticated analysis employed to reduce errors of measurement in using difference scores. Three sets of congruencies were used—personal incentive–job opportunities, personal incentive–organizational culture, and job opportunities–organizational culture. In the second regression analysis, scores of each person on the eight personal incentive scales, the eight job opportunities scales, and the four organizational culture scales were entered into the multiple regression equation in a stepwise fashion to determine the maximum linear relationship between the set of these 20 predictors and each of the two measures—job satisfaction and organizational commitment.

The results of the stepwise multiple regression analysis for job satisfaction, shown in table 5–8, indicated that ten of twelve congruencies made sig-

Table 5–8
Significant Congruency and Component Variables for Predicting Job Satisfaction

Congruency Variables	Component Variables
Personal Incentive–Job Opportunities	*Personal Incentive*
3 Power	9 Excellence
5 Excellence	10 Task
6 Competition	*Job Opportunity*
7 Financial	2 Affiliation
10 Affiliation	3 Task
Personal Incentive–Organizational Culture	4 Financial
2 Ego	5 Recognition
8 Task	6 Competition
Job Opportunities–Organizational Culture	*Organizational Culture*
1 External	1 External
4 Ego	7 Social
9 Social	8 Task
$R^2 = .50$	$R^2 = .61$

Note: The number preceding each variable represents the relative order in which it contributed to the squared multiple correlation. *Personal Incentive–Job Opportunities* is the difference between a person's Personal Incentives scale score and Job Opportunities scale score on the same dimension. *Personal Incentive–Organizational Culture* is the difference between a person's average Personal Incentives scale score and Organizational Culture score in each of the four major areas. *Job Opportunities–Organizational Culture* is the difference between a person's average Job Opportunities scale score and Organizational Culture scale score in each of the four major areas.

nificant contributions and, in sum, were able to explain over 50 percent of the variance of satisfaction. Of the ten congruency variations considered, five of the personal incentive–job opportunities congruencies were included in the final list of congruencies that are related to job satisfaction: power, excellence, competition, financial, and social concern.

If we contrast the two multiple regression analyses reported in table 5–8, we can conclude that congruency variables, as a group, do not predict as well as the scales themselves, which are labeled *component variables* ($R^2 = .50$ versus $R^2 = .61$). The major set of predictors among personal incentives, job opportunities, and organizational culture are the job opportunities scales, because they represent the second through the sixth place in the order in which they entered the regression analysis; that is, they significantly increased the multiple correlation. However, the two analyses lead to slightly different conclusions. When congruencies are employed, job satisfaction is most closely associated with the ego dimension, in which leadership and power are stressed. That is, when people perceive a greater similarity between the importance they place on succeeding through competition—by having positions in which they can exercise leadership—and what their job offers them in these dimensions, they express a greater degree of job satisfaction. If we use the component variables (actual scales), external rewards (financial and recognition) offered in their jobs become the most important incentives. It is interesting that only the two incentive variables related to task are related to job satisfaction.

The same two analyses were conducted to determine the relationship between these congruencies and organizational commitment. Table 5–9 presents the congruencies and component variables that were significant in predicting organizational commitment. If we use congruencies, we can conclude that the ego dimensions are the most predictive of the eight congruencies involving incentives and job opportunities. The capacity of the employees to find ways to exercise leadership and influence in their jobs is related to satisfaction in their work.

In comparison to congruency measures, the significant component variables also included the ego dimensions, but only as personal incentives. In contrast, opportunities to establish warm and supportive working relationships with their co-workers and supervisors are an important predictor of commitment. If we examine the differences between the significant predictors of job satisfaction and of commitment to the organization, we can conclude that affiliation is more closely associated with commitment than with satisfaction.

These findings are similar to those of other studies of the correlates of commitment. Drake and Mitchell (1977) concluded that workers who perceived that they held greater power in the organization relative to others were more committed to the organization. Pennings (1976) and Azim and Bosiman (1975) also found that people who possessed high levels of influence within an organization expressed a relatively high commitment to the organization.

Table 5–9
Significant Congruency and Component Variables for Predicting Organizational Commitment

Congruency Variables	Component Variables
Personal Incentive–Job Opportunities	*Personal Incentive*
2 Competition	3 Excellence
6 Affiliation	4 Power
7 Power	6 Social Concern
9 Excellence	*Job Opportunities*
10 Financial	1 Affiliation
Personal Incentive–Organizational Culture	9 Financial
1 Ego	10 Recognition
5 Social	*Organizational Culture*
11 Task	2 External
Job Opportunities–Organizational Culture	5 Social
3 Social	7 Task
4 External	8 Ego
8 Ego	
$R^2 = .54$	$R^2 = .60$

Note: The number preceding each variable represents the relative order in which it contributed to the squared multiple correlation. *Personal Incentive–Job Opportunities* is the difference between a person's Personal Incentives scale score and Job Opportunities scale score on the same dimension. *Personal Incentive–Organizational Culture* is the difference between a person's average Personal Incentives scale score and Organizational Culture score in each of the four major areas. *Job Opportunities–Organizational Culture* is the difference between a person's average Job Opportunities scale score and Organizational Culture scale score in each of the four major areas.

However, commitment is also associated with interpersonal relationships among the workers. Workers who can assist others in their work feel a greater loyalty to and express a greater sense of ownership of the organization. Although the two opportunities of influence and affiliation are sometimes viewed as contradictory, this may not be the case. The two orientations may, in fact, be viewed as complementary. Those with the greatest formal authority often are in the best position to assist others and to be supportive, at the same time being able to direct others toward the organizational goals. In a sense, this is what managers feel is their job—to influence others and to help make their subordinates maximize the organization's productivity.

Finally, a multiple regression analysis was run that included the eight personal incentives, three sense-of-self measures, and the eight job opportunities scales, the advancement and marketability scales and the four organizational culture scales. As shown in table 5–10, of the 25 potential scales, 12 were statistically significant predictors of job satisfaction and 10 predicted organizational commitment. Both sets of significant predictors resulted in multiple correlations exceeding .60. Task and external rewards incentives were included as important variables in predicting job satisfaction and commitment.

Table 5-10
Significant Predictors of Satisfaction and Commitment

	Satisfaction	Commitment
Personal Incentives	Excellence	Excellence
	Recognition	Power
		Social Concern
Sense of Self		Self-Reliance
Job Opportunities	Task	Affiliation
	Competition	Recognition
	Affiliation	
	Recognition	
	Financial	
Advancement/Marketability	Advancement/Marketability	Marketability
Culture	Task	Task
	Power	Social Concern
	Rewards	Rewards
	$R^2 = .62$	$R^2 = .65$

However, the pattern of significant personal incentives is not identical for satisfaction and commitment. Job satisfaction is more closely aligned with task and power dimensions, whereas commitment is more closely associated with the interpersonal dimensions of social concern and affiliation. Also, commitment is more closely associated with a high sense of self-reliance than job satisfaction is.

Conclusion

It is sometimes assumed that some individuals have a certain orientation that causes them to throw themselves into work regardless of setting or circumstance. No one assumes that work motivation has *no* situational basis, but we might wonder about the possibility that a certain personal incentive profile and patterns of sense of self might make individuals more inclined toward investing themselves in work, even as the nature and structure of the job and its context vary broadly. The assumption here is that some people are less situation-bound—more able to structure the situation to their own predilections or somehow adapt more readily to a broader array of jobs. Even if the job does not match their particular predilections, they make the most of it. Operationally, this may be interpreted to mean that certain meanings (personal incentives and sense of self, in particular) would relate to job satisfaction and job commitment, apart from the job situation or organizational context. We cannot rule out this possibility absolutely, but our research indicates that it is the opportunity to pursue valued personal incentives effectively in a specific job or organizational context that is important. This suggests that one does not simply select "motivated people" to have a motivated work force; one must also take into account the work and the organizational climate. The organization must provide opportunities for workers to effectively pursue personal incentives that are salient to them. It is not just the meanings (personal incentives, for example) that a person brings to a job that are critical; rather it is the meanings that arise as the person perceives opportunities for himself or herself within the job and in the organizational setting. That simple but basic point is underscored in the results presented here, which indicate that a particular construction of meanings brought to the situation by the person, when complemented by specifiable job-associated perceptions, make a difference. Thus, the constructs of personal investment suggest more than a general idea of how things might work; they show specifically what types of meanings and job perceptions work together in encouraging personal investment in a work setting. The constructs of personal investment theory are, if we may use the term, *meaningful* in analyzing and defining person and situation matches that effect personal investment.

More generally, the data gathered with the aid of the IWI have provided further confidence that meanings held by people as they confront the work situation are importantly related to and likely are a cause of work investment.

Implications: A Step Beyond the Data and A Look Ahead

In earlier chapters (particularly chapter 3), we reviewed rather tightly controlled experimental studies that led us to the conclusion that personal investment was a function of certain meanings held by the person. We also suggested more specifically how certain meanings were likely to have particular effects. Beginning with chapter 4, however, we have begun to move beyond the limited confines of laboratory studies to expand our theory and make it more applicable to the real world of personal investment. In this chapter, in particular, we have applied the theory to the real world of jobs and careers. In a series of field studies, we have shown that our model has relevance to how people invest themselves in important areas of their lives. Moreover, the theory set forth here and the measurement instruments that have evolved out of the theory can be applied in answering very practical questions.

This assertion will be put to further test in subsequent chapters. For now, however, we wish to underscore the point that meanings, as we define them, are associated with specific personal investment patterns. If people hold certain meanings, they are likely to choose to invest their time, talent, and energy in situations that are compatible with those meanings. For example, if financial rewards are salient, it is likely that the person will not aspire to be a teacher. Similarly, a person with a strong sense of competence who also holds a strong competitive personal incentive will be led to perform in situations that challenge his or her ability; and a person who readily relates to people will seek out social situations. Some managers are tied to their desks and isolate themselves from all but a few staff members; others can't be tied to an office, let alone a desk.

All in all, meanings held by a person in any given situation guide personal investment in a variety of predictable ways. Having outlined the ways in which meanings likely affect behavior, however, we must conclude with an important caveat. Not every facet of the theoretical structure we have erected has been fully tested, and we cannot be fully confident of the workability of each and every implication of the theory in practice. But what we are saying about meaning and personal investment is based on considerable evidence. The evidence has not all been gathered in accord with the theory and procedures outlined here, but there is a strong empirical base to the theory. Although many of our statements have not had as extensive and controlled a test in real-life settings as would be desirable, we contend that they are as defensible as any hypotheses currently available and that they are better supported than most.

6
Organizational Culture, Meaning, and Personal Investment

We have asserted that meaning and motivation are inextricably linked—that the meaning of the situation to the individual determines personal investment and that knowing the meanings individuals hold allows us to predict how and when they will invest their time and energy—in their jobs or in any other activities. We assume that this assertion has now been established as a credible hypothesis—perhaps a viable principle—for understanding personal investment. But the utility of this hypothesis depends to a significant degree on the answer to a follow-up question: How do these meanings emerge? That is, how are they formed?

Of course, we are not confronting that question for the first time in this book. We set forth a firm basis for answering that question in chapter 3, where we presented an overview of the antecedents associated with personal investment. Important among these antecedents was the nature of the performance situation itself, the nature of the task to be performed, and the context in which it is performed. Generally, what the person does depends significantly on where the person is. People come to any situation with a set of biases based on their past experiences, and these past experiences color their perceptions of any task or situation. But the nature of the situation itself is at least as important as personal history in affecting meaning and personal investment. Jobs are not all alike, nor are all work settings alike. They differ in the skills demanded and the variety and autonomy offered; they vary in how performance is evaluated and rewarded; and they differ especially in the nature of the social relationships that exist. Such variations in job and work contexts affect the meaning of the work situation to the person and thereby determine personal investment. Thus, the structure of the job and the context in which the task is performed are critical variables affecting work performance. This is fundamentally true whether the person is an executive, a line supervisor, or a worker at the bottom of the employer–employee hierarchy.

In chapter 3, we provided a comprehensive summary of contextual factors that are likely to affect the meaning of the task to the person, and we outlined how they were subject to management and manipulation to enhance motivation. We build on that foundation in this chapter. Accepting the relevance of a broad range of situational causes of personal investment, we will focus on the role of what has come to be called *organizational culture.* Specifically, we intend to show that organizational culture can be a critical determinant of personal investment.

The Concept of Organizational Culture

The concept of organizational culture has become popular in recent years (Kilman, 1985). As Pascale (1984) has put it: "What corporate strategy was in the 1970s, corporate culture is becoming in the 1980s" (p. 28). To some extent, the use of this concept has evolved out of considerations of the work environments and organizational climate in U.S. and Japanese companies. Ouchi's (1981) popular anlaysis of the differences and similarities in work climates across the United States and Japan and Peters and Waterman's (1982) best-seller seem to have reinforced what may have been an already emerging tendency to describe organizations as cultural entities (see also Pascale & Athos, 1981; Schein, 1984, 1985; Wilkins, 1983).

Probably one reason that organizational culture has become a popular idea is that it addresses a burning question of executives at all levels: Can I do anything to enhance the overall motivation and productivity of workers? In workshops and conversations with managers of large and small organizations, this question first became salient for us.

Most managers of large organizations have very little direct contact with the people who do the basic work for which the organization is designed. They seldom see the workers or talk to them about their jobs, and they are hardly in a position to have much direct control over what goes on at the various work stations. Indeed, it is probably safe to assume that many really don't concern themselves with such matters, perhaps hoping that they will be handled by the personnel department or by automation. Yet they are and must be concerned about the overall productivity of the organization they head. They are held accountable for any decline in worker productivity or loss of morale. Recent popular studies on excellent companies (Hickman & Silva, 1984; Peters & Waterman, 1982) have indicated that when the corporate leadership is concerned with what workers do, it is likely to have positive effects on worker productivity. And as Pacale and Athos (1981) have indicated, the "art of Japanese management" revolves around this special concern with the worker.

Is there anything that can be done at all levels of management to affect what goes on "in the trenches"? Recently, considerable discussion and some research has been devoted to defining and understanding this thing called organizational culture (Jelinek, Smircich, & Hirsch, 1983). Moreover, a growing body of literature—some of it anecdotal, but some of it systematic and scientific—indicates that changes can be made at the organizational level that can and do affect the overall psychological climate of a large social system. In addition, it is argued that as one affects the culture of the organization, one will affect the productivity and overall performance of that organization (Deal & Kennedy, 1982; Peters & Waterman, 1982).

In this chapter, we will concentrate on presenting evidence from our own research regarding the existence, variety, and possible effects of organizational culture on personal investment. As we will soon see, our evidence and that of others argues that organizational culture has to be taken seriously as an important variable. The evidence also strongly suggests that those in leadership positions can do something to create a motivated work force through changes that affect the organizational culture.

Defining Culture

It is not surprising that there is no unified agreement regarding what an organizational culture is or might be. The term is often used in a rather nonspecific, nontechnical way. As with many popular terms, it has value in referring to a more or less shared observation on the nature of things, but it is not used with precision. It is clear, however, that if the term is to have utility in assessing the nature of a business organization or in forming management policy and procedure, greater definitional precision must be forthcoming.

There is considerable precedent for specifying the concept of *culture*, which has been around for some time. More important, it is an established concept within the realm of social science theory and research. Although that is not meant to imply that there is universal agreement on the use of the term, there is a firm basis for establishing a working definition that can ultimately prove useful in measurement and research. Following our own previous work (Maehr, 1974a), we suggest that culture is properly viewed as a complex of norms extant within a particular social organization or group. These norms, in turn, might be viewed as shared answers to basic questions confronting the social group—"answers" in the sense that they reflect a response to problems confronted by the group and the people who compose that group and a choice that must be made in organizing individual and group behavior. But it should not be concluded that individuals are fully cognizant that problems are being solved or choices are being made regarding which norms are followed. Often, a norm represents an unquestioned assumption about how things are to happen; it is an answer that is seen as inevitable. Drinking the blood of a live animal is as *normal* for the Masai (an African tribal group) as eating the meat of a dead animals seems to most of us. Drinking "live" blood and eating "dead" meat both solve the problem of hunger, but each represents a different choice that has been made by different social groups—a choice that becomes, in effect, the virtually inevitable way of behaving and believing for people who hold membership in those groups.

Defining culture in terms of shared answers or norms is straightforward. But if that approach is to prove useful, there must be an understanding of the nature of norms and normative behavior.

Norms and Normative Behavior

In discussing the concept of culture, one must keep in mind a critical and oft-observed characteristic of human behavior—the person as a social being. When people are involved in situations with other people, their behavior invariably begins to follow certain predictable patterns after a while. Rules, regulations, customs, and preferred styles emerge—that is, *social norms* evolve—and to a considerable degree, all involved are expected to give recognition if not exhibit subservience to them. The first principle of social interaction concerns the emergence of such guidelines for action. The second principle is that, within limits, individuals tend to conform to these guidelines; when they do not, they are likely to pay some price. That is, social groups create norms and, within limits, individuals conform. This happens in play groups and work groups; it happens in families, societies, and work organizations. Moreover, the existence and nature of these norms account for a major portion of the observable variation in human behavior in any given setting; that is, norms are a major cause of behavior. As indicated in earlier chapters, norms are also a major determinant of personal investment: People make their investments from a set of known and acceptable options. Whether a given option is acceptable or not depends significantly on what a given group considers acceptable.

Culture as a Complex of Norms

Culture may appropriately be viewed as a complex of norms and prescriptions that are extant in a given situation for a given group of people. Implicit in the concept of *norm* is the notion that these guidelines are to some degree shared. That is, the culture of a group consists of the commonly understood and shared beliefs and expectations that exist for people who compose the group. Of course, individuals vary in the degree to which they conform, and groups vary in the degree to which a common set of guidelines is salient to the various members. Such variations in understanding and conforming to any set of guidelines are important in themselves in analyzing group behavior.

The use of the term *culture* then, assumes that a certain group of individuals has been functioning in an interdependent fashion over a period of time. When such social interaction exists, there will be normative products;

that is, the group will arrive at ways of organizing itself, regularizing the behavior of its members, coordinating their functions, minimizing conflicts, and so on. In sum, the group members work out ways of getting along among themselves. The answers the group arrives at in this regard are a first type of normative product. A second type of normative product evolves out of concerns regarding how the group will relate to its environment: How will it handle the basic questions of what to eat and how to defend against the elements and enemies? Each social group arrives at some more or less agreed-upon answers to such basic questions of existence; it produces guidelines or *norms* for dealing with, thinking about, and acting in reference to the problems of living. These *shared answers* to life's challenges and problems are perhaps *the* critical feature of a culture. When the term *culture* is used to describe a particular society or societal group, such as in a reference to "Japanese culture," it often refers to a broad array of shared answers—ways in which the group structures certain experiences, assigns causes, explains events, and generally gives meaning to the worlds experienced by group members. Most important, however, culture involves guidelines regarding what people should strive for or aspire to. In other words, values and goals are a critical feature of that complex of norms referred to as culture (see chapter 8).

It is important to add that within any culture—if the culture is to persist and have relevance as a guideline for behavior—there is a need to communicate what the culture is. This is done in a variety of ways. Myths exist to describe heroes and, not incidentally, to define what is worthy of emulation and worth striving for. Greek school boys in Alexander the Great's time read Homer and not only found their heroes but also found the values of their heroes. They learned of goals that were worth pursuing. Similarly, young boys and girls who read Horatio Alger stories—or even read about Dick and Jane and Spot—pick up indications of what is of worth for them and for their social group. Such heroes essentially define options—a range of possible behavior—and suggest what one can hope for.

In a similar fashion, rituals and observances are designed not only to reinforce a view of the world in general but also to encourage a notion of purposes in particular. This is what much of so-called religious life is about, but secular rituals are often every bit as important as those found in churches and temples (Boje, Fedor, & Rowland, 1982).

Through informal and sometimes nonplanned events in the life of the society, members can learn much about what it is all about. These activities become opportunities for the leaders to describe the society's image of itself, thereby saying to all participants: This is what we are striving for, this is what we want to be, and this is what will be recognized and rewarded. Thus, ritual and rite reinforce meaning, particularly as they establish goals and define options with a society.

In terms of personal investment theory, we emphasize that a culture provides general guidelines for establishing meanings. It defines options; it establishes the availability and desirability of goals—what is worth striving for; and within limits, it suggests ways in which the person should define himself or herself as a member of the society. In this sense, we can say that the culture provides meaning for the individual. Furthermore, as culture establishes such meaning orientations, it influences personal investment.

The Culture of the Organization

Whetten (1984) has defined the culture of an organization as "taken for granted assumptions about shared beliefs, values and norms about the way things are (or should be) done around here." Thus, he has stressed the normative role of culture and has noted that within an organization, shared expectations and guidelines for actions tend to exist that are in an important sense specific to and uniquely characteristic of that organization. Deal and Kennedy (1982) noted this feature of organizations but also stressed that these norms are communicated through rite, ritual, and myth. Not only societies sponsor rituals and create heroes for such purposes; organizations also do so. Example after example is given of rituals that are standard in various companies, heroes that are promoted, and rites that are observed. As Deal and Kennedy have pointed out, these events serve to define the guidelines for all who participate in the organization. In a special way, they define what is worth striving for within this context, what is expected, and what will be rewarded. For example, Friday afternoon "beer busts," which apparently existed at Tandem Corporation (Deal & Kennedy, 1982), can express the value of social interaction and the worth of all in the organization. Birthday lunches or coffee hours in an office can have similar effects. Such social events point up the importance a company places on cooperative and effective social interaction among all members of the organization. When such activities cut across levels of power and authority, the organization can communicate the meaning not only that all members of the organization are important but also that all have a contribution to make. It may also communicate or reinforce the belief that mobility within the organization is a possibility. When these events occur in coordination with achievement or with the striving to attain production goals, the organization can also encourage the belief that productivity is valued. To this we would add that organizational culture may be thought of as providing a meaning base that guides personal investment. This occurs, particularly, as options are defined and incentives are stressed. It also occurs as roles are assigned and status is conferred.

One major reason for considering organizational culture as a variable is to develop a perspective of the organization as an entity that can be readily grasped by managers and leaders in such a way that they can operate effectively in terms of it. Thus, the use of the concept of organizational culture relates especially to an intention to describe an entity to which all of management can relate. The chief executive officer and senior level management of a corporation are particularly concerned with what they can do to enhance motivation and productivity. They are also concerned with commitment and morale. In most cases, however, they cannot or do not see the relevance of concerning themselves with a specific job situation, nor can they concern themselves with selecting all the "right" people. At best, they can select and directly affect the behavior of those with whom they must deal on a day-to-day, face-to-face basis. Since senior level managers cannot really expect to affect workers in a direct and immediate way, their attention is drawn to the effects of *organizational* changes on behavior. Basically, their concern is with how they can affect the overall context in which persons work, therby influencing morale and productivity. It is this problem of affecting the overall organizational context that the concept of organizational culture presumes to address.

We use the term *culture* to reflect the nature of an organization as a holistic entity. With others (for example, Goodenough, 1963, 1971; Schein, 1984, 1985), we consider that this nature is best revealed in the norms that can be identified by the employees themselves. In our analysis of organizational culture, we concentrate primarily on a limited set of norms that we feel are especially important in determining personal investment. Specifically, we focus on the shared perceptions of purposes and desired ends. Although our assessment procedures closely parallel procedures for assessing what has sometimes been called work climate, we prefer the term *organizational culture* precisely because it suggests a stress on meaning—particularly on values and goals.

Assessment of Organizational Culture

The foregoing discussions of culture in general and organizational culture in particular may prove useful for providing a perspective on mangement. However, their usefulness for understanding what goes on in organizations depends to a significant degree on assessing the existence of such a thing as a *culture*—or, more accurately, on assessing cultural variation in nature and salience.

How does one go about assessing organizational culture? Is there any way one can assess critical facets of organizational culture that truly indicate the essence of the differences that exist among the ways different corporate entities or units operate?

One can, first of all, follow an ethnographic approach—a tried and true way of studying culture. This is essentially what Deal and Kennedy (1982) did. They lived and worked in the corporate environment for an extended period and observed what was going on. On the basis of their field notes, they constructed a regular sequence of happenings and described patterns that served as guidelines for behavior. Their observations were usually complemented by structured and unstructured interviews through which they probed further the existence and importance of the behaviors they had observed. Then they attempted to portray the interlocking relationships in a coherent story of the workings of the corporation.

The value of such "thick" descriptions of human social behavior is self-evident but questionable. In reading a portrayal of a company that is based on such field observations, one has the feeling of experiencing the situation very directly. The corporation comes alive; it seems to have flesh and bones. For that and other reasons, ethnographic descriptions are interesting to read.

The ethnographic portrayal of any cultural entity, including a work organization, certainly has value. At the very least, it serves as a heuristic device—a source for questions about critical variables that might be examined to understand how corporate life might differ from company to company. It also provides a "big picture"—an overall portrayal that allows one to see a social organization as a coherent entity that possesses a kind of personality. Particularly in Deal and Kennedy's work, one can sense the importance of rites, rituals, myths, and heroes as formative factors within any work organization. Indeed, it is easy to overlook the symbolic significance of many activities without an ethnographic perspective. Stories can become myths, which can define company direction, goals, and style. They express a way of viewing the corporate world and the work place. They provide meanings for those who behave in this environment. They help to express what the company stands for, thereby communicating to all what the options are and what the rewards are likely to be. They serve as a frame of reference for defining oneself within the corporate context. Such insight into the existence of and meaning of myths, even slogans, is an important product of an ethnographic approach to the study of corporate life. These facets of corporate life cannot easily be uncovered through computation of production figures or "objective" assessments of the quality of work environments.

But there are difficulties in following an ethnographic approach, at least exclusively, in the analysis of corporate life. Ethnography is time-consuming; it is not a procedure that lends itself to a quick analysis of the workings of any particular social group, corporation, or work place. Moreover, the insights that are to be obtained from ethnography depend significantly on the quality of the people doing the ethnographic research. They must not only spend a considerable amount of time and effort working and observing in the society or corporation under study, but they must also possess an understanding of organizational behavior. They must also have the ability to effectively portray what is going on. Many social groups and business organizations simply cannot afford and are not interested in having someone hanging around for a considerable period of time, listening to and observing what is going on without any clear knowledge or expectation of what the results will be. Moreover, there is a problem in relating ethnographic observations directly and reliably to measures of morale and productivity. Equally relevant, it is difficult to compare different organizations of similar natures in a standard fashion. Although we may find ethnographic analysis of a corporate culture most interesting and insightful, few managers can afford the necessary patience to wait for tangible results that provide guildelines for action.

We have selected an alternative approach to assessing organizational culture—or at least certain critical facets of corporate culture. We are interested in efficiently assessing corporate culture variables that are associated with and perhaps determinative of motivation and personal investment. Our attempt to assess corporate culture represents a psychometric approach; that is, it involves gathering data through standardized questionnaires. Actually, the notion of assessing culture in a more systematic and objective or standardized fashion is not new. Triandis and his colleagues (Triandis et al., 1972) have developed sophisticated procedures for assessing whole societies, and these procedures have been widely employed. The notion of assessing the quality of environments, particularly work environments, is also not new. There are many precedents to guide us in this regard (see, for example, Campbell et al., 1970; Cook, Hepworth, Wall, & Warr, 1981; James & Jones, 1974; Lawler, Hall, & Oldham, 1974; Schneider & Synder, 1975; Stern, 1970). Thus, we are not exactly stepping in where angels fear to tread, and we trust we are not stepping in as fools.

In the course of our early work on motivation and personal investment, it became clear that people not only were willing to talk about themselves and their work, they were even more able and willing to talk about their work place. Moreover, they seemed to be able to describe their work place in terms of whether or not they could pursue options and incentives that were of importance to them. Often spontaneously, they could tell us not only about the incentives, rewards, and opportunities that existed in their specific job but also about what the company as a whole seemed to be promoting or not emphasizing. When they talked about incentives available in their job, these incentives seemed to parallel their statements about events that gave rise to a sense of success or satisfaction on their part. They expressed a degree of knowledge of what was stressed by the firm or company, and they also expressed how they personally related to company goals and incentive structures.

Goals and incentives available within a corporate context are not the sole features of what has come to be called corporate culture, but they are arguably the most important features. When we discussed the nature of cultures in general and organizational culture in particular, we referred specifically and at some length to the establishment and promotion of guidelines regarding what was worth striving for. We concluded that the personal incentives we had identified for individuals could be matched by goals and purposes as an important feature of organizations. We considered it logical to assume that different organizations would emphasize different purposes and goals for working.

Following this line of reasoning, we began to construct a series of questions about what was available to the worker in the organizational context, focusing especially on the pursuit of incentives and their availability. This eventuated in the development of a set of organizational culture scales, the technical features of which are set forth in chapter 4. We were able to assess reliably the perceptions that individuals have of the company in which they work. Our work also indicated that the perceptions of the company paralleled the personal incentives that we had found to be associated with the behavior of individuals. That is, organizational values were found to match the personal incentives of individuals. This complementarity of culture and person scales was not an altogether accidental finding, of course; we doubtless were biased in designing items that would reflect compatible person and culture goals. But it is important that we could reasonably claim that individuals recognize categories of company goals that are comparable to the personal incentives that guide their personal investment.

Besides identifying incentive dimensions that described organizations as they were perceived by workers, we also developed another type of scale for assessing organizations. There was reason to believe that the very saliency of an organizational culture might be a critical factor. That point was often made in ethnographic and other nonpsychometric studies (Deal & Kennedy, 1982; Peters & Waterman, 1982). It also seems logical that companies not only may stress certain incentive possibilities or affirm certain purposes, goals, and values but that they also may stress, to a greater or lesser degree, what the company stands for. They may be more or less effective in communicating the *mission* (i.e., goals and purposes) of the company or organization. We chose to assess the saliency of the culture directly by asking people about their awareness of what the company stood for and what it promoted. As it turned out, this was a wise decision; the responses on the saliency scale proved to be quite interesting as well as useful in predicting certain patterns of behavior.

However, it is one thing to develop a set of scales that are reliable, but the real question is what is being assessed. We therefore proceeded to explore the validity of these scales in analyzing organizations and in predicting the behavior of people in these organizations.

Validation of Procedures

The first step in this validation process was obvious enough. If the organizational culture scales we had developed had any validity and utility, they should be able to differentiate between organizational cultures. That is, if one organization seemed to treat their employees quite differently from others, we should be able to detect it. At the least, different organizations should have different organizational culture profiles based on our measures. If there is no such distinction between organizations, we really have nothing to talk about. If other independent observations indicate that Company A has a different way of doing things—a different organizational culture—from Company B, our scales should distinguish the two. In addition, the scales should add a degree of specification to the differences observed, which would complement other observations of the company. In test development jargon, we employed a "known groups" method of test validation.

Besides determining whether our scales could reasonably and reliably distinguish between companies, we also explored the uniqueness and integrity of the construct as it was assessed through these scales. For example, we considered whether the organizational culture scales assessed something different from what one might obtain by averaging the personal incentive patterns of the people who worked in the organization. More informally, we inquired whether the "personality" of the organization was something other than a mere summation of the personalities of the people who happen to compose it.

Finally, we considered the pervasiveness of a perception of organizational culture across various levels in the work organization. The organizational culture construct implies some degree of generality across a social group, but the degree to which the participants in this group adhere to a definition of the culture is in itself an interesting issue. For example, although there may be a broad base of agreement regarding what IBM or Procter and Gamble are about, is there a slightly different understanding of these cultures in different organizational units within each organization? Does the perception of organizational culture vary with the job held? Does it vary with status in the corporate hierarchy? Does it vary with being central or peripheral to the essential operations of the company?

In summary, three questions were asked to further define or refine the validity and integrity of the concept of organizational culture and its assessment with the aid of the IWI:

1. Do different organizations have different organizational cultures?
2. Is an organizational culture profile distinguishable from the averaged personal incentives of the participants in that organization?
3. How and to what extent does the perception of organizational culture vary across employees with different job responsibilities in the organization?

Different Organizations, Different Cultures

Six different organizations were selected for study. They were selected not only because they represented different types of organizations but also because they represented an array of differences in norms and operating procedures. That is, our preliminary and informal assessment of "the way things are done here" indicated that these companies would provide the cultural contrasts needed to determine the discriminant validity of our organizational culture scales.

The six organizations are briefly described in table 6–1. Even with the brief descriptions provided, it should be clear that we had reason to believe that these companies might represent different organizational environments. If our approach to defining and assessing organizational culture made any sense at all, we should be able to show differences among these six different groups.

As can be seen in figure 6–1 and table 6–2, differences do exist in the organizational culture profiles of the six organizations. The most readily distinguishable differences were found in the airline, consulting, and fast-food organizations. Several characteristics of these results are especially noteworthy. The consulting firm is viewed by its workers as a place that promotes challenging and interesting work, that stresses a strong family feeling among its workers, and that is generous in its rewards, especially recognition. The employees also know they can make excellent salaries if they do good work, as well as receiving recognition for their good work.

In many respects, the organizational culture profile of the airline company represents a striking contrast to that of the consulting company. Overall, the profile for the airline company suggests that this organization did not provide opportunity for fulfilling the aspirations of workers in any of the four personal incentive areas. Differences in profile shape across the six organizations are perhaps most evident in the social and external reward areas. Unlike the consulting firm, the airline company does not seem to promote a family feeling. It is a family-owned company, but the family feeling is not present among employees to the same degree as in the consulting company. According to the employees, it also is not a company in which rewards are distributed to its workers in a satisfying manner.

As shown in figure 6–1, the six companies also differed on the culture saliency scale, with the fast-food company employees expressing the greatest awareness of a culture and the airline company employees the least. It is interesting that the saliency dimension is related to the content of the organizational culture, as assessed by the four organizational culture scales (see table 6–3). Specifically, saliency is especially related to the task, social solidarity, and external rewards dimensions. A company is arguably most evident as a viable entity to its workers when it stresses these dimensions. However, this generalization does not apply universally. As shown in figure 6–1, the fast-food firm had the highest score on both ego and saliency. This small firm was known for its competitive spirit and aggressiveness. The company is young and determined in its desire to get a significant share of the fast-food market in a number of cities along the East Coast.

Table 6–1
Summary Descriptions of Six Sample Organizations

Type of Company	Brief Description of Company	Types of Personnel Included in Sample
Commuter airline (Air)	A family-owned company with 200 employees and $30 million annual revenue; headquartered in a relatively small midwestern city; long history of safety.	Executives, mechanics, customer service personnel, flight crew
Health care center (Hos)	A general-care hospital of 200 beds; located in a midwestern town of 35,000; recently initiated an aggressive marketing campaign to increase its status within the community.	Executives, department directors, middle managers, supervisors, nursing coordinators
Consulting firm (Cons)	A management consulting company that has grown to over $25 million annual sales in 20 years; employs 360 people; headquartered in a suburb of a large western city; and has many affiliate offices throughout the world.	Executives, sales personnel, research/product development personnel
Trade association (Trade)	An established association that represents producers of a farm commodity; headquartered in a large midwestern city, but branches are located throughout the world; the staff totals nearly 180, and the annual budget exceeds $15 million.	Executives, middle managers
Manufacturing firm (Man)	A company, located in a small midwestern city, that began as a family firm 60 years ago; currently has 600 employees and has revenue in data processing products exceeding $100 million; in the past 10 years, the company has increased sales by over 300%.	Executives, middle managers
Fast-food chain (Food)	A firm that owns more than 40 fast-food restaurants under a franchise agreement with one of the largest national restaurant chains; headquartered in a large East Coast city, but owns restaurants in more than ten cities in three states; the firm is 10 years old, and the original three owners still hold the leadership positions.	Executives, middle managers

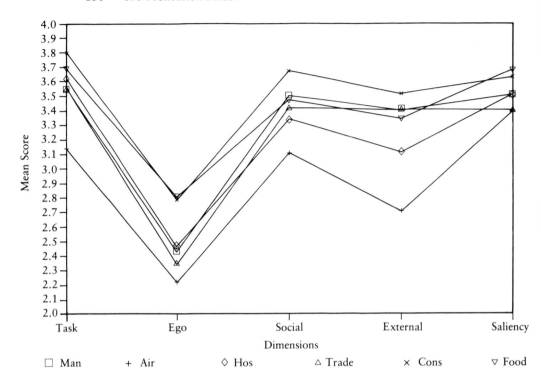

Figure 6–1. Average Scores of Employees in Six Organizations on Organizational Culture and Saliency Scales

Although general observations about the substance of the results with the companies in question have value, we first turn to the central point of reporting these results. It will be recalled that we initially entered into this series of analyses because we wished to determine whether or not we could distinguish companies through a psychometric index of organizational culture. In this regard, we have been successful. Not only have we demonstrated that we can differentiate companies in terms of organizational culture, but we can do so in a way that is plausible. In short, we have taken the first step in validating our research procedure.

It is important to note that the organizational culture scales of the IWI do distinguish companies that are apparently quite different. In addition to administering our questionnaire, we gathered qualitative data to assure ourselves that we were, indeed, sampling organizations that were likely to vary in organizational culture. Based on our qualitative data on the airline company, we knew that this organization was in a period of transition, with accompanying organizational problems. The consulting company, on the other hand, was generally known to be an extremely effective, productive,

Table 6–2
Significant Differences in Organizational Culture among Six Organizations

Dimension	Overall Probability[a]	Significant Comparisons[b]
Task	.0001	2–3, 2–5, 2–6
Ego	.0001	2–5, 2–6
Social Solidarity	.0003	2–5
External Rewards	.0001	2–1, 2–3, 2–4, 2–5, 2–6

[a]Probability level of observed differences under tested hypotheses of no differences.
[b]1 = manufacturing firm; 2 = airline; 3 = health center; 4 = trade association; 5 = consulting firm; 6 = fast-food chain.

and successful organization. Thus, we expected to find differences between the two companies.

Moreover, the kinds of differences that were found with the psychometric scales are very much in accord with what we learned about these companies through our observations, interviews, and open-ended questionnaires. Workers in the consulting company could readily state what the company stood for, and they agreed almost unanimously on a few significant figures or "heroes." In a number of different ways, they left little doubt that they knew that a certain value system pervaded their work place. Equally important, they believed that the firm, which had a very strong leader and was still run by the founder, provided a supportive, family-like environment for encouraging individuals to "self-actualize." It is interesting that the term *self-actualize* was used repeatedly by employees in describing their possibilities within the company in which they worked.

In the airline company, on the other hand, employees expressed a range of opinions on the goals of the company, with a significant number of individuals feeling essentially alienated from the leadership. Some remembered a rather glorious past and a few past heroes, but there was considerable comment on how the past differed from the present, focusing particularly on how employees were now inappropriately rewarded and recognized. The family atmosphere was used to describe the past rather than the present.

These data indicate that the members' experiences in the organization, as stated in their own personal ways, conform with the kind of results obtained with the psychometric scales. Thus, these data help support our contention that organizational culture as defined by the IWI is a viable construct. It can distinguish organizations—and it can distinguish them in ways that are consistent with other types of evidence.

Organizational Culture and Personal Meanings

Does the organizational culture scale assess characteristics of an organization that are similar to the sum of the orientations exhibited by the employees?

Table 6–3
Correlations among Organizational Culture, Saliency, Commitment, Marketability, Advancement, and Job Satisfaction

	Organizational Culture				Saliency	Commitment	Marketability	Advancement	Satisfaction
	Task	Ego	Social	External					
Organizational Culture									
Task		0	.81	.76	.65	.64	.43	.42	.67
Ego			-.07	.07	-.12	-.05	.02	-.06	-.05
Social				.81	.67	.67	.43	.51	.69
External					.62	.67	.45	.57	.70
Saliency						.61	.33	.44	.54
Commitment							.52	.51	.64
Marketability								.58	.46
Advancement									.52

If this were the case, then the culture of an organization, particularly the values and goals assessed by the IWI, is merely the sum of the personal incentives of the members of that organization. To consider this question, we also examined the collective personal incentives of the employees of each organization. The collective personal incentive profiles of employees in each of the six organizations are portrayed in figure 6–2. When these profiles are compared with the organizational culture profiles displayed in figure 6–1, it is evident that organizational culture is different from a mere representation of the summed personal incentives of the members of the organizations. In other words, organizational culture as we have assessed it is more than an aggregation of personalities.

This visual impression is also confirmed by more technical statistical analyses. Correlations between workers' personal incentives and their perceptions of the organization as indicated by responses on the four organizational culture scales were all low and were not practically significant. Therefore, we can conclude with some assurance that perceived organizational culture is not a mere reflection of the employees' personal incentives. There is independence in the constructs and in the scales used to assess them.

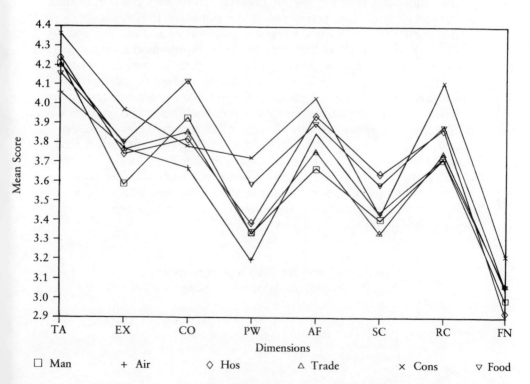

Figure 6–2. **Average Scores of Employees in Six Organizations on Personal Incentives Scales**

Different Jobs, Different Perceived Culture

Having found that the construct of organizational culture has some degree of integrity because it can assess differences in various organizations, we then asked whether employees' perceptions of an organizational culture supersede their perceptions of their own immediate job environment. Do people in different positions in the organization perceive a different organizational culture?

The answer to this question is a qualified yes. The relationship between employees' perceptions of the opportunities their jobs provide for fulfilling their personal incentives and their views of the organizational culture tends, overall, to be moderately large and positive (see table 6–4). The one exception is found in perceptions in the ego domain. Opportunities to pursue power and competition personal incentives on the job are not associated with the perception that the organization stresses power and competition. The social personal incentive dimension is only moderately related to the complementary social dimension on the organizational culture index.

In general, however, these findings do suggest that to an important degree, employees tend to view the organization through the eyes of their jobs, or vice versa. Their perceptions of the immediate job environment are related to their perceptions of the organizational culture as a whole, especially in the area of external rewards. But this is by no means the whole story. There is reason to believe that organizational culture exists as something distinctly different from job perceptions. As we summed the perceptions of job opportunities in each organization (figure 6–3), we found patterns quite different from the organizational culture profiles. Thus, the organizational culture construct as assessed here not only is different from the collective personality (personal incentive profile) of the employees but is also different from the kinds of jobs and job opportunities that exist within any given organization. One could not say that Company A had a different organizational culture from company B simply because a different kind of work was done there. To a significant extent, organizational culture seems to reach beyond both personalities and jobs.

Table 6–4
Correlations between Job Opportunities and Organizational Culture on Similar Dimensions

Dimension	Correlation
Task	.58
Excellence	.51
Competition	.21
Power	.06
Affiliation	.54
Social	.45
Recognition	.71
Financial	.64

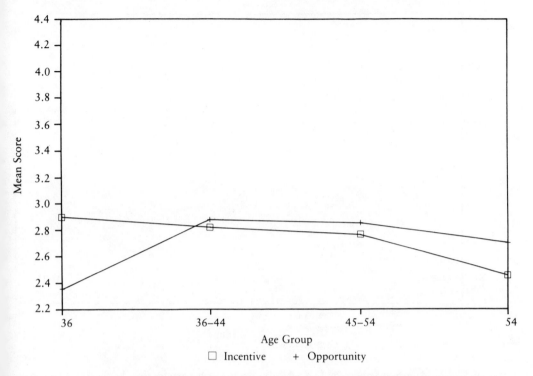

Figure 7-11. Average Scores of U.S. Adults on Financial Incentive and Opportunity Scales, by Age Group

across age, with higher scores on some scales and lower scores on other scales. Of most interest is the change in sense of self. The nonselected group consistently exhibited a lower sense of competence across age. This differential in sense of competence increased with age, as the nonselected group had an accelerated decline in sense of competence at the older ages.

The two groups also exhibited different patterns on several personal incentives. With increasing age, the high-achieving group tended to become less extrinsically oriented—that is, less concerned with recognition for work and financial rewards but more concerned with helping others. The comment of one of the people we interviewed in depth early in our research is illustrative. This interviewee, an executive with one of the Fortune 500 companies, simply but nicely expressed the altruism that may be exhibited in these results: "I have been treated well; it is now my turn to help others." Many of people's goals of individual accomplishment may have been accomplished by their later years, so they can more readily give their attention to others—people, institutions, civic organizations—as they near the end of their careers. In this regard, we are reminded of Erik Erikson's (1950, 1959, 1968) concept of

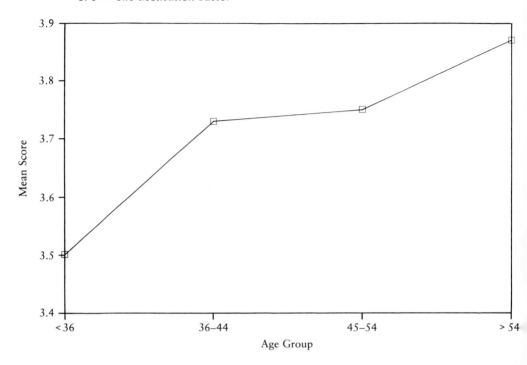

Figure 7–12. Average Scores of U.S. Adults on the Job Satisfaction Scale, by Age Group

"generativity," which he hypothesized to characterize later stages of adult development.

When we specifically queried some of our outstanding achievers about why they continued to work as they did, they typically gave us two kinds of responses. One response could be simply phrased, "I simply enjoy what I'm doing," reflecting the kinds of intrinsic interests that are perhaps more operative at later career stages. The other response could be readily associated with Erikson's concept of generativity: "I want to leave a legacy."

Thus, the data from our interviews and the questionnaire converge in presenting us with a picture of high achievers who, on the one hand, are less concerned about the extrinsics—the financial rewards, the perquisites, the status, and the recognition—and, on the other hand, express a concern for how their work contributes to something beyond themselves. Perhaps there is egotism here; perhaps they simply believe (and rightly so) that what they have accomplished has lasting importance and wish to play a role in making their accomplishments serve others.

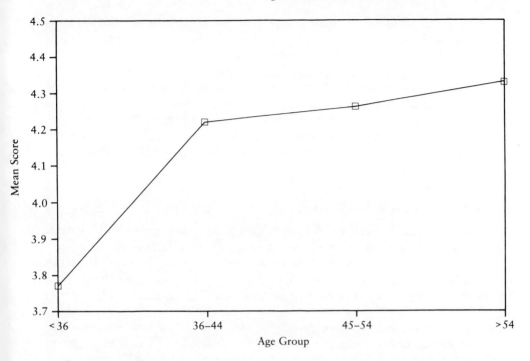

Figure 7–13. Average Scores of U.S. Adults on the Organizational Commitment Scale, by Age Group

Some Concluding Thoughts about Motivational Changes throughout the Life Span

Few studies have been specifically concerned with motivational changes in adulthood, and these studies generally have not followed from nor integrated easily with any specific theoretical framework. In addition, the studies that have been conducted, including our own, have had methodological problems that prevent us from concluding with complete confidence that the differences found are attributable to age cohort or cultural shifts. Yet we can make some generalizations that can contribute to development of a more meaningful framework for dealing with these important but extremely difficult questions.

Age and the High Achiever

Our results suggest that people who excel in their youth will exhibit high-achievement patterns throughout their lives. Of course, high achievers may not choose to excel in the same areas throughout their lives. However, although they may retain similar motivational patterns throughout life, there is some reason to believe that the exigencies of aging do have motivational effects (Braskamp, Fowler, & Ory, 1984).

We use the term *exigencies of aging* advisedly. The point we are trying to stress is that age-graded events seem very likely to play a role in affecting motivation. For example, it seems that retirement eventuates in a role change for most people at a certain age in their lives. Although age 65 may not be critical for affecting motivational change, it is a time for considering or examining new roles associated with retirement (George, 1980; Kelly, 1982b; Kleiber, in press).

Age and the Average Achiever

What about the more typical person in a more typical career path or work role? It is one thing to find that outstanding individuals retain a strongly achievement-oriented type of personal investment throughout their lives, but is this true of people in general? We cannot answer this question with finality, but our results do yield some suggestions worth considering.

Work Investment. It was especially interesting to us that task and excellence personal incentives remain high across the older ages. There is no dropping off in the attraction to doing something well and in the intrigue with challenge and novelty. This has two possible implications about the motivation of older workers. First, they are likely to be internally motivated—less tied to the extrinsics of the job in performing the tasks at hand. Correlated therewith is the finding that they apparently are less concerned with financial rewards and exhibit a greater commitment to the work orgnaization. As discussed earlier, their station in life is such that it allows for this increase in intrinsic motivation and decrease in extrinsic orientation, which naturally leads to greater organizational commitment. Nevertheless, according to our results, age does not bring about any real decrease of investment in the person's place of work or job. We have found, as others have, that it is the younger, not the older workers, who are likely to create "motivational problems."

Second, in our sample, we were dealing largely with reasonably successful, skilled workers. Conceivably, a slightly different picture can be drawn in the case of the unskilled and marginal worker. Yet there is no reason to expect that all employees in our sample had all they wanted from their jobs. Many must have experienced burnout, disillusionment, "plateauing." They were an unselected group of largely middle-class workers. Thus, we might have observed a decrease in personal investment in the work sphere—if this were really the typical pattern at the older age levels. The chances are that we have sometimes overestimated the negative motivation of older workers by concentrating on the few who seem to be "dead wood." Does this possibly suggest that there is really no motivational reason why people cannot continue to work effectively into their later years? We cannot nor will we attempt to answer that question for every person or every context. We simply note that meanings that should lead to a positive personal investment in the work sphere remain very salient at the upper age levels in our sample.

Age and Retraining. A second implication of the pattern of meanings found, particularly the change (or lack of change) at the senior levels, relates to what is increasingly becoming a major social issue of our times: the capacity of the older person to benefit from training, retraining, and continuing education.

As we write this chapter, the U.S. economy remains a subject of some concern. Even though there is a feeling of optimism in some quarters, there are also reasons for concern, one of which relates to workers and employment. Many workers who have lost their jobs will not regain them. It is widely predicted that such major industries as steel and automobile manufacturing will not regain their former status nor be structured in the same fashion. Robots are replacing the assembly line worker at the same time that auto and steel manufacturing are decreasing in importance in the overall U.S. economy. "High-tech" industries are in vogue, and it is predicted that the worker of tomorrow will be involved in these and in service capacities rather than in so-called heavy industry. In short, it is rather generally assumed that, in the United States at least, we have reached the postindustrial age. This may also be true in many other Western countries, portending a significant change in the economy and working patterns of the world as a whole.

This analysis of the situation may not be altogether correct, but it is probably not altogether wrong, either. Even if it is only partially correct, it appears that a massive adjustment in the labor force will be necessary. Those who worked with lathes and welding torches may have to learn the intricacies of handling a silicon chip or perhaps acquire the subtleties necessary for providing a service. All of this requires learning. New skills, knowledge, and techniques must be acquired, and this must occur well beyond the age when most people would be inclined to think of themselves as students. Certainly, adult education in some form or another is likely to be increasingly impressed on an ever-widening number of our citizenry.

This is not to suggest that education was ever a matter to be left solely to the young, although the educational establishment has characteristically thought of it in that way. Departments of adult education are few and are not particularly noteworthy for their prominence or prestige in major colleges of education. Yet adult education has been around for some time, though it may not always have been recognized as such. Training, retraining, updating, and continuing education have been part of the business world for some time, comprising a multibillion-dollar enterprise. Continuing education is now mandatory for many professions, and few communities cannot boast a readily available adult education program.

The point is that the ability to learn new skills or enhance old ones is becoming an absolute necessity if people are to remain in the work force. The question we pose here is whether there are motivational factors that make older people less or more ready to benefit from education, more or less able to experience retraining?

First, we should make the point that is made repeatedly in treatises on adult development: People can and do learn at all ages. Perhaps no one over 40 has doubted the possibility that learning occurs well beyond the customary age of leaving school. Until recently, however, systematic evidence on the capacity of adults to learn has been more a matter of anecdote than science. With the increasing interest in development at all ages and the increasing concern with continuing education, new knowledge relevant to adult capacity has been forthcoming (see, for example, Knox, 1977, 1980, in press). Although there is still considerable room for debate on the matter of age and intellectual capacity, it is certainly clear that adults can and do learn at all ages. Significant detrimental decline does not typically occur until quite late in life, and even then it can be compensated for. Putting this in very practical terms, training and retraining of older workers is possible. Indeed, one might even say that, for all practical purposes, it is just as sensible to assume that we can retrain or update older workers as it is to assume that we can train younger workers. Furthermore, there is nothing to suggest that intellectual capacity prevents learning at all ages, so education can be an appropriate leisure-time activity not only after retirement but into the seventh and eighth decades of life and beyond!

Having stressed this very important and basic point, there is a second and equally basic question: Granted that adults at all ages *can* learn, are they equally motivated? At the outset, we do well to recall the basic conclusions reached in our discussion of motivational changes throughout the life span. We have argued that aging per se is not the only critical factor in motivational changes that occur throughout life. Rather, situational and contextual conditions are also of primary importance. In many important respects, motivational patterns remain relatively stable and constant. Those who are highly motivated to achieve as children remain highly motivated to achieve as adults. In our study of adults and their personal investments, it was likewise noted that an older person is just as likely as a younger one to be concerned with the development of competence or with excelling—incentives that are likely to be associated with a positive orientation toward learning. Therefore, at the very least, one should not take age by itself as an indication that the will to learn has dissipated. There are reasons, in special instances, why adults may be more or less inclined toward learning, and it is likely that different incentives will attract them. But aging does not necessarily reduce capacity or will to a degree that warrants writing off the possibility of retraining older workers. Contrary to the old saw, one *can* teach an old dog new tricks, provided that the conditions to do so are present.

The Aged and the Loss of Incentive

Thus far in this chapter, we have discussed how personal investment changes—sometimes with age but more specifically with changing life circumstances. We have not emphasized the possibility of increases and decreases in overall personal investment per se but instead have stressed the quality, direction, and changes in personal investment. Throughout much of human activity across the life span, we can think of motivation primarily in terms of the different ways in which resources can be distributed, and the question of availability can be conveniently ignored. Certainly, when one is primarily talking about children and youth, the concept of motivational deprivation is, for all practical purposes, inappropriate (Maehr, 1974a). But there are certainly cases in which such a concept is not only convenient but also appropriate—even necessary. There is reason to believe that, in some circumstances, aged people experience or exhibit what can only be called a loss of motivation. Nothing seems to interest them anymore; even living itself may seem to have no appeal, and they essentially give up. Not that the aged are alone in this experience, but it seems that certain situations confronting older people are especially likely to eventuate in such a loss of personal investment. Thus, Klinger (1977; see also Langer & Rodin, 1976; Schulz, 1976) has pointed out that depression at all ages may be attributed to a loss of incentive—nothing seems worth doing.

Focusing particularly on the aged, we raise the question of whether we can sense in our results any hint that a loss of incentive is beginning to occur at the older ages that could anticipate the development of a passive, even depressed lifestyle. To examine the possible loss of incentive in old age, we compared the overall profiles of the people in the four age groups. When the sum of the personal incentives was calculated for each person, no decrease was found in the overall levels. Thus, despite shifts in the importance given to specific personal incentives across the four age groups, there was no overall decline in incentive level. Perhaps our adults were not old enough or in a desperate enough situation to exhibit any such loss of incentive, but this particular tendency was not found with our sample. The age differences we found were all a matter of redistribution of emphasis in motivational orientation. Moreover, the redistribution was not such that one would expect a kind of giving up on life or, for that matter, on work.

Conclusion

Our consideration of the effects of age on personal investment should be considered only a preface to further study of this increasingly important area. The concluding generalizations, hypotheses, suggestions—and speculations—may stimulate a perspective for considering a number of important issues in this regard. Throughout this chapter, however, several important themes emerged that can be taken seriously in dealing with questions of age and motivation. First, and perhaps of overriding importance, is the finding that age does not inevitably bring about a lowering of the will to achieve, to excel, or to invest oneself in the work activities of life. Second, it seems that age per se is not the critical factor driving human behavior and development; rather, certain circumstances, perhaps often associated with age, are primary. Research for the future must go beyond noting that these circumstances are correlated with age and must determine whether this is necessarily so.

8
Sociocultural Context, Meaning, and Personal Investment

Personal investment in work or in any other situation is affected by the wider sociocultural context in which the individual lives. It is obvious that people who are members of different cultures often view life and work quite differently. They also define success, failure, achievement, and happiness in different ways—they live by different rules and are guided by different expectations.

Anyone who has lived in or visited another country for an extended period has a story to tell about relating to less cosmopolitan members of the country in question. Often, it is a matter of a simple repair to an auto or a pair of shoes. It is not only a language difficulty that impedes transactions between the representatives of two very different cultures—it is the way things are done or are expected to be done. Perhaps it is also a matter of time perception. It is not uncommon for the well-socialized U.S. businessman to inquire about exactly when an agreed-upon repair will be completed—*and* to think that he has an agreement regarding the price—only to return and learn that the understanding was not mutual. Of course, such misunderstandings not only occur across widely different societies and cultures; they also occur within a society. Although they are certainly not always attributable to cultural differences, cultural differences are often a factor in prompting a different view of how things should be done. For example, the college-educated professional who has moved where job and career beckoned finds it difficult to understand the employee who must drop everything to take care of a sick cousin. Such differences in perceptions of how things should be done are a sign of the existence of different cultural networks in which people exist. The point we wish to examine in greater detail in this chapter is that the wider sociocultural context in which people exist is significantly involved in determining the meanings they hold and the personal investments they will exhibit. Although we examined this issue to some degree in earlier chapters, this chapter will specifically examine recent research that is directly related to how the wider sociocultural context affects meaning and personal investment.

The Sociocultural Matrix

When we use the term *sociocultural matrix*, we refer to the general social and cultural environment in which the person and the work organization exist. For the most part, it consists of the norms, guidelines, and prescriptions that any group of individuals holds in common. In chapter 6, we presented a brief description of culture when we focused on the concept of organizational culture. However, as we now wish to consider the effects of the wider sociocultural context on worker behavior, we must expand that discussion.

Workers and work organizations do not exist in a social vacuum. That point, which is virtually self-evident, is also most salient at this point in the book. For our purposes, the sociocultural matrix may be viewed as varying along six dimensions: knowledge and technology, style and preference, beliefs and values, social organization, artifacts, and ritual. A brief word about each of these dimensions should be sufficient to provide an overview of the sociocultural worlds that exist for workers and work institutions.

Knowledge and Technology

We begin with what may be the most obvious differences in work behavior and work institutions—differences in knowledge and technology. One could not talk about sociocultural influences in the twentieth century without mentioning television and computers; nor could one ignore supersonic jets, automobiles, and industrial pollution. Work life is drastically different in an isolated Middle Eastern village from what it is in the Silicon Valley—and traditional Middle Eastern villages are hard to find because of the oil industry and the ubiquitous transistor radio.

In an important sense, the sociocultural matrix is characterized by the knowledge and technology shared by the participants in this matrix. It is not only that different cultural groups have different knowledge; such differences may affect the way work can be carried out and may determine overall productivity. In terms of personal investment theory, knowledge provides options and defines acceptable alternatives, thus setting forth the range of options for personal investment (see chapter 3).

Theoretically, at least, in the global village that is our world, it is possible to disseminate any given knowledge base broadly, and comparable technologies are found around the world. However, there is a question regarding whether there is equality in preparation for dealing with, incorporating, and utilizing any given knowledge base or technology. Different societies or social groups may do a better job of disseminating the knowledge base that is necessary for participating in the world of computers and robots. One might wonder about the likelihood of establishing a Saturn plant in a remote area in the inner reaches of Africa, where there has been very little preparation for the kind of work that is required in such a complex and highly sophisticated work environment. Aside from the social problems that would likely ensue if one were to impose a culturally alien work context and style, there is the simple fact that workers do not have the requisite skills. Such an industrial creation of another culture is not likely at this point to elicit the best efforts of citizens of remote African villages. Their education possibly limits them, and they may be lacking in technical know-how. But equally important, their culture may actually bias them against feeling comfortable with the "impersonal" nature of a Saturn plant.

One does not have to reach for exotic comparisons to illustrate the importance of the dissemination of knowledge among the participants of a particular social group. The quality of education offered is increasingly considered a factor in gaining a competitive edge in the world market. Moreover, at the local level, the choice to locate a work organization depends significantly on the availability of knowledgeable and technologically skilled workers.

Thus, one important feature of a culture regarding work and work organizations is the knowledge base that exists within the sociocultural matrix. Just what do the people who are likely to be workers know? Just how prepared are they for meeting the demands and requirements of the work that will be done? Current discussions on the relative quality of schools in the United States (see, for example, Bunzel, 1985; Kirst, 1982; Marcuccio, 1983; Tyler, 1983) are hardly trivial. Although we may often expect too much from our schools, the fact is that the knowledge base of a society and the degree to which this knowledge is disseminated and utilized are critical features of the society. They are especially important in that they significantly determine how the society will perform in meeting the needs of its members and, often, whether it will survive.

Style and Preference

Equally obvious, perhaps, are the different ways in which various cultural groups handle basic human needs. Some concrete and readily understood examples should suffice. The necessity to eat and protect the body against the elements is universal, but *what* one eats and *how* one dresses are matters of style and preference as well as necessity. The three-piece suits worn by certain groups contrast sharply with the veils, robes, or loin cloths of others. To the experienced gourmet's delight, various groups have arrived at acceptable alternatives to fried chicken, mashed potatoes, and gravy. Even hamburger and hot dogs are not the same the world over. All in all, it is clear that there is not just one way to eat, dress, or take care of basic bodily needs. The sociocultural matrix in which a person exists promotes certain styles and preferences while repudiating others.

To some, differences in style and preference seem harmless, but people have been known to fight over them. Long hair annd beards, topless bathing suits, and tie-less shirts have been regulated at one point or another in one place or another. And as pragmatic as business institutions can be, some of the more difficult conflicts arise in attempts to regulate preferences and styles. Thus, when a work supervisor from one cultural group deals with workers from another group, style and preference often emerge as bones of contention. In the effort to reinforce an organizational culture that may or may not be compatible with the wider cultural world of the employee, work organizations often make specific attempts to control dress.

A friend of ours, a budding young bank executive freshly blessed with an MBA, is fond of telling the story of her attempt to wear a red suit occasionally at work. For a while, she was able to resist the pressure to conform to the expected style. She wanted to maintain her independence in such matters, but the seemingly casual but carefully aimed comments of her superiors were enough to make her retreat to basic blue, gray, and black for her work dress.

Social Organization

A third facet of the sociocultural matrix is the particular way in which behavior happens to be organized. When people are placed in situations where they interact with each other on a continuing basis, their behavior comes to take on an orderly and predictable character. Rules, regulations, customs, and styles emerge to which all are obliged to give recognition, if not subservience. In addition, certain patterns and relationships among group members can be seen to evolve. Some members seem to have more power than others; there are those who lead and those who follow. If the group is in existence for any length of time, different people assume different work assignments or functions. Thus, social organization might be viewed as consisting of a number of important facets, each of which is worthy of comment.

Roles. Social intereaction seems to breed norms automatically. Such guidelines for behavior not only provide answers when experience cannot but also greatly simplify the individual's relations to others. Therefore, they are the crucial factor of group behavior and an integral part of the social network into which people are born, grow, learn, develop, and work. Among the most important norms are those particularized norms known as *roles*. When a person occupies a certain position in a group, there are certain expectations for him or her. For example, consider the position of mother. In most social groups, there are certain things that we expect of mothers. Traditionally, mothers have a primary responsibility for selected family functions, such as exercising control over the children. There are similar expectations for fathers, children, teachers, and bosses. Each society identifies positions, and a social *role* is the societal expectations regarding the manner in which each position is to be filled.

What is particularly interesting and important about roles is that the identification of positions, the assignment of individuals to these positions, and especially the expectations for those so assigned are all ways in which social groups mold behavior. As is clear from such comparative studies as Margaret Mead's (1935) *Sex and Temperament in Three Primitive Societies*, different things are expected of men and women in different societies. As a result, there seems clear evidence that men and women exhibit differences in personal orientation and in behavioral patterns. Not only do they think of themselves differently; they act differently.

Status. Any group of people is more than rules and roles. Even in the smallest and most ephemeral of groups, a status system of some sort will emerge; that is, some individuals will be accorded greater honor and prestige than others. Sometimes this status is theirs by virtue of birth or without any real achievement on their part; it is *ascribed* to them. For example, the rich man's son is accorded more status than the laborer's son—not because of his own efforts but by virtue of his birth. In other cases, *achievement* is the basis of status, as in the case of a self-made millionaire. What is important about status is that power is often associated with it. For example, the foreman has greater status in the work group than the newly hired laborer. A foreman typically controls the distribution of resources and rewards to a greater degree than most workers. Thus, the flow of influence in the work group tends to be from the foreman to the worker. The new worker must conform, quit, or be fired.

Mechanisms of Control. Every social group exercises some control over its members. We have repeatedly emphasized the role of behavioral norms and have noted the cultural variations in beliefs and values. Different social groups evolve different mechanisms for exacting conformity from their members. Anthropologists such as Ruth Benedict, Clyde Kluckhohn, and Margaret Mead have often talked about "shame" and "guilt" cultures. In the guilt culture, the person's behavior is controlled primarily by internal sanctions—that is, by a highly developed conscience. In the shame culture, there is less evidence of internal controls; rather, external sanctions seem to be more important. In a similar vein, Whiting (1959) has proposed that three types of control systems are used in the various societies of the world. The first involves "exaggerated and paranoid fear of retaliation from humans"; the second type proceeds "from a sense of sin deriving from the projected dread of punishment by gods or ghosts"; and the third control derives from "the sense of guilt and readiness to accept blame deriving from a sense of personal responsibility for one's actions." Cultures differ in their dependence on internal controls; presumably, members of these various cultures likewise differ in the degree to which they are internally controlled.

We must add a word of caution here. Although there is evidence of a differential orientation toward internal control across cultures, internal and external sanctions coexist in all cultures. As Ausabel (1955) pointed out some time ago, guilt and shame exist side by side in all cultures and reinforce one another in the maintenance of moral and social order. Nevertheless, it is quite possible that certain cultures—as a result of child-rearing practices, different training methods, or whatever—produce individuals who exhibit greater internal control than those in other cultures. The point of interest for us in this volume is that different groups have come to rely more or less on individual responsibility and self-control. Western-educated managers have come to expect people to have a highly developed sense of conscience and self-control. That is, they expect their employees to operate independently and without external control. In some cases, they will not sense the importance of the group as a controlling force in the behavior of the individual, particularly in cultures that are alien to the managers.

Beliefs, Values, and Goals

Given the essential thrust of this book, perhaps the most important facet of the sociocultural matrix relates to the beliefs, values, and goals that are extant within and regularly enforced by social groups. A wide variety of beliefs, values, and goals exists for the individual by virtue of membership in a particular social group. There are beliefs that allow and provide a frame of reference for the interpretation of information our senses bring us. They range from the highly developed theories of the scientist through the speculation of the layperson to the unformed notions of the primitive or young child. People seem to need to make sense of their world, but the way they do this varies. Furthermore, such variations in beliefs about the world are inevitably followed by variations in behavior. Thus, individuals who readily accept the importance of demons and spirits in their world are more likely to see evidence for the existence of such phenomena than those who reject demonology and spiritualism. It seems absurd to most of us to attribute the death of a child after a long fever to the act of an offended deity. We would likely accept only explanations that have justification in terms of our knowledge of science—the existence of a viral infection, a congenital disorder, a malfunctioning organ, or some other physiological cause. Even if the empirical facts were contradictory or confusing, we would shrink from demon talk, because that is not *our* way of explaining things. Yet it is *one* way of explaining things, and it is understandable that such explanations may play an important role in the practice of medicine.

Besides the beliefs that help us make sense of our world, there are ethical beliefs—that is, beliefs that relate to how we should regulate our lives. For a sick person, there might be variations in the beliefs regarding cause and treatment, but there would be less disagreement regarding whether the person should be treated. Life is valued among all people, although specific norms regarding the taking or preserving of life may vary. In addition to such universals, there is considerable disagreement regarding how life should best be lived. In fact, when we go beyond a few basic universals, the possibilities seem virtually unlimited. Florence Kluckhohn (1961; Kluckhohn & Strobeck, 1961) has provided a systematic way of considering the possibilities that exist in the development of these various lifestyles. Briefly, she has suggested that people are confronted by all kinds of questions, the answers to which will determine their lifestyle. She has suggested, further, that there are five basic questions that people in all places and circumstances must answer.

The first such question involves the individual's relationships to others. Is it individualistic, with greater stress on what someone accomplishes and with emphasis on personal rights and freedom? Or is perhaps a greater emphasis placed on the importance of belonging to a group, be it a family or a gang? Obviously, the beliefs that are held in this regard will shape many facets of people's lives and will doubtless also have a special effect on their style of achievement. The individualistic mode of achievement that David McClelland (1961) ascribed to the Western entrepreneur is not readily accepted within cultures in which the father is master of the children until his death. Similarly, an emphasis on individual achievement—sometimes to the detriment of one's fellows—may elicit less than the best efforts among cultural groups that place prime value on cooperation and compatibility.

A second basic question concerns the significant time dimension—past, present, or future. Much of what we do in American work organizations is based on thoughts about the future. We lay out plans, assess production goals, promise ultimate bonuses, and so forth. One must keep in mind that not all cultural groups are equal in their future orientation. The anthropological literature contains numerous examples, but perhaps no one has made this point better than Oscar Lewis (1961) in *Children of Sanchez*. This book, a fascinating first-person account of what it means to be poor, contains poignant descriptions of the belief system that characterizes not only the Sanchez family but possibly poor people in general (Valentine, 1968). One finds in this poor Mexican family a notion about time that may be different from yours and mine—if we are indeed futuristic, middle-class Westerners at heart. Throughout the dialogue, it is either implicitly or explicitly affirmed that the significant time dimension is the present. One doesn't save what little income one receives now to purchase something in the future. One does not lay up a store for future bad times. It is tacitly assumed that denying oneself now will have little effect on future happiness. Admittedly, sacrificing in the present and planning for the future probably does not make a great deal of sense if one is unsure of even today's basic needs. In any event, futuristic beliefs typically do not emerge as dominant features of the lifestyles of the poor.

They simply do not have the luxury of planning for the future and delaying present gratification to make extensive gains at some vague future point. Thus, a culture consists, in part, of concepts of time. Such concepts are also likely to play an important role in molding an orientation to life generally.

A third basic question suggested by Kluckhohn regards what the valued personality type is. Is it simply *being*? Is it *becoming*? Or is it *doing*? There may be other possibilities in this regard, but the point is that different social groups place varying value on different styles of life and personality orientations. Whereas spending the day loafing may be an acceptable mode for one group and contemplation may be a desirable mode for a second group, a third group may espouse activity—busyness, even for its own sake. It is difficult for many Americans to understand and appreciate how someone could devote his or her life to meditation and contemplation. Medieval monks and Oriental holy men are really quite foreign to our culture. We are doers, and we get nervous when there is nothing tangible to keep us busy. Our need for activity to fill time is probably equally inscrutable to Oriental holy men.

A fourth basic question involves people's relationship to nature. Are people subjugated to nature? Are they seen as existing *in* nature or *over* nature? Western science and technology are based on the assumption that people can, indeed, control nature. Pestilence and drought can either be prevented or controlled. For example, the farmer in Illinois calls the agricultural extension service at the onset of corn blight and expects something to be done about it. The Middle Eastern peasant is likely to accept such matters as "God's will" and shows a surprising lack of interest in the advice of a Western technician. If we extend such views on people and nature to life generally, it is interesting to note the role that fatalism and the feeling of personal responsibility can play in molding behavior in various spheres.

The final question each group must answer involves people's innate predispositions. Are they evil? Are they good? Are they neither good nor bad? Are they suitable to the culture or to the role the individual is expected to play? Can they be changed? If so, to what extent? Although people around the world exhibit various shades of opinion in this regard, one does not have to move outside one's own neighborhood to become aware of the variations that can and do exist. The accepted beliefs about people have formed the basis for establishing institutions, enacting legislation, and designing social programs. They are also directly related to how work will be organized and directed. Thus, as Schein (1985) has suggested, McGregor's (1960) Theory X and Theory Y are based on different assumptions about the inherent nature of people. In Theory X, workers are seen as essentially "bad"; that is, they don't really want to work, and they are trying to take advantage of the situation whenever possible in a way that is bound to be detrimental to the organization as a whole. Management exists largely to control such bad tendencies of workers. In Theory Y, workers are seen to be positively motivated, given the right context and opportunity. They are worthy of trust. Instead of establishing various control procedures, managers attempt to estalish a work environment that capitalizes on workers' basic willingness to contribute to the organization by giving a fair day's work for a fair day's pay.

Thus, an individual's sociocultural background is composed of assumptions regarding the nature of the universe, the way to live, the purpose in being. It may well be that such beliefs, rather than any other single factor, are what most clearly define a culture.

Artifacts, Myth, and Ritual

Finally, we turn to one of the more obvious differences between cultures—differences in what is produced by cultural groups. These differences are primarily on the surface; they are obvious to the eye, but their importance often can be discerned only as one understands the thoughts and beliefs that are associated with them. If one visits Bangkok, one is impressed with the temples and the statuary there. One looks around and quickly realizes that something is different from Main Street, U.S.A. One visits a household and not only sees different ways of sitting and eating but also quickly notes different rituals. There are also different stories to be told—stories that relate to the meaning of life or the reason for work or study or play. There are stories about heroes, stories about despicable characters, and stories about spirits and gods and devils. One cannot begin to describe and define that sociocultural context without at least mentioning these factors. However, as we have already implied, the essence of the sociocultural matrix is not these products of the culture but the meanings they suggest or reflect. One can look at artifacts, examine myths and stories, and note the role of rituals—but the essence of culture lies beneath all this. Not that people don't care about these cultural products; indeed, they often fight to preserve them. But it is the way of thinking and doing that underlies these cultural artifacts that is important. Thus, when we consider these products, we must remember that they merely reflect what the culture is about. The essence of a culture lies in its normative structure. Myth, ritual, and various cultural artifacts are ways of communicating the nature of life and how it is to be lived; they are important only as instruments for conveying this meaning, suggesting the essence of the underlying culture. Thus, the way of *thinking* about focal life questions is the basic ingredient of the sociocultural matrix.

Culture as an Answer to the Meaning of Life

All in all, we would like to stress that one can appropriately define culture or the sociocultural matrix as a complex of answers to certain regularly asked questions among a group of people. These are answers that they hold in common in regard to the problems that daily living presents. Some of these answers are of highest priority; people defend them to the death. Some are especially salient; others are held more or less unconsciously. But what binds these answers together into something called culture is that they order and regularize the behavior of people. They make group living to some degree predictable, they reduce the number of decisions to be made, and they provide answers where intolerable ambiguity exists. In an important sense, they establish meaning for the person and the group. Moreover, in view of the special concerns of this book, we would stress that they establish the kinds of meanings that determine personal investment. These answers define available and acceptable options in the world of work as well as in life generally. These answers specify what is worth striving for and believing, thereby defining what we have termed personal incentives. They also establish a basis for defining a sense of self, as they provide models of competence and standards of excellence. A culture defines whether the measure of a person is intellect or physical agility or social skill or faithfulness. A culture defines whether self-reliance is good or whether planning for the future is desirable. Being active, reflective, energetic, or relaxed may all be goals to emulate or standards against which people can judge their worth, depending on the answers that are found within their culture. Such meanings are critical in determining how personal investment is likely to vary cross-culturally, so we can expect that the sociocultural context will play a crucial role in determining how work is approached, how it is done—and with what degree of investment.

Keeping this broad framework in mind, we intend to examine the effects of the sociocultural context in a much more limited fashion in this chapter. We will consider, first, the patterns of motivation and personal investment that are exhibited by clearly diverse cultural and subcultural groups. We will discuss these patterns according to our understanding of the workings of cultures—in terms of normative patterns and expectations. More specifically, we will review a recent study on cultural differences in achievement-related meanings. This study represented a first stage in our own thinking on meaning and motivation.

Next, we will examine a recent study comparing the United States and Japan in terms of the meaning dimensions assessed by the IPI. We will present a picture of how divergent groups might differ in meanings that are associated with personal investment in the world of work.

Following this consideration of the effects of broadly divergent cultural groups on personal investment meanings, we will look at the effects of membership in a particular subcultural group—specifically, being male or female. In this regard, we will review recent analyses of the IPI/IWI data that have focused on gender differences.

Although we will not be able to examine all the intricacies of socio-cultural membership and personal investment, we will show whether and how such membership is associated with meanings that likely lead to differential personal investment patterns.

Cross-Cultural Differences in Achievement-Related Meanings

A number of years ago, we set out to understand the varying meanings of achievement in different cultural groups. With the collaboration of numerous colleagues and students, we used multiple methods and techniques to explore the meanings of success, failure, work, play, and leisure to a wide variety of individuals (Duda, 1980, 1981; Farmer, Vispoel & Maehr, 1985a, 1985b; Fyans et al., 1983; Maehr & Nicholls, 1980). Although our approach incorporated diverse procedures, we quickly became fascinated with the use of the semantic differential by our Illinois colleague, Charles Osgood.

In a truly massive endeavor, Osgood, Miron, and May (1975) gathered data on the meanings of various concepts across 30 different cultural groups. The cultures involved are specified in table 8–1. Among the concepts employed were some that seem to be related to the meaning of achievement. Although Osgood and his colleagues did not specifically set out to study the meaning of achievement cross-culturally, their data might prove suggestive in this regard. Thus, much as the human relations area files (Barry, 1980) provide a source for testing cross-cultural hypotheses, so might the semantic differential data gathered by Osgood and his colleagues be similarly employed. Indeed, in many respects, the Osgood et al. data seem to provide a veritable storehouse of archival data waiting to be discovered by the cross-cultural researcher. We and our colleagues initiated a secondary analysis of the achievement-related meanings assessed by Osgood and his coworkers. Selection of concepts was systematic: judges from a variety of cultural groups who were knowledgeable about achievement theory reviewed the concepts available in the Osgood et al. data set and identified achievement-related concepts. We selected those concepts in which there was a convergence of opinion, and this turned out to be a rather inclusive list. The major categories and concepts are presented in table 8–2.

Cross-Cultural Commonalities in Achievement Meaning

Through a series of analyses, Fyans et al. (1983) first attempted to determine whether there was a convergence of meaning for achievement across the 30 cultures. That is, they attempted to identify a core set of meanings related to achievement that was apparently held in common by the 30 different cultural

Table 8-1
General Indices for 30 Language/Culture Communities

Location, Language	Site of Collection	Language Family	Geographic G
Afghanistan, Dari	Kabul	Indo-European (Iranic)	West Asian
United States, American English	Illinois	Indo-European (Germanic)	North Americ
Afghanistan, Pashtu	Kabul, Kandahar	Indo-European (Iranic)	West Asian
United States, Black English	Trenton, Chicago	Indo-European (Germanic)	North Americ
Belgium, Flemish	Brussels	Indo-European (Germanic)	West Europea
India, Bengali	Calcutta	Indo-European (Germanic)	South Asian
Costa Rica, Spanish	San Jose, Liberia, C. Quesada	Indo-European (Romance)	Central Ameri
India, Hindi	Delhi	Indo-European (Indic)	South Asian
Finland, Finnish	Helsinki	Finno-Ugric	North Europe
France, French	Paris, Strasbourg	Indo-European (Romance)	West Europea
West Germany, German	Munster	Indo-European (Germanic)	West Europea
Greece, Greek	Athens	Indo-European (Greek)	Mediterranean
Hong Kong, Cantonese	Hong Kong	Sino-Tibetan	East Asian
Hungary, Magyar	Budapest	Finno-Ugric	Central Europ
Iran, Farsi	Teheran	Indo-European (Iranic)	West Asian
Italy, Italian	Padu	Indo-European (Romance)	Mediterranean
Japan, Japanese	Tokyo	Japanese	East Asian
Lebanon, Arabic	Beirut	Afro-Asiatic (Semitic)	Mediterranean West Asian
India, Kannada	Mysore City, Bangalore	Dravidian	South Asian
Malaysia, Bahasa	Kelantan State	Malayo-Polynesian	Southeast Asi
Mexico, Spanish	Mexico City	Indo-European (Romance)	North Americ
Netherlands, Dutch	Amsterdam, Haarlem	Indo-European (Germanic)	West Europea
Poland, Polish	Warsaw	Indo-European (Slavic)	East Europea
Romania, Romanian	Bucharest	Romanian	East Europea
Sweden, Swedish	Uppsala	Indo-European (Germanic)	North Europe
Thailand, Thai	Bangkok	Kadai	Southeast Asi
Turkey, Turkish	Istanbul	Altaic	Mediterranean West Asian
Chiapas (Mexico), Tzeltal	San Cristobal las Casas	Mayan	North Americ
Yucatan (Mexico), Spanish (Mayan)	Ticul, Chablekal, Kom Chiem	Indo-European (Romance)	North Americ
Yugoslavia, Serbo-Croatian	Belgrade	Indo-European (Slavic)	Mediterranea East Europ

groups. Thus, the question was whether one could identify a limited set of concepts that accounted for most of the variation in response to the various achievement meanings across the 30 cultural groups. If so, what might the components of this set be? The components of this general factor, presented in table 8–3, account for approximately 77 percent of between-culture differences in achievement concepts. In short, the factor is highly generalizable. Whereas there may indeed be considerable variation in the meaning of achievement

Table 8–2
Concepts Chosen to Reflect Achievement Meanings

Sense of Self		Achievement Options			Achievement Situations	Achievement Goals		Miscellaneous	Sex Role
General Self-Regard	Internality-Externality	Instrumental Behavior	Interpersonal Style	Modernism		Affective	Abstract		
I-myself	Taking initiative	Education	Cooperation	Big family	Game	Success	Power	Courage	Male (gender)
	A choice	Questioning things	Devotion	Automation	School	Reward	Progress	Need	Woman
	Purpose	Work	Respect	Space travel	Business	Failure	Development	Determination	Masculinity
	Accepting things as they are	Illiterate	Sympathy	Tradition	Examination	Punishment	Knowledge	Laboratory	Girl
	Free will	Saving money	Love	Future	Play	Shame	Wealth	Growing	Man
	Luck	Lotteries	Follower	Present		Pride	Beauty	Worker	Boy
	Fatalism	Revolution	Leader	Authority		Defeat	Freedom	Problem	Female (gender)
		Playing cards	Aggressive	King		Pleasure	Religion	Poor people	Femininity
			Competitive	Time		Fear	God	Rich people	
			Duty	Past		Pain	Sin	Down	
			Independent talk talk	Charity		Sadness		Up	
			Servant	Caste				Most people	
			Master	Tomorrow				Conflict	
			Champion	Today				Hope	
			Hero	Yesterday				Servant	
				Family					
				Relatives					
				Master					
				Mother					
				Father					
				Brother					
				Sisters					
				Automobile					
				Middle class					

Table 8–3
Cross-Cultural Factors of Achievement

Concepts	Vector Loading
Progress	.86
Father	.85
Worker	.84
Success	.82
Knowledge	.92
Masculinity	.80
Work	.75
Power	.75
Courage	.73
Cooperation	.73
Freedom	.70

$\varrho^2 = .77$.

across persons and groups, there seems also to be an interrelated set of achievement meanings that these very diverse cultural groups hold in common.

Cross-Cultural Variation in Achievement Meaning

Considering this convergence of meaning, a second series of analyses was run to see how cultures that scored high on the cross-cultural factor differed from those that scored low. In this case, low-scoring cultures are Mysore-India, Romania, Poland, Black-English United States, and Sweden. High-scoring cultures are the United States, prerevolutionary Iran, Afghanistan-Pashtu, and West Germany. These further analyses involved computing multiple regression analyses separately for low and high cultures in reference to certain presumably critical criterial words. The prediction variables were the meaning scores on all other concepts. The goal of this analysis was to determine whether high and low cultures would associate different concepts with a given criterial concept. For example, would different sets of predictors be associated with the concept of *success* for cultural groups scoring high or low on the cross-cultural factor? From the full list of achievement concepts, concepts were selected that, according to preliminary analyses, might lead to interesting differential patterns. Some of these concepts and the associated patterns are presented here.

Personal Incentives. Four concepts thought to be broadly related to achievement goals (here termed personal incentives) were selected for consideration. Tables 8–4 and 8–5 present summary data showing the differential patterns exhibited by language communities scoring high or low on the cross-cultural factor.

As shown in table 8–4, the high-scoring cultures tend to associate success with self, initiative, freedom, education, work—and masculinity. For low-

Table 8–4
Achievement Concepts Most Associated with Affective Goals

Criterial Concepts			
Success		Reward	
High-Scoring Cultures	Low-Scoring Cultures	High-Scoring Cultures	Low-Scoring Cultures
Free will (.94)*	Girl (.46)	Saving money (.85)	Lotteries (.90)
Boy (.96)	Devotion (.96)	Aggressive (.93)	Follower (.96)
Father (.94)	Female (.95)	Leader (.65)	Master (.96)
School (.92)	Yesterday (.91)	Future (.97)	Tradition (.90)
I, myself (.89)	Illiterate (.85)	School (.64)	Play (.96)
Authority (.87)	Charity (.89)		
Brother (.86)			
Initiative (.73)			
Work (.65)			
Playing cards (.57)			

*Values in parentheses indicate beta weights in the regression weights.

scoring cultures, the meaning of success clearly takes on a different, almost contrasting form. The association of success with feminity in these cultural groups is particularly interesting. The analysis of the criterial concept of *reward* tends to reinforce and complement what was found in the case of *success*. Note, for example, how *future* is associated with *reward* in high-scoring cultures, whereas *tradition* is associated with *reward* in low-scoring cultures. The complementarity of reward and success meanings is not surprising. Somewhat unpredictable and, therefore, specially intriguing, is the view that *play* leads to reward.

Table 8–5 presents the data for *progress* and *knowledge*. Again, the findings generally reflect a distinction between societal groups that hold what can only be described as a Weber-McClelland concept of the way to achievement, supporting the patterns previously described.

Table 8–5
Achievement Concepts Most Associated with Abstract Goals

Criterial Concepts			
Progress		Knowledge	
High-Scoring Cultures	Low-Scoring Cultures	High-Scoring Cultures	Low-Scoring Cultures
Education (.88)	Lotteries (.90)	Father (.99)	Future (.95)
Father (.92)	Follower (.96)	Brother (.94)	Female (.96)
Middle class (.87)	Tradition (.91)	Education (.89)	Devotion (.93)
Business (.87)	Sympathy (.91)	Masculine (.89)	Girl (.91)
Independent (.84)	Female (.86)	Examination (.87)	Family (.91)
Automation (.80)		Pride (.85)	Defeat (.82)
Servant (− .80)		Servant (− .68)	

Perceived Options. Concepts that we have classified as representing perceived options were also considered. The results in the case of three of these (*education, competition,* and *champion*) are presented in tables 8–6 through 8–9.

Even a cursory glance at table 8–6 will indicate that *education* means very different things to the groups scoring high and low on the cross-cultural factor. What stands out particularly is the apparent view of low-scoring cultures that *education* confirms the old ways rather than ushering in the new.

Table 8–7 summarizes the results associated with *competition* and *champion.* Low-scoring cultures view both *competition* and *champion* negatively. *Competition* is associated with *punishment* and *sin* and *champion* with *fear* and *defeat.* In the high-scoring cultures, *competition* and *champion* are not only *not* seen as negative, but such avenues of achievement as *school* and *work* are intimately tied up with these concepts. Apparently, these are arenas in which one can get ahead or through which one can excel. In short, they are perceived as options on the way to achievement. Investing in these areas is associated with success, progress, and excelling over others.

Table 8–8 presents the meanings associated with selected achievement situations: *school, business, examination,* and *game.* There is a recurring theme in the results: Low-socring cultures apparently do not see the school as a positive environment, and a distinct note of negativism is expressed toward each of the selected achievement arenas. Thus, low-scoring cultures associate *pain* with school and *defeat* with business.

Sex Role. The final cluster of perceived achievement options is sex role. The importance of sex role in determining motivation and achievement has been researched extensively, though not always with consistent or readily interpretable results (see, for example, Steinkamp & Maehr, 1984a). Cross-cultural research on this topic is limited (see, for example, Maehr and

Table 8–6
Achievement Concepts Most Associated with Achievement Options: Instrumental Behavior

Criterial Concept: Education	
High-Scoring Cultures	*Low-Scoring Cultures*
Competition (.97)	Yesterday (.89)
Hero (.95)	Family (.80)
Progress (.88)	Devotion (– .77)
Male (.81)	
Success (.73)	
Feminity (– .96)	
Playing cards (– .95)	
Poor people (– .99)	

Table 8–7
Achievement Concepts Most Associated with Achievement Options:
Interpersonal Style

	Criterial Concepts		
Competition		Champion	
High-Scoring Cultures	Low-Scoring Cultures	High-Scoring Cultures	Low-Scoring Cultures
Up (.97)	Punishment (.95)	School (.94)	Knowledge (.93)
Work (.95)	Power (.85)	Space travel (.92)	Fear (.87)
Purpose (.90)	Sin (.84)	Determination (.86)	Defeat (.81)
Free will (.85)	Rich people (.92)	Power (.80)	Growing (.97)
Lotteries (− .90)	Luck (.86)	Courage (.70)	Devotion (.94)

Nicholls, 1980; Quinn, 1977). Accordingly, these results have special value. The data in table 8–9 provide an interesting perspective, as they suggest ways in which the construction of sex role may differ in societies that are high or low on a cross-culturally generalizable achievement factor.It is interesting that in the high-scoring cultures, achievement seems to be associated with masculinity but not femininity. Any suggestion of a relationship of femininity with achievement is to be found in the low-scoring cultures. This finding is simultaneously perplexing and intriguing. Fyans et al. (1983) had difficulty explaining it—and so do we. However, in an exhaustive review of studies on gender differences in science achievement, Steinkamp and Maehr (1984b) found that in lower socioeconomic groups in the United States and in certain so-called developing countries, girls were sometimes more likely to be positively oriented toward science achievement. Otherwise, boys were regularly more likely to exhibit higher levels of science achievement. Perhaps the most important explanatory factor is that the cross-cultural factor is decidedly masculine, based as it is on a male sample.

Sense of Self. Two clusters were classified in the sense-of-self category: *general self-regard* and *internality-externality*. For general self-regard, the criterial concept was *I-myself*. As can be seen in table 8–10, in high-scoring cultures, *I-myself* is not only seen more positively than it is in low-scoring cultures but is tied to concepts that suggest that one can achieve success if one tries. Moreover, in high-scoring cultures, *self* seems to be intimately tied to achievement; in low-scoring cultures, it is tied to *family, cooperation,* and *love.* Following earlier notions (e.g., Atkinson, 1958) high-scoring cultures appear to stress achievement and low-scoring cultures stress affiliation, which is quite in accord with McClelland's (1961) suggestion in *The Achieving Society.*

The *internality-externality* cluster of concepts may well stand with *I-myself* as the most important cluster in terms of current theoretical concerns,

Table 8–8
Achievement Concepts Most Associated with Achievement Situations

Criterial Concepts			
School		Business	
High-Scoring Cultures	Low-Scoring Cultures	High-Scoring Cultures	Low-Scoring Cultures
Courage (.94)	Saving money (.97)	Success (.92)	Knowledge (.93)
Success (.84)	Future (.75)	A choice (.87)	Boy (.86)
Free will (.84)	Tomorrow (.91)	Progress (.86)	Defeat (.81)
Determination (.82)	Pain (.86)	Illiterate ($-.78$)	Luck (.76)
Progress (.76)	Failure (.99)	Playing cards ($-.75$)	Illiterate (.95)
Boy (.76)		Relation ($-.85$)	

since this cluster seems to relate rather directly to the achievement construct of causal attribution (Weiner, 1977). As seen in table 8–11, *taking initiative* and *a choice* were selected as representative of this domain. Some of the same basic themes are illustrated with these concepts. For example, *a choice* is associated with *school* in high-scoring cultures but with *lotteries* in low-scoring cultures. In high-scoring cultures, *initiative, desire,* and *freedom* are associated with work and school, but they are associated with *play* in low-scoring cultures. High-scoring cultures apparently see *freedom* in work and in work-associated activities such as school. Low-scoring cultures, in contrast, look to the realm of play for any such freedom.

Conclusions

The semantic differential analyses reported here initially set out to consider variability in the meaning of achievement across varying cultural groups. Certainly, the data presented show an obvious variation in the meaning of achievement from culture to culture. Achievement—its meaning and possibly also its actualization in behavior—is a many-splendored thing.

Having paid heed to such apparent variations in the meaning of achievement, however, there is a more important finding in this collection of data matrices. A pancultural meaning of achievement is possible that is not unlike the Protestant ethic of Weber (1904/1930) nor at variance with McClelland's (1961) concept of achievement motivation. More specifically, the cross-cultural achievement motivation factor uncovered in these analyses stresses work, knowledge, and freedom and deemphasizes family, tradition, and interpersonal concerns. Those who have been especially concerned with recently proposed cognitive interpretations of motivation will be pleased that freedom and possibly also initiative and effort emerge as associated conditions. In all, there appears to be something like an achievement ethic that is possibly pancultural or at least evident in all the cultural groups sampled by Osgood et al.

Criterial Concepts			
Examination		Game	
High-Scoring Cultures	Low-Scoring Cultures	High-Scoring Cultures	Low-Scoring Cultures
Growing (.92)	I, myself (.82)	Lotteries (.99)	Illiterate (.82)
Knowledge (.87)	Work (.98)	Cooperation (.92)	Pain (.89)
Reward (.83)	Family (.82)	Wealth (− .72)	Courage (.87)
Knowledge (.73)	Cooperation (.90)	Up (− .93)	Failure (.72)
Freedom (.72)			

(1975). School and work are important components of that ethic, as is a perception of an open system in which initiative leads to success. Those who participate in this achievement ethic believe in *themselves* as an avenue to success, and they appear to be distancing themselves from traditional ways as well as from the family and interpersonal ties.

Also intriguing is the fact that freedom, initiative, and work cluster together in relationship to achievement in the high-scoring cultures, whereas this tendency is *not* evident in the low-scoring cultures. One is tempted to speculate that high-scoring cultures have essentially broken the barriers between work and play. Work can be fun, not just a burden. It is a domain for personal fulfillment as well as a place to earn one's daily bread. In low-scoring cultures, work remains enslavement; freedom and fun occur only outside the work sphere.

In sum, our analysis of the Fyans et al. (1983) study leads to the conclusion that what Weber labeled the Protestant ethic reflects a general set of

Table 8–9
Achievement Concepts Most Associated with Sex Roles

Criterial Concepts			
Masculinity		Femininity	
High-Scoring Cultures	Low-Scoring Cultures	High-Scoring Cultures	Low-Scoring Cultures
Success (.98)	Question theory (.81)	Religion (.96)	The present (.99)
Middle class (.98)	Leader (.95)	Future (.91)	Examination (.85)
Progress (.96)	Tradition (.96)	Defeat (.85)	Conflict (.73)
A choice (.95)	Family (.79)	Growing (.75)	
Brother (.94)		Free will (− .77)	
Worker (.90)			
Wealth (.89)			
Education (.79)			

Table 8–10
Achievement Concepts Most Associated with the I-Myself Concept: Sense of Self

Criterial Concept: I-Myself	
High-Scoring Cultures	*Low-Scoring Cultures*
School (.99)	Family (.99)
Leader (.99)	Cooperation (.95)
Worker (.96)	Love (.94)
Success (.89)	Pain (.94)
Work (.87)	Failure (.86)
A choice (.87)	
Free will (.71)	

assumptions and beliefs that is widely recognized. It is intriguing to consider the possibility that such assumptions and beliefs—such meaning—affect personal investment in similar ways regardless of culture.

The United States Versus Japan: A Cross-Cultural Study of Personal Investment Meanings

The remarkable accomplishments of the Japanese, perhaps more than anything else, have prompted popular soul-searching on the work ethic in the United States. How can this tiny, island-bound nation do it? Many remember the day when Japanese products were laughed at, when the label "Made in Japan" was an occasion for derision. Many who do remember now worry about whether their new American-made Honda will prove to be the high-quality car that their old Japanese-made one was. Despite almost a decade of

Table 8–11
Achievement Concepts Most Associated with Internality-Externality: Sense of Self

Criterial Concepts			
Taking Initiative		A Choice	
High-Scoring Cultures	*Low-Scoring Cultures*	*High-Scoring Cultures*	*Low-Scoring Cultures*
Examination (.93)	Play (.98)	Male (.95)	Lotteries (.91)
Work (.91)	Sympathy (.87)	Masculinity (.95)	Automation (.93)
Freedom (.91)	Authority (.86)	Courage (.93)	Play (.92)
Brother (.88)	The past (.81)	School (.90)	Game (.88)
Defeat (−.99)	Need (.92)	Success (.86)	Power (.92)
	Fear (.92)	Illiterate (−.86)	
		Caste (−.99)	

discussion on the topic, there remains considerable interest in the success of the Japanese, apparently at almost anything. What is it about Japanese people, their way of life and work, the way they believe, and what they value that spells success? Not surprisingly, such questions lead to discussions of motivational patterns. Perhaps the Japanese are simply more motivated than most people. But that simple answer is actually a nonanswer—unless we specify what we mean by motivation and unless we can provide some findings about how the Japanese differ in terms of some specific definition of motivation.

With these issues and questions in mind, and with the assistance of various colleagues (Harnisch & Maehr, 1985; Mayberry, 1984; Schwalb, Harnisch & Maehr, 1985), we initiatied an exploration into possible differences in personal investment meanings in a sample of Japanese roughly similar to the sample employed in our early research with the IPI in the United States (see chapter 4). The purpose of this study was twofold. First, our goal was to examine whether the personal investment meanings identified in the United States were represented in a similar manner in Japan. For example, would we obtain similar personal incentive factors? Second, if we should obtain some similarity in personal investment meanings, how might our samples compare? For example, might our Japanese group exhibit different personal investment meanings from our U.S. sample, possibly indicating that there are significant differences in motivation and personal investment in the two societies? In making this type of comparison, we focused especially on the differences in U.S. and Japanese workers. We did this, in part, for methodological reasons. That is, we wished to compare groups in the two societies that held positions of comparable status and role to the degree that this is possible. In addition, however, we were especially interested in the worker role, in view of its possible importance in influencing overall productivity patterns in the society as a whole.

Although much has been said about differential work and achievement orientations in the two societies, most of these reports are anecdotal. A few studies have considered motivational differences following accepted social science procedures (Azumi & McMillan, 1976; DeVos, 1973; Pascale, & Maguire, 1980; Uneo, Blake, & Mouton, 1984), but most comments on the differences in motivation have not proceeded from the framework of contemporary motivation theory. As a result, there is surprisingly little evidence on the question of Japanese–U.S. differences in motivation and achievement in the world of work.

Procedures

One of the researchers (David Schwalb) had been living and working in Japan for about a year at the time the study was initiatied. He was reasonably fluent in the language and conversant with the culture. Through the collaboration of Japanese colleagues and his entrée to various groups in Japan, Schwalb was able to learn how data could be gathered and what they might mean. His impressions were employed, first, as a corrective for or prevention against gross procedural errors. In addition, his participation and experience were valuable in developing interpretations of the data.

The IPI was used in much the same way it had been used in the United States. That is, the goal was to compare a representative sample of Japanese adults with the U.S. sample to see what type of "objective" results might be obtained—and then to interpret these results in terms of a broader knowledge of U.S. and Japanese cultures. To do this, we were faced with two major problems.

First, we had to assure ourselves that, in some sense, we could indeed assess personal investment meanings from the two societies in a comparable fashion. As a first step in this direction, we translated the IPI into Japanese, following accepted practices in conducting cross-cultural research; that is, the usual translation and back-translation procedures (Barry, 1980; Irvine & Carroll, 1980; Pareek & Rao, 1980) were employed in constructing the instrument. It is interesting that there was no need to delete items because they were inappropriate within Japanese society. Some items did not translate readily, but because there were, by our count, fewer than five such items, translation posed no real problem in employing the IPI with a Japanese sample.

As a further check on the comparability of the IPI for assessing personal investment meanings in the two cultural groups, we also conducted factor analyses separately for each of the groups and compared the factor structures. Because this tactic was designed not only as a validation procedure but also as a procedure that would provide substantive information on the conceptual worlds of U.S. and Japanese adults, we will report the results of these analyses as we present the results of our comparisons of personal investment meanings in the two cultural groups.

A second procedural problem involved the comparability and representativeness of samples from the two societies. This problem is seldom completely surmounted in cross-cultural research (cf. Triandis & Brislin, 1980), and we cannot claim to have fully surmounted it either. Table 8–12 presents a brief description of the Japanese sample, and table 8–13 shows the differences

Table 8–12
Profile of 522 Japanese Adults in Sample

Average age	37
Percentage males	57
Educational level (percentage)	
High school	41
Junior college	11
College	48

Table 8–13
Comparison of U.S. and Japanese Adults by
Occupational Group
(percentage)

Occupational Group	United States	Japan
Sales, service, professional	8	9
Clerical, technical	22	60
Manager, administrator	64	9
Owner, executive	6	21
Total	100	99

between the two samples in terms of occupational group membership. It may be noted that the samples differ somewhat in occupational level, age, and gender proportions, but both samples represent a wide range from the two societies. Thus, it is unlikely that any results obtained are limited to an idiosyncratic few in either of the societies. This heterogeneity enhances the likelihood of sampling broadly generalizable traits representative of the two societies. All in all, we were reasonably successful in selecting a Japanese sample that overlapped with the range of occupational and status categories associated with the U.S. sample.

In addition, we selected vocationally comparable U.S. and Japanese subgroups (575 U.S. and 467 Japanese workers) for systematic comparison of IPI profile characteristics.

Do Japanese and Americans Think about Personal Investment in the Same Ways?

At the outset, we considered how Japanese and U.S. adults might construct meanings associated with personal investment. Do Japanese exhibit a similar complex of meanings? Specifically, are the personal incentive dimensions found for the U.S. adults the same or similar to those found for the Japanese adults?

Various analyses were conducted to determine whether the basic meaning factors (personal incentives and sense of self) obtained from the U.S. sample were also present in the Japanese sample. Is there an underlying factor structure that accounts adequately and similarly for the variances in the two cultural groups? In less technical terms, this statistical exploration was designed to determine the adequacy of the instrument in comparing Japanese and U.S. adults in a way that goes beyond simply selecting and translating items properly. This procedural emphasis on the adequacy of the IPI allowed us to ask whether we could logically compare U.S. and Japanese adults on task, competition, or other personal incentives assessed by the IPI. Could we make comparisons of the ways in which the two cultural groups view themselves?

The first stage of our efforts involved conducting a series of analyses focused on determining the general validity of the data obtained by the IPI. These analyses were conducted by and reported in more technical detail by one of our students, Paul Mayberry (1984). Here we will simply summarize the more general and substantive findings of this research. Generally, all of the personal incentive and sense-of-self dimensions associated with the IPI in our earlier analyses transfer readily to the Japanese sample. Thus, the set of factors obtained with the earlier U.S. sample was substantially replicated with the Japanese sample.

One may simply take this as evidence that one can employ the translated version of the IPI in conducting research with Japanese subjects and make rather direct comparisons with U.S. samples. The emergence of similar personal incentive and sense-of-self categories in the two societies does make it possible to use the IPI in comparing motivational patterns in the United States and Japan and prepares the way for discussion of possible differences in meanings and personal investment in the two cultures.

However, there are also theoretical implications in this finding. The two cultural groups utilize similar dimensions of meaning, and the meanings held by U.S. adults appear to be also operative in Japan. Also implicit in this procedural exercise is an interesting substantive issue: Factor structures not only demonstrate the extent of adequacy of a questionnaire but may also detect the structure of thought in a culture. These analyses indicate that the two cultural samples are similar in organizing their thoughts about meaning and personal investment. It may be recalled that we did not argue (in chapter 3) that the same set of meanings should or would be operative in different cultural groups or even across different situations, but finding that they *are* operative in two diverse cultural groups in particular reference to the work situation is most interesting. Perhaps the set of achievement-related and work-related meanings is not so diverse as we had first surmised it might be.

Personal Incentives and Sense of Self

Granted that the IPI provides a reasonably defensible yardstick for comparing the two groups along certain personal incentive and sense-of-self dimensions, how, if at all, does the Japanese sample differ from the U.S. sample in terms of these meaning dimensions? To approach an answer to this question, Schwalb et al. (1985) first conducted a series of multivariate anlayses designed to determine whether the profiles of personal incentives and sense of self of the two groups were different statistically. These analyses also controlled sample differences associated with age and gender and focused on profile differences of the overall sample groups taken to be generally representative of Japan and the United States. The Japanese and U.S. samples did exhibit clearly different profiles, which cannot be readily attributed to demographic or other idiographic features of the two samples. Indeed, Schwalb et al. (1985) made a strong argument that the results indicate an important difference in motivational orientation in the respective societies. The analysis best summarizes the factors that distinguish the two samples when such sample characteristics as age and gender are controlled.

Overall, the U.S. and Japanese samples (1,011 U.S. adults and 500 Japanese adults) had statistically significantly different personal incentive and sense-of-self profiles. Over 55 percent of the variability among people in the four age groups from each country can be attributed to the differences in scores on the personal incentives and sense of self scales. The largest differences were due to country affiliation. The personal incentives scales that contributed most to the differentiation between countries were affiliation, recognition, and social concern. The U.S. adults placed more importance on these personal incentives than the Japanese did. Also important were the financial, task, and excellence personal incentives scales, with the Japanese exhibiting higher scores than the U.S. sample. The power and competition scales did not discriminate between the samples. By comparison, age was not generally an important discriminator once country affiliation was taken into account.

In some respects, these results are a bit surprising. A greater stress on power and competition in the U.S. sample might have been expected. Using thematic measures of motivation and operating out of a different theoretical frame of reference, McClelland (1961) found that power motivation was greater in U.S. adults than in Japanese adults in 1950. However, in the present case, power and competition are not important in determining possible societal influence on personal incentives. The finding that Japanese place a greater stress on task and excellence conforms to the commonly accepted picture of the Japanese—namely, that they are concerned with doing their job well. However, the results in the case of affiliation, social concern, and recognition are not in accord with McClelland's findings nor with generally accepted stereotypes of the two societies. Characteristically, discussions of the differences in Japanese culture and business stress the group-oriented nature of behavior in Japan and the individualistic orientation in the United States (DeVos, 1973; Morsbach, 1980; Pascale & Athos, 1981; Plath, 1983). This does not necessarily mean that affiliation, for example, must be high in one case and low in the other, but it certainly would lead to that expectation. Perhaps the difference in social orientation in the two societies has been overstressed in many respects.

Thus, our results do not reflect the presumed greater social orientation of the Japanese. Parallel to that finding is the indication that the Japanese sample stressed financial rewards to a greater extent, whereas one might have expected the opposite. Presumably, the United States is the more materialistic culture—or is it? The findings in the external rewards scale placed alongside the social scales, particularly social concern, indicate that this generalization may no longer be warranted. One way of interpreting this is to suggest that the Japanese sample seems to reflect better the kind of personal incentive profile that is likely to lead to high achievement in the world of work. A greater stress on external rewards and a lesser stress on social concern seems well designed to foster achievement on the job or in a career.

Although the Schwalb et al. (1985) study cannot stand as definitive at this point, neither should it be automatically dismissed. What emerges in the comparison of the two profiles is a general impression that the Japanese ethos is characterized by certain personal incentives (task and excellence) that should encourage an achievement orientation. Similarly, the Japanese stress on financial rewards and the relative lack of stress on social concern may well combine to encourage achievement in the world of work. Financial rewards, not social relationships, are probably the most reliable indicators of achievement in the world of work. Moreover, social concern is an orientation that is likely to detract from a single-mindedness in pursuing achievement in the realm of work—or in many other realms, for that matter. Thus, for every workaholic businessperson, there is the totally absorbed scientist or artist who likewise puts his or her work above the concern with the well-being of others, except perhaps in a very abstract sense. Perhaps Schwalb et al. (1985) did, in fact, uncover a basic motivational orientation that better explains Japanese productivity and achievement than the rather simplistic analysis of the role of groups and family in the two societies. Certainly, it is most interesting that whereas McClelland (1961) did not really find the Japanese higher than Americans in achievement orientation in 1950, the present results reveal a pattern indicating that the Japanese are very likely more achievement-oriented today than U.S. workers are.

Sense of Self

Only one of the sense-of-self factors—self-reliance—figured importantly in the multiple regression analyses. The U.S. adults placed considerably more stress on self-reliance than the Japanese adults did. These findings are not altogether surprising, in that they reflect what has been a regular observation of the two societies. That is, they seem to reflect the "rugged individualism" that is thought to be characteristic of the United States in contrast to Japan (Morsbach, 1980). It is interesting that the results in the case of self-reliance do not seem to mesh well with some of the findings in the case of socially oriented personal incentives. For example, why are affiliation and recognition apparently more important for the self-reliant North Americans than for the less self-reliant Japanese? Looking more closely at the items in each of these scales, Schwalb et al. (1985) found some basis for asserting that North Americans might wish to achieve social recognition for what they do. Although they express a fondness for being with others, when they think of accomplishing something, they see it as a task they must do on their own. The Japanese, on the other hand, seem to express slightly less interest in social interaction for its own sake but believe that achievement is not necessarily an individual effort.

This may or not be the appropriate interpretation of the results, but it has a significant degree of plausibility. Of course, this interpretation can only be constructed as a hypothesis to be pursued further in subsequent research; the present results cannot speak definitively to this most interesting and important set of questions.

Does Motivation Explain Japanese Success?

The results obtained with the IPI in the two societal samples are interesting and suggestive. At the very least, they suggest directions for future research, and they may also raise some questions about the validity of certain assumptions that have figured prominently in comparisons of U.S. and Japanese achievement patterns. At this point, we cannot be certain that these results are truly representative of broad orientations in the two societies that logically explain possible differences in work and achievement orientations. One can readily note that these results might simply exhibit a bias in our samples that has not been specifically controlled for through the statistical controls we exercised. However, it is equally plausible to argue that the results do, in fact, properly reflect the state of affairs and suggest why the Japanese are currently exhibiting a competitive edge over the United States. Certainly, the relatively greater stress on task and excellence should facilitate an achieving society. Moreover, the greater stress on financial rewards and the lesser stress on social concerns are more than likely to facilitate achievement, particularly in the world of work. As we have repeatedly pointed out, financial rewards are critical motivators for work motivation. When a person is highly oriented toward attaining financial rewards and relatively unencumbered by social concerns, it is reasonable to assume that he or she will concentrate more on work and on career.

Lest we be misunderstood, the emphasis on pursuing financial rewards is not to be associated pejoratively with mere greed. The fact is that reward, recognition, and most of the symbols of excellence in the world of work are tied in with this incentive. As David McClelland (1961) pointed out long ago, money means more than financial wherewithal to the entrepreneur. It is a way of scoring points, of keeping track of career progress, of defining success. In short, it has symbolic significance for the person that goes beyond the

210 • *The Motivation Factor*

the hedonistic enjoyment of what money can buy. It is a *measure*—a very concrete measure—of one's success in realizing one's goals. Therefore, by pointing out that the Japanese are focused on financial rewards as well as on task and excellence personal incentives, we are simply stressing the possibility that they are very much like the Protestants described earlier by Max Weber and later by David McCLelland. By calling attention to the parallel relative lack of social concern, we are simply stressing that achieving in almost any area requires a certain amount of single-mindedness. It is reasonable to assume that social concern might detract from the pursuit of achievement in the business world. Thus, one might surmise that an orientation that stresses financial rewards and a relative lack of social concern is in fact well designed to foster a heavy personal investment in one's work in the world of business.

We are not unaware of some broader questions regarding whether we want a society to be especially oriented in this way. Will a price be paid in the quality of life? Certainly, it is possible that goals that are most compatible with success in the world of work may not be altogether compatible with creating a happy existence or enhancing the quality of life. A too-focused emphasis on what is good for business may ignore what is good for society—that is a well-known and oft-told story. We recognize the dilemmas here, but we are constrained to leave the issues without a resolution, if indeed a resolution is really possible. After all, such questions have been around for a long time, and answers have seldom proved durable.

Comparisons of U.S. and Japanese Worker Subgroups

Although comparisons of the two samples as a whole are very suggestive of certain interesting differences that may exist in the two cultural groups represented by our samples, we have chosen to portray a more focused set of comparisons—comparisons of similar types of U.S. ($N = 575$) and Japanese workers ($N = 467$). We do this for at least two reasons, the first of which is methodological. That is, the selected subsamples are arguably more comparable than the larger, more heterogeneous samples. Second, the subsamples are especially interesting in that they concern specific workgroups in the two countries.

Table 8–14 presents the results of the comparisons of comparable U.S. and Japanese vocational groups on the eleven scales of the IPI. It can be seen that the two groups do differ, and in fascinating ways. The two workgroup subsamples had differing profiles of personal incentives and sense of self, specifically reflective of the larger samples. Thus, what was said earlier in regard to the more heterogeneous larger samples also obtains in the workforce samples. It appears that what was said about general motivational orientation in the two societies applies to workers at all levels.

Table 8–14
Standardized Beta Weights in Regression
Equation to Predict Country from Personal
Incentives and Sense of Self

Scales	Standardized Beta Weights
Personal Incentives	
Task	.14*
Excellence	.16*
Competition	− .06
Power	− .00
Affiliation	− .23*
Social Concern	− .15*
Recognition	− .24*
Financial	.14*
Sense of Self	
Goal-Directedness	− .17*
Self-Reliance	− .40*
Sense of Competence	− .02

Note: Level of significance equals .01. A positive weight means that the Japanese subsample scored higher on the scale than the U.S. subsamples.
*p < .01.

Conclusions

The varied comparisons conducted by Mayberry (1985) and Schwalb et al. (1985) are of general interest in considering the larger questions posed at the beginning of this chapter. Generally, these studies strongly suggest two important findings.

First, one can appropriately employ the theoretical framework and assessment procedures developed with U.S. adults in studying Japanese adults. Similar factor structures were found in the Japanese and U.S. samples, indicating that individuals from the two cultures are likely to understand the personal incentive and sense-of-self items in similar ways. The similar factor structures, as well as the overall nature of the results found by Schwalb et al. (1985), indicate that one can use the associated items for further comparative studies of motivation and work patterns in the United States and Japan.

Second, in focusing on the comparisons of responses of Japanese and U.S. adults, a series of interesting conclusions seems possible. The observed differences in the two samples cannot readily be attributed to the vagaries of sampling, response bias, or other methodological factors. We have reviewed some of the problems that ensue with cross-cultural comparisons, and this study has not escaped these problems. Yet the results should be taken seriously.

They present a differing picture of the two societies as their citizens approach the world of work, and it is possible that this picture suggests why the two societies exhibit different degrees of productivity at this time.

Gender Differences in Meanings and Personal Investment

An important aspect of the wider sociocultural context is the social roles that individuals play. Indeed, some roles can be thought of as participation in a subculture. One such social role that is considered particularly important in terms of personal investment is that associated with gender. There is a wide and extensive literature on gender and social motivation—and especially in terms of achievement (see, for example, Alper, 1979; Spence & Helmreich, 1978; Steinkamp & Maehr, 1984a). As highly industrialized societies turn their attention to the roles of women in the world of work, it is interesting to consider gender differences in personal investment. Again, we will turn to data gathered with the IPI and the IWI as a basis for considering these issues in terms of personal investment theory.

Gender Differences in Personal Incentives and Sense of Self

To consider the effects of gender role on meaning and personal investment, Harnisch and Maehr (1985) recently conducted a reanalysis of all data gathered on the IPI and IWI scales. Although gender had been used as a control variable in previous analyses, the focus in this series of analyses was especially on the role of gender in modifying meaning and personal investment. Thus, such questions were considered as whether any gender differences that were found to exist in one society, such as the United States, would exist in another society, such as Japan. Also considered were patterns of meaning and personal investment as they vary differently for the two sexes, depending on age. For example, do women show an increased stress on excellence and self-reliance in the middle years, after the child-rearing demands on their time and energy have been reduced?

To consider such questions systematically in terms of personal investment theory, a series of statistical analyses and focused quantitative comparisons were conducted. First, multivariate analyses (multiple regression and discriminant analyses) were run in which gender was defined as the criterion variable. In these analyses, the focal independent or predictor variables were taken to be the eight personal incentive scales and three sense of self scales of the IPI/IWI. In addition, country, age, and occupation level were incorporated in the anlaysis—largely to serve as control variables. The essential question asked in the discriminant analysis was whether males and females differ in terms of personal incentives and sense-of-self judgments across the two societies? The answer to that question was yes, but the difference was not especially large ($R^2 = .12$). This difference appeared to reside mainly in responses to the power and task scales and, to a lesser degree, in the affiliation and excellence scales. Males were higher on power but lower on task; females were higher on affiliation but lower on excellence.

Gender and Perceived Job Options

Harnisch and Maehr (1985) also gave further consideration to how males and females viewed their jobs. Using the IWI data available on U.S. male and female employees ($N = 188$), they conducted a series of analyses to determine whether and how males and females differed in their perceptions of the opportunities available to them in their current jobs. In these analyses, an attempt was made to control for occupational level and age—variables that might figure strongly in job perceptions. The only difference found here—but it is an important one—was that males and females were clearly distinquishable in terms of their perceptions of affiliation opportunities in their job. The females expressed more opportunities to assist others and to be friendly and supportive to others than the males did. Note how this complements the earlier finding that females apparently place greater stress on the affiliation personal incentive. Now we learn that they also see their job as providing opportunities to pursue this incentive.

Meaning and Personal Investment in the Cultural Context

We began this chapter with a sketch of the ways in which sociocultural factors might be important in affecting meaning and personal investment. We moved on quickly to show how different cultures exhibit variation in the meanings they associate with achievement, work, success, and failure. Perhaps most interesting, however, is that we raised the serious question of whether or not there might be a certain pattern of meaning that is more facilitative of achievement regardless of culture. In somewhat general terms, one does have to consider the possibility that something like the Protestant ethic is a cross-culturally generalizable set of values that tend to be related to a commitment to achievement. Frankly, in the past (Maehr 1974a), we have questioned that possibility in criticizing the work of David McClelland (1961). We now are beginning to wonder whether he and Max Weber were right in general principle, though perhaps incorrect in some of the details.

Perhaps of greatest interest in terms of understanding the world of work are the apparent personal incentive and sense-of-self differences found in the

U.S. and Japanese samples, as reported by Schwalb et al. (1985). These results push us to consider the possibility that differences between U.S. and Japanese productivity and achievement—so often talked about and occasionally documented—rest significantly in the motivational patterns of individuals in the two societies. The patterns that Schwalb et al. (1985) found in the Japanese and U.S. samples are such that we would expect the Japanese to be more involved in work and achievement. To put this in lay terms, the Japanese are simply more motivated to work hard, to achieve, and to excel. They tend to exhibit the kinds of meanings that lead to productivity to a greater extent than those held by U.S. adults. At present, they are the better exemplars of *The Achieving Society*.

9
Managing Personal Investment

W hen we are asked to talk about motivation to people who are in the business of motivating others, we find them generally receptive to the concept of motivation as personal investment. That is, most people find it easy and useful to think in terms of such questions as: How do I use my time, talents, and energy? What can an organization do to promote the investments of its employees to meet the goals of the organization? What are the effects and outcomes of the investment of time and energy? It makes sense that people are guided by personal incentives as well as by judgments about self and perceived options. Moreover, it also makes sense to people that their investment in their work or some other activity is guided by the nature of the activity itself and the rewards derived from it as well as by their social environment, including the expectations of the organization and peer support and encouragement. Indeed, we have found it easy to engage practitioners in thinking up examples of behavior to illustrate what we are talking about. However, at some point, the question is inevitably asked: But what do we *do* to direct personal investment? It is one thing to present a logical scheme; it is quite another to suggest how the scheme might be useful. In this chapter we will endeavor to show how personal investment theory might be useful to those who are in charge of motivating others. Although personal investment theory can also be used as a conceptual scheme to examine one's own motivation, as evidenced in the questions listed earlier, the focus of this chapter is on how a manager or human resources director can enhance the investment of employees in the organization. How can a supervisor motivate those under his or her supervision? What strategies can the director of human resources in a firm suggest to enhance the motivation and personal investment of employees in their work? What can a chief executive of a large company do to increase the general level of motivation, job satisfaction, and commitment not only of his or her immediate staff but of company personnel as a whole? Just how does one create a "culture" to increase personal investment that is in accord with the purposes of the organization?

We cannot answer all such questions with finality, of course, but we will try to demonstrate how personal investment theory provides a useful perspective for answering them, and we will endeavor to present certain principles that can be followed in enhancing motivation in the work setting. Personal investment theory represents a broad perspective on human motivation. It is a way of viewing how people make life choices and devote their time and energy to a variety of tasks. But the research reviewed in this book gives us confidence in the belief that it provides an especially useful perspective for understanding people and their work and, thus, implies how work can best be organized and managed.

A Personal Investment Perspective

Before attempting to identify principles that may be employed in the development and mangement of personal investment, we should review the basic ingredients of personal investment theory. In particular, we need to review what we have learned about the antecedents of personal investment. Later, we will also define what we understand by the term *management* and consider the roles that leaders at any level in an organization play and how they influence the motivation and personal investment of others in the organization.

Motivation as Choice

At the outset, it may be noted that a unique perspective on managing motivation is implicit in the term *personal investment*, which we have proposed as an alternative to the term *motivation*. This difference is more than stylistic. The use of the term *personal investment* is designed to stress that motivation is particularly indicated by the kinds of choices people make in their lives. Therewith, we stress that motivational "problems" are not, in the main, attributable to a *lack* of motivational potential but, rather, are a matter of how people choose to invest their time and energy. Thus, when one considers a worker "unmotivated," one probably is only observing that he or she is not choosing to direct attention to the task at hand. In another context or situation, this same worker might show all the energy that would elicit the characterization "motivated." The point is that there is not really anything "wrong" with such people—they are not lacking in drive or lazy. Rather, they are either attracted or not to a task. In such cases, managers may be well-advised to ask what there is about the job or the job context that does not serve to elicit workers' investment.

Meaning as a Determinant of Personal Investment

The burden for change is placed especially on the situation. More particularly, the focus is on the *meaning* of the situation to the person—the critical determinant of how or whether the person will invest himself or herself in it. We suggest, also, that situations and their meanings are more easily subject to change than people are.

As discussed in earlier chapters, meaning is appropriately viewed as consisting of three components or dimensions: (1) certain perceived options or action possibilities available to the person in the situation; (2) certain views of oneself in relationship to the situation, including particularly one's view of oneself as being able to perform competently; and (3) reasons for or personal goals in performing the task. We refer to these components as personal incentives.

Antecedents of Meanings and Personal Investment

Many factors affect the meaning of the situation to the person. To simplify this complexity of causes, we refer to two basic causal categories: the *person* and the *situation*. As we concentrate specifically on personal investment in the world of work, we find it convenient to subdivide situation into *job* and *organization*.

Person. The first consideration is the nature of the *person*. Individuals arrive at situations with experiential baggage—personal histories that have given them certain meaning biases. They arrive with preferred personal incentives, a defined sense of self, and an awareness of perceived options. The meanings people bring to a situation may, of course, be subject to change as the result of what happens in the situation, but they may also have not only an initial but an enduring effect on how people behave. For example, it might be predicted that a person who scores high on the IPI/IWI competition scale is generally likely to seek out competitive situations, to perform well in them, and to be happy in such situations. Moreover, it is possible that, given half a chance, the person will redesign a situation in competitive terms. We do not go so far as to say that a high score on the IPI/IWI competition scale indicates that the person is competitive in nature. We suggest, however, that this person has a predisposition with which he or she is likely to confront any new situation. Such qualities are not fixed in stone at an early age—but they are reasonably durable. They are also likely to be pervasive, and people may exhibit such characteristics across a wide variety of situations.

Situation. Personal investment is not just a function of "personality" or "character"—established irrevocably at an early age and generalizing across all work and achievement contexts. Although it is sometimes tempting to suggest that some people are simply more motivated than others and leave the discussion at that point, such a simplistic analysis is misleading at best. In our opinion, it is downright wrong. People's motivation depends, to a considerable degree, on the situation. Thus, such features of the work context as the nature of the task to be done, with whom it is to be done, and how it is to be done play a critical role in determining personal investment. Regardless of who the person is—despite his or her "personality"—certain job features can be real "turnoffs" or real "turnons." As discussed earlier (chapter 3), one can design and redesign jobs to affect the motivation and personal investment of workers. For example, if a task is designed such that the worker has a wide degree of choice on how it will be done, a task personal incentive orientation is likely to emerge. Such an orientation should lead, in turn, to "internal motivation" (Hackman & Oldham, 1980) and to "continuing motivation" and commitment (Maehr, 1976). Thus, not only what the person brings to the situation but the nature of the situation itself is of importance. Awareness of these two types of causes is most important in designing intervention strategies, as we will soon see. More broadly, this general perspective on motivation must be kept firmly in mind as we consider what managers can do to enhance workers' personal investment in specific situations.

A Perspective on Management

The term *management* includes a variety of behaviors and responsibilities, as authors of good introductory texts quickly point out (see, for example, Feldman & Arnold, 1983). Focusing particularly on its use in an organizational setting, it incorporates such behaviors as decision making, resolving conflicts, exercising leadership, organizing work, and exercising power. Basically, management focuses on the development and implementation of plans for the optimum use of available resources in furthering the purposes for which the organization exists. In this book, we are especially concerned with the optimum use of *human resources*. More specifically, the issue is how management can enhance the personal investment of employees in accord with the organization's goals.

It should be evident to anyone who has read the preceding pages that motivation is not a topic that management can ignore. In reviewing our studies of successful companies and those of others, it has become clear that such companies are successful largely because they manage to attract and retain the personal investment of their employees. Moreover, such a fortunate state of affairs need not be left to chance. Previously reviewed research and theory have indicated what can be done to elicit such personal investment. Managers and supervisors at all levels *can* do something to enhance the motivation and personal investment of employees; indeed, this may well be their primary task. Among the many tasks of managers, the most important is to lead, and the corollary to that is to motivate. But how?

Strategies for Enhancing Motivation and Personal Investment

Over the years, a variety of strategies for initiating motivational change have been discussed, developed, and implemented (see, for example, Maehr & Kleiber, in press). A review of all that has been said and done suggests that, in general, there are three pressure points for change: the person, the job, and the organization. Figure 9–1 summarizes the critical variables associated with each category and suggests possible antecedents of these variables.

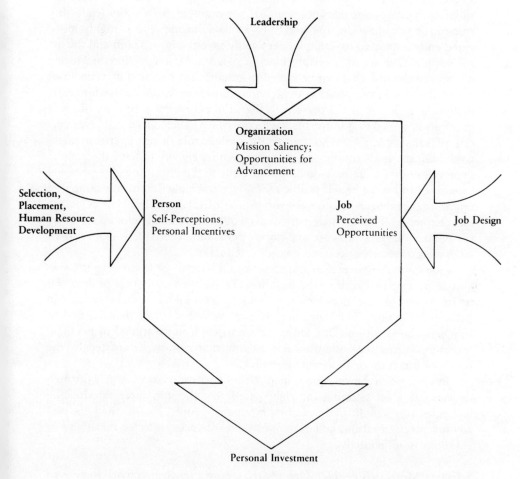

Organization
Mission Saliency;
Opportunities for
Advancement

Leadership

Selection,
Placement,
Human Resource
Development

Person
Self-Perceptions,
Personal Incentives

Job
Perceived
Opportunities

Job Design

Personal Investment

Figure 9–1. Pressure Points for Changing Personal Investment in an Organization

Person-Focused Strategies

We can readily identify three motivation enhancement strategies that focus exclusively on the person—that is, on the relatively enduring and pervasively important characteristics that the person might bring to any situation. These strategies are *selecting* motivated people, *placing* the right person in a given task or job, and *developing* selected meaning and personal investment orientations in individuals.

These strategies share the operational assumption that the situation is stable, constant, or relatively unimportant. Perhaps one cannot change the situation; perhaps one does not want to. For example, for a major leadership role in the organization, one certainly wants someone who is highly motivated and committed to—that is, personally invested in—the job and the organization. One wants a certain kind of *person*. Although there are surely features of the task that can be varied to enhance the personal investment of the incumbent in the position (e.g., salary and bonuses), one cannot really design the task to suit the person. Rather, the person must fit the task. It is generally assumed that individuals who are to play such a role will bring certain personal orientations to the role that will enable them to perform effectively. On the basis of our previous discussions, we would have the general expectation that such individuals would come to the position with a personal incentives and sense-of-self profile that might resemble that of our sample of upper-level managers or perhaps the profile of the so-called high achievers (see chapter 5). That is, such individuals would be especially characterized by the importance given to task and power personal incentives, a high sense of competence, self-reliance, and goal-directedness.

However, this general expectation would have to be tailored to the specific leadership demands of the situation. Thus, a company that prides itself on its "family feeling" may look for a leader who is high in social concern and perhaps affiliation. The point here is that the focus is on what the person brings to the situation. One looks for a particular motivational or personal incentive orientation; one does not assume that it must be created by the board of directors or by company policy.

In sum, when the decision is made to enhance motivation largely through concentrating on selecting the right people for the job, three interlocking strategies may be followed: *selecting* motivated people, *placing* the right person in a given situation, and *developing* and enhancing selected meaning orientations in individuals.

Selecting Motivated People. One way to secure a motivated work force is to hire motivated people. That is easy enough to say, of course, but how does one go about doing this? There is no one simple answer to that question—a variety of procedures can be and are followed. Employers assess the motivational characteristics a given worker is likely to bring to the job in several ways. Often, they seek letters of recommendation and interview the prospective employee. Sometimes they employ standardized tests or questionnaires. We wish to make four basic points about selection that are relevant regardless of the specific procedures used.

Motivational Stability. When selecting motivated employees, those who select make an assumption that motivation and personal investment are determined by reasonably stable traits of the individual that operate across a wide variety of situations. They often sample behavior or characteristics exhibited by people in one situation with a goal of predicting to a substantial degree what will happen in a different time and place. Of course, it is the business of theory to suggest what one should sample to make such predictions, and in previous chapters, we have made a special case for examining what we have termed personal incentives and sense of self. In our judgment, these cognitions are likely to be the most stable indices of when and how a person will invest himself or herself in any situation. People do tend to bring such meanings to any new work situation, and these meanings do predict work investment. Moreover, one can readily assess these meanings before the people enter the situation. Thus, to an important degree, "motivated workers" can be identified. More accurately, we can identify those who are likely to be motivated in a specific context or work situation. The assessment procedures described in chapter 4 provide a framework for developing such a selection program.

The Predictive Validity of Assessments. The second point is obviously related to the first. It is important not only that stable characteristics of the individual can be assessed but also that these characteristics can be shown to be related to the nature and quality of the necessary or desirable personal investment. They also must be demonstrably nondiscriminating in terms of relevant performance criteria. A personal experience may help make our point.

As any old hand in the area of human resources knows, there are people who think they can choose good workers without tests or formal procedures of any kind. We recall a manager who regularly spoke of his "sixth sense" for choosing the right man for the job—and it almost always was the right *man*. He never recognized his gender bias, and it ultimately did him in. He had never really tested his selection criteria—if indeed he could specify them— against performance in any objective or systematic fashion. The point is that such informal, intuitive, nonexplicit, and nonobjectifiable procedures are sometimes guided more by prejudices than by evidence that they work effectively. Stereotypes and prejudices might guide one successfully in enough cases to keep them operative, but they also lead to mistakes—and to considerable damage. Explicit criteria, procedures, and tests of effectiveness reveal the process—warts and all, thereby making the necessity for change more quickly evident.

The Correctability of Procedures and Criteria. The third point builds on the second: Whatever personnel selection procedures or systems are used, they must be correctable. Again, this presumes specification of criteria and procedures. Indeed, it is essentially another argument for such explicitness, for it is obvious that when one is unaware of selection criteria, it is impossible to determine whether these criteria are valid predictors of job performance. The advantage of a standardized survey or test lies precisely in this explicitness of criteria and procedures. The test or survey automatically notes characteristics that determine judgments in such a way that one can later check on whether the judgments were valid.

The Transferability of Procedures and Criteria. The fourth and final point is that the procedures used in selection should be transferable. One of the problems with informal selection procedures, even when they seem to work, is that they work only when certain people are doing the selecting. That is, the selection process resides solely in the particular people who make the choices and cannot be readily transferred to others. When these "experts" go, so does the selection process. Standardized procedures, because they are designed to be explicit, also assist the transfer of selection decisions to others. The value of this, too, is virtually self-evident.

Toward Systematic Personnel Selection. To meet the foregoing basic selection criteria, one needs a good theory of what motivation is. The theory must be both specific and explicit, so that it can be readily translated into indices that predict personal investment in specifiable situations. This book is directly focused on providing such theory, and we are bold enough to suggest that those who select employees can apply it in formulating ways of judging who has what they want. More operationally, this theory, or any comparable one, suggests how one might "test" for personal investment before the fact. The testing may take different forms. For example, one can use an instrument such as the IPI/IWI more or less as it has been constructed, interpreting the results to the specific situation as needed. The procedure for doing this is quite straightforward, as we shall illustrate.

First, one must decide what kinds of motivation or personal investment characteristics are needed for the job or role in question. To do this, one could simply look at the normative data in chapter 4 and decide that one wants a profile much like that of the high achievers or any other group described there. It would be better, however, to consider the specific situation in question and identify people in that or similar situations who are doing very well and a contrasting group of people who are not doing well. Having identified these two groups, one could then administer the IPI/IWI and obtain separate personal incentive and sense-of-self profiles for the groups. Having determined that the two groups are distinguishable in terms of personal incentives and sense-of-self judgments, one could then set the scores of the high-performing group as a standard for judging the acceptability of new candidates.

Once standards have been established in this manner, one could assess prospective candidates by comparing them to the separate profiles, using these profiles as important evidence in selecting among the applicants. Moreover, having established such procedures for selection, one can subsequently follow up on the accuracy of the selection process. Thus, one could readily compare selected candidates after a designated period of time, determine how they are performing, and decide whether the predictions made with the instrument should be adjusted.

What we are describing here in a very brief and cursory fashion is, in fact, a time-honored way of employing standardized measures in selecting employees. The implied technical features are all well developed and readily available. Perhaps most important of all, the data processing can all be handled by a computer. Parenthetically, it may be noted that a version of the IPI/IWI is currently being used in precisely this manner (Braskamp & Maehr, 1985).

If for some reason one chooses not to use a standardized instrument of some kind, one can nevertheless follow an analogous procedure—simply applying the theoretical principles explicit in the IPI/IWI in constructing an interview or in conducting a review of a worker's resume. The point is that the selection should be a planned, self-conscious process that is explicit enough to allow for replication.

In summary, even at this early stage of research on personal investment, one can be quite objective about selecting motivated people for jobs. Whether one chooses to use the instruments that have emerged out of our work or those developed by others (e.g., Atkinson, 1958; McClelland, 1985a; McClelland & Boyatzis, 1982), the logic is basically the same, and the approach is well worth trying.

Matching People to Situations (Placement). What should be evident in both our theory and our suggestions for practice, is that one does not typically select "motivated people." Rather, one must select people for particular tasks. All people are motivated in some sense, but not all will be equally motivated in a particular job or in a particular setting. Thus, one must examine and assess both workers and the characteristics of jobs. But how does one go about doing this?

One can readily imagine that individuals characterized by a given personal orientation may be particularly attracted to certain jobs and minimally interested in others. For example, a new president of a bank once consulted with us on how to handle his bank teller problem. Briefly, the problem was that morale tended to be low and turnover high. Close supervision was thought to be necessary, because quality of performance varied beyond what was acceptable. The first solution attempted by the president was a series of meetings, which involved "inspirational talks" by himself and so-called motivational experts. We believe he initially contacted us because he thought we, too, could provide some kind of inspirational talk. As people involved with the study of motivation at a major university, we certainly should be able to give a good talk. After all, a good pep talk can inspire everyone from football players to insurance salesmen—and isn't that what motivation is all about? Certainly, enough managers must believe in the value of inspirational talks or the motivational lecture circuit would not be so prominent a feature of the business world.

After some discussion, this manager—the president of a medium-sized bank—began to wonder aloud about the value of inspirational talks and suggested that the problem might revolve around the match between the job and the people hired. As he expressed it, the problem was primarily one of hiring "overqualified people," who quickly became frustrated in the job and whose frustrations were compounded when they realized that their entry-level jobs really went nowhere. Further discussion yielded the insight that the job was and had to remain one in which individuals were not motivated by the chance for advancement, career development, personal growth—or the opportunity to earn large amounts of money. Security was high and fringe benefits adequate, but compensation was minimal, with little possibility of developing a work-incentive system oriented around financial rewards.

What was ultimately decided was that people high in socially oriented personal incentives rather than power or task incentives would likely fulfill this role most adequately. Their social orientation would be an asset on the job ("friendliness" is highly prized in tellers) and might be something an employer could capitalize on in enhancing morale. What eventuated was a concerted and direct effort to enhance the social dimensions of the job. Parallel to this, plans were laid for selecting new employees with stronger social orientation. In this case, enhancing the social dimensions of the job involved encouraging employee luncheons, recognition dinners, and opportunities to share leisure opportunities. The bank president also made a special point of regularly dropping around "to be friendly."

All of these conclusions and decisions occurred more or less informally—that is, through discussion and armchair analysis. Because no systematic evaluation was conducted, we cannot be absolutely sure of the results. Nevertheless, the process seemed to yield a viable plan: Put people in jobs where they can pursue desired personal incentives.

Although the idea of matching workers to jobs has some degree of support (see, for example, Wanous, 1980), in our own research, we found some reason for moving cautiously. In chapter 6, we reported an extensive study of personal incentive and job opportunity congruency, which was defined as the difference between a person's score on a personal incentive scale and the corresponding score on a job opportunities scale for each of the eight dimensions. Only partial support was obtained for the proposition that such congruency was a primary factor in determining personal investment. Certainly, one of the problems is the difficulty of developing precise measures of person–job congruency. Reflecting on our results, however, we suggest now the importance of realizing that although person–job congruency may be important, it is not the only important factor in determining personal investment. We found that facets of the wider organizational culture could outweigh personal incentive–job opportunities congruency in predicting personal investment, as indicated by job satisfaction and organizational commitment. That makes sense. Certainly, other things being equal, a good overall work climate can make up for what is missing in one's job. It is clear, however that in attempting to get people to be personally invested in their work, one should examine the degree of personal incentive–job opportunities congruency and, if possible, work toward enhancing this congruency.

Motivation Training Programs. Most organizations attempt to encourage their participants to hold appropriate beliefs, values, and behavioral patterns. More specifically, they endeavor to ensure that employees possess the "right" motivational orientations. In this regard, they sometimes attempt to use motivation training programs. Perhaps no one has more systematically considered the development, implementation, and analysis of motivation training programs than David McClelland (1965, 1978; McClelland & Winter, 1971). These programs have tended to focus on the development of achievement motivation (see chapter 2) in managers and executives of large companies as well as in independent businesspeople. Some have concentrated especially on the development of entrepreneurship. But motivation training programs have been applied to a wide variety of other activities as well (see, for example, Alschuler, 1973), and even if they were specifically designed to enhance achievement patterns, particularly entrepreneurial behavior, they appear to be broadly relevant to motivation in general. Thus, if one wishes to influence the personal investment of employees in the work organization, one should examine the work of McClelland and his colleagues in this regard, for this work has identified several basic features that are likely to be at the base of any program that is effective in achieving enduring motivational change in people.

Knowledge of Motivation Patterns. The first aspect of such programs involves, logically, the presentation of models of the behavior that is to be emulated. Thus, in the McClelland program, the trainee is instructed in how the highly motivated person thinks, talks, and acts. There are many ways in which this could be done.

McClelland and his colleagues have centered such activities on the writing and analyzing of achievement themes that they have uncovered in their research with highly motivated people. Besides providing an opportunity for the trainer to describe the achievement motivation patterns, this technique stimulates the trainees to think about themselves—to analyze their feelings, goals, and aspirations. Case histories and biographies are examples of ways in which the desired patterns can be modeled. We have even found that a summary of research on the "achievement-motivated personality" not only captures the interest of business-oriented groups but can also serve effectively as the first step in an achievement motivation training program. Such stories of achievement model the behavioral patterns that are to be reproduced, but they probably do not stimulate the kind of soul-searching that McClelland implies is necessary in the early stages of a training program.

The important point here is that a motivation training program should begin with a description of what motivation is or is not. And such a program should quickly get to the specifics of the kinds of responses or behaviors that are desired. In terms of personal investment theory we think of this stage as one in which behavioral options are laid out for the individual. It is assumed that before individuals will invest their behavior in a certain way, they must know about some investment possibilities. Thus, early on in any motivation training program, it is important to be quite specific about investment possibilities, to present concrete models and plans, and to lay out behavioral alternatives.

Encouraging Commitment. As already implied, motivation training programs involve some self-analysis. This self-analysis is not only directed at evaluating one's characteristic feelings, thoughts, and behavior, but it also focuses on personal goals, purposes, and aspirations. A specific question that is asked and must be answered is: Do I really want to be like this? Ethical reasons alone would encourage trainers to confront trainees with such a question. In addition, this type of question encourages commitment to motivational changes. Such commitment is a necessary precursor to change, as the trainee presumably must make a conscious choice to pursue a course of action.

Practicing Motivational Patterns. After the motivation behavioral patterns have been presented and a degree of commitment has been attained, the third step involves actually engaging in the kinds of patterns that have been modeled and described. That is, the trainee actually tries to engage in the kinds of patterns that are characteristic of the highly achievement-motivated person—or the person who happens to be investing his or her time and energy in a certain way. This may be done through role-playing or through simulation games.

Decision-making exercises can also be used, with an emphasis on encouraging participants to take the moderate risks of the entrepreneur. Goal-setting exercises might be employed, and exercises in time management might be presented. The point is to give the individual some sort of "behavioral feel" for what it means to exhibit a particular kind of motivational or personal investment pattern so that he or she can begin practicing it as a matter of course.

Establishing Normative Patterns. Such practicing may be important for a number of reasons. First, it helps build certain behaviors into the individual's repertoire, making them available for ready use. However, as such practice occurs in a group setting—in interaction with peers and with a present or potential reference group—it may have additional value. Briefly, as the pattern of behavior is practiced, normative patterns begin to emerge to indicate that this is an appropriate, indeed the "accepted," way to act. This adds further force to the practice and helps ensure that the *capacity* to act becomes a *predisposition* to act. Moreover, because such training seminars tend to establish enduring interpersonal ties between the participants, these normative patterns attain a power that lasts beyond the experience.

Enhancing Sense of Competence. Finally, there is the ubiquitous point that primary among the factors related to achievement motivation or personal investment is a sense of competence. Although most motivation training programs suggest that some form of change in sense of competence is necessary to effect motivational change, it is typically not clear how this change in sense of competence occurs. For example, there is usually considerable stress on "thinking positively" but little analysis of how such positive thinking is engendered. In this regard, one could derive certain basic principles from research on self-concept change (Haas & Maehr, 1965; Ludwig & Maehr, 1967; Maehr, Mensing, & Nafzger, 1962) or on changes in causal attribution (Andrews & Debus, 1978; Dweck 1975) or self-efficacy (Bandura, 1977, 1982). In all of these cases, however, one will quickly learn that changes in a person's sense of competence will not occur quickly and probably will not occur through persuasion alone. Rather, such changes are most likely to occur in the performance of tasks—for example, when people perform challenging tasks (i.e., those whose outcomes are initially uncertain) and manage to demonstrate that they can, indeed, accomplish such tasks, as indicated either by feedback inherent in the task or by the evaluation of "significant others."

Thus, in addition to telling people to think positively, they can be given techniques for establishing desired but achievable goals and encouraged to pursue these goals with the hope that a reasonable degree of success will be attained. The workshop setting might be the place to get things started—it might serve as a support group to encourage the person in pursuing a goal—

but it is the pursuit and attainment of goals in real-life settings that are likely to create changes in sense of competence.

The principles discussed here are basic for initiating programs to enhance motivation. Derived largely from McClelland's work on changing achievement motivation, they have rather wide applicability as general principles to be employed in designing programs for changing people's motivational and personal investment patterns. McClelland and his colleagues have indicated that they can be used to design effective motivation change workshops that have been found useful for managers and entrepreneurs. Without denying this use of these principles in a workshop setting, we suggest that their major use might well be in a somewhat different context: career planning and organizational socialization.

Career Planning. In recent years, there has been considerable interest in career planning, particularly for individuals who have plateaued or have reached a point where their personal investment in the work organization—or perhaps work itself—seems to have leveled off—or dropped. There are, of course, other circumstances when career planning and self-analysis related to career choices and goals are likely to be important. To help individuals in such circumstances, workshops and conferences are often organized, materials are developed, and speakers are hired. In this context, we would like to risk a proposal and outline a specific suggestion for action.

It seems likely that many of the basic principles that we identified in the work of McClelland (and others) on motivational change can also help in designing career self-analysis programs. In particular, we suggest that the underlying importance of self-analysis in these programs is the examination of oneself in relationship to one's present job and in relationship to other options.

Although there are a variety of ways in which this can be done, we suggest that it most certainly can be done by employing the theory and procedures reviewed in this volume. The IPI/IWI provides diagnostic information regarding the degree to which the individual's desired goals (personal incentives) can in fact be fulfilled in a given work setting. It not only provides a general diagnosis regarding how a person thinks about himself or herself but also portrays how this thinking relates to his or her job and work organization. When such information is provided to employees, it often stimulates insights regarding why they are dissatisfied or looking for other alternatives. Moreover, the IPI/IWI can provide information regarding what people might look for in a job—specifically, what kinds of job opportunities and incentives give them satisfaction (see Braskamp & Maehr, 1985).

Organizational Socialization. As we immersed ourselves yet again in McClelland's work, we came to a new conclusion: The principles that seem to be basic to his motivational change programs not only apply in motivation training programs; they are also applicable to any program designed to socialize new recruits into an organization.

For the past few years, there has been increasing interest in what might be called organizational socialization (see, for example, Pascale, 1984). This interest has increased, in part, because of the new interest in organizational culture (see chapter 6). We argue that a major goal of organizational socialization is to engender the right personal investment patterns in new recruits. Moreover, rather than letting this happen either by chance or without analyzing the programs and procedures that carry this burden within the organization, one might well structure a program systematically around motivational change principles. In other words, the overall goal of the program would be to affect motivation and personal investment in a desired fashion. The procedures for doing this could be derived from the motivation enhancement principles we have reviewed. That is, the manager who is concerned about bringing new recruits along might do well to reflect on the theory of personal investment and on principles associated with motivation and endeavor to build such features into the socialization program.

Organizational Expectations. There is, first, a need to communicate to new recruits in an organization what is expected of them—not just on their jobs but as members of the company. Of course, this can be done only if the company has some sense of mission, some set of shared goals. As we found in our research, companies that have a strong organizational culture are likely to be able to communicate effectively to members, including new recruits, what they care about. Moreover, companies with a strong organizational culture appear to be strong on the socialization of new employees (Pascale, 1984; Schein, 1985). Conversely, it is likely that a strong culture cannot be developed or retained unless it is communicated effectively to new recruits.

In any event, the first stage in the socialization process involves specifying what the organization is about. This orientation may be done by describing models and heroes and presenting myths (see chapter 6), or it may be done more prosaically by simply defining company goals and expectations for employees. The orientation also involves description of opportunities that are or will be available to employees.

Encouraging Commitment. As we mentioned in discussing motivational change programs, it is not enough to describe opportunities and options. People have to examine whether or not these options are appropriate for them. Only if the organization is seen as providing opportunities for fulfilling themselves—pursuing desired personal incentives—is commitment to the organization, its goals, and its mission likely to be elicited. It is important that the socialization process include opportunities for individuals to examine their own motivational or personal investment orientations in relationship to the expectations of the company. Such examination not only may weed out those who will not fit in but also may engender commitment in those who will become part of the organization's mission. The opportunity to make a conscious choice to stay with the company when other options are available is likely a factor that enhances commitment.

Experiencing Roles and Styles. In discussing motivational change programs, we noted that these programs tend to involve opportunities for the individual to try out various ways of acting and behaving. We suggest, now, that socialization programs also give recruits an opportunity to experiment with various roles and opportunities in the organization. This experimentation might involve short-term internships with various work or project groups or internships at different levels in the company and in different jobs. As in the motivational change programs, this practice should be done in an atmosphere where evaluation and feedback is given but where failures are not fatal. There are several reasons to give new recruits a broad range of experiences within the company, not the least of which is that it is one way of learning about the workings of the company—including its values, goals, expectations, and opportunities—from a variety of perspectives. We stress particularly, at this point, that such experiencing of roles provides an opportunity for people to test themselves in pursuing what are presented as company ideals. They are provided concrete instances to determine whether this is how they want to be—in a context that is supportive and encouraging.

Identifying with the Company. The aforementioned behavioral experimentation presumably also may help individuals see how they may fit in with the company. It is a chance to view their competencies and match them to opportunities in the organization. Throughout the preceding chapters, we have emphasized that people are not likely to be personally invested in something if they feel they lack the ability to perform adequately. Only as people succeed in new and novel challenges are their sense of competence and sense of commitment or personal investment in an endeavor likely to grow. No one can succeed in everything. The goal of the socialization process is to help people find some niche in which they experience competence, develop a sense that they are contributing, and thereby acquire an identification with the organization.

Norm-Sending. Clearly, the socialization process is concerned in a special way with what might be called norm-sending. The goal is to make the organizational expectations salient to new recruits and to attract them to accepting these norms and living by them. Much of what we have already said in this regard relates to how this might be done. We would add, however, a suggestion that derives directly from motivation training programs—namely, that norms seem to be most potent as individuals interact with other individuals. It is probably not enough to *tell* people what the norms are; they need social interaction to reinforce the norms. Thus, opportunities to work with well-established senior members early on are often critical in socializing new recruits into the organizational culture. New recruits need models and mentors and the chance to interact with groups that will give them feedback on whether their behavior is appropriate in the organization.

Socialization and Motivation. It should be clear that a concern with the motivation and personal investment of members of the organization will eventuate in a concern for the socialization process. How new recruits are socialized into an organization is a topic of considerable discussion at the moment, although the theory and research are by no means definitive. We have suggested that besides looking at various models of the socialization process (Pascale, 1984; Schein, 1985), one might also examine the principles that are implicit in the work on motivational change. These principles, which definitely overlap, suggest some approaches to designing the socialization of new recruits into the organizational culture. In particular, they suggest how organizations might encourage certain acceptable personal investment patterns in new recruits.

Conclusion. A number of what we have called person-focused programs or strategies can be employed with the goal of enhancing personal investment of employees. We have attempted, primarily, to sketch the principles that undergird these strategies. Each situation will demand its own particular adaptation of any given approach. It is difficult, perhaps even impossible, to fully standardize any motivation enhancement procedure, but one can readily adapt available models and build a specialized system from established generalizable principles.

Although a person-focused strategy is useful, it is clear that any serious concern with motivation enhancement must also give special attention to the nature of the situation in which the person is to be motivated. Thus, we turn next to features of the situation that must be considered in designing strategies for enhancing personal investment.

Job-Focused Strategies

In our review of the antecedents of personal investment, we argued that some of the factors are present and operative in the immediate situation. These factors include characteristics of the activity (job) itself, the organization of the activity, its social nature, and its place within a particular organization. Insofar as personal investment is influenced by such antecedents, it can be changed by altering these situational factors.

In our earlier designation of situational antecedents of personal investment (chapter 3), we considered an array of factors that might affect motivation and personal investment. As we consider now what can be done to enhance motivation, we would like to simplify the matter somewhat by suggesting that there are two readily identifiable, though not separable, pressure points for change: the job itself and the larger organizational network in which the job is performed. We will discuss, in turn, how each of these aspects of the situation can be considered for change in attempting to enhance motivation and personal investment.

In considering how one might enhance motivation, it is natural and logical to focus on the job—the task itself. What has to be done? How is the work designed? Under what social and physical conditions is it accomplished? Three facets of the task should come under special scrutiny in this regard: the social aspects, the task's inherent attractiveness, and the feedback provided to the employee performing the task.

Social Aspects. The social aspects of a job include the norms, expectations, roles, and interpersonal relationships that are associated with performing the task. Included also is the status assigned the job by the organization or the wider society. Each job has a social value as it is viewed as more or less important or prestigious by each society.

One of the major conclusions of our extensive study of personal investment in work organizations was that the social aspects of the job, collectively, are one of three major factors that determine the degree to which a person will become personally invested in the job. Job satisfaction and organizational commitment, especially, are related to the quality of the social climate associated with the place of work.

Certain social aspects of the job are best handled on a case-by-case basis. For example, many instances of interpersonal conflict cannot be solved by a general change in the work environment or in the nature of the job. They require attention to the specific nature of the conflict. To solve them may require individual job transfers, redefinition of tasks, or counseling.

However, the social environment of a job situation can often be improved on a more general basis. For example, activities that establish personal bonds between workers seem to enhance the attractiveness of the job—at least for most people at most jobs. Related to this is the special importance of the perception that those who run the company care about the workers. Social activities that allow workers to get to know one another as individuals may help establish such bonds, and activities that encourage managers to interact personally with workers may elicit the desirable perception that management cares. In the bank teller example presented earlier, we were impressed with how much the workers appreciated the fact that the organization provided an opportunity for social events. But we were most impressed that the bank president's attempt to show a personal interest in the workers seemed to enhance motivation not only among the bank tellers but among other units in the organization as well.

Our research and that of others also indicates a potential major problem that can arise in work organizations—a problem that evolves from interpersonal competition. In our society, it is regularly assumed that competition is a good thing. The research evidence indicates that it can be—sometimes. If effective job performance demands cooperation and harmonious interpersonal relations, the job must be so structured that it does not foster competition between fellow workers. If harmonious, joint effort among workers is not needed, then competition may not be a problem. Thus, it is likely that competition will not have negative effects on salespeople working rather independently and on a commission basis, but fostering a competitive orientation may be devastatingly counterproductive in an office staff where cooperation is crucial for efficient and productive work. Earlier (chapter 3), we suggested how a task or job can be designed to enhance or reduce its competitive nature. The burden rests on managers to assess the existence and desirability of a competitive orientation.

Inherent Attractiveness. The second job-related aspect is the attractiveness, challenge, and inherent worthiness of the task to the employee. Earlier, we identified a number of variables that have been associated with the inherent attractiveness of the task: task identity, skill variety, challenge, autonomy, and task significance. At times, a manager or supervisor may have difficulty manipulating these variables in such a way that personal investment will be enhanced. Also, the workers involved may simply not want the task to be other than what it is (Hackman & Oldham, 1980). But one should be wary of assuming too soon that the task is what it is and that change is impossible. Recently, Hackman (1985) has illustrated how one can redesign the way jobs are done in a variety of settings to enhance worker responsibility and commitment. Principles of self-management seem to be broadly applicable in the work place, and increasingly so in the high-tech world of business and manufacturing.

Evaluation. Before one can change the job structure and requirements to enhance motivation and personal investment, one must engage in performance appraisal. It can hardly be avoided, and, most important, it is the facet of the situation that often has the most important effects on personal investment. This very basic point has been made repeatedly throughout this volume; it is explicit in the numbers and graphs that portray our results; and it is broadly pervasive in the wider literature. It is also a point that has not escaped the scrutiny of managers who turn out to be successful (Spady, 1984).

We are using the term *evaluation* here to include both performance appraisal of people and evaluation of units or programs. In practice, it is often difficult to separate the two. Management often looks at programs not in terms of organizational charts and structural arrangements on paper but in terms of the performance of the people in charge of the programs. There is also the issue of assessing organizational effectiveness—that is, determining the overall health of an organization. Organizational health is variously defined, ranging from the annual financial report to shareholders to the quality and employment of human resources. In short, evaluation consists of assessing how well an employee is performing the assigned responsibilities and of determining the overall effectiveness of a firm. To answer the question of when a company is excellent requires a discussion of different approaches to the study of organizational effectiveness, utilizing different criteria (Cameron, 1981; Goodman & Pennings, 1979). In our treatment of evaluation here, we limit our discussion to the issue of how a firm can optimally utilize its human resources—most often the most important resource. Thus, we focus primarily on how to deal with the internal management problem of working with the employees, rather than on the issues of how an organization relates and responds to its environment. This adaptability of an organization is an important key to organizational effectiveness (Goodman & Pennings, 1979).

There are several reasons why evaluation of performance is so important. At the very least, our research and that of others has made it undeniably clear that the evaluation process is crucial (see chapter 3). First, we emphasize that through the evaluation process, the organization can clearly—perhaps most clearly—articulate what it is about. Through written and spoken statements, corporations articulate their goals, expectations, values, and beliefs. But these messages really take their most effective form as they are tied to recognition and reward. Ideally, the evaluation process is the tie that binds. As many others have pointed out (e.g., Pascale, 1984), if a company wants excellence and quality, it must do something to ensure them. What we would add is that the organization does this best through regular and systematic evaluation of programs and the people running them. William Spady (1984) made a similar point in his review of the book by Peters and Waterman (1982), where he noted that the managers of successful organizations are characteristically data-oriented. They build into their management procedures the gathering of data on how things are operating (a point also made by Bennis, 1984). Also, they have a commitment to change and modify things in response to those results. That is, they take the results of the evaluation data seriously. Effective performance appraisal or program evaluation says to all, simply and directly: We are very serious about our goals and expectations. We want to know whether they are met. This attitude takes concrete form when it serves as the basis for reward and recognition.

Second, employees are likely to be most personally invested if the evaluation process is done effectively. In the results reported earlier, two interesting and parallel findings on personal investment were uncovered. If a company makes it clear what it wants and expects—what it is about—it most likely can elicit the personal investment of its employees, especially their organizational commitment. The personal investment of employees is also tied closely to whether they are recognized and rewarded for doing a good job. As we examined these data more closely, we also examined work organizations in more detail and realized that these two findings were really two sides of the same coin. On the one hand, if the workers are to be personally invested in activities that are in accord with broad organizational goals, they have to know what these goals are. On the other hand, if management does not reward in terms of what the organization wants, these wants—these organizational goals—become meaningless. Meaning—not meaninglessness—elicits personal investment.

In many ways, then, evaluation is at the heart of influencing the personal investment of employees. But, how does one do it? Work on the motivational effects of performance appraisal has yielded many and varied findings, and we cannot presume here to reflect adequately the wealth of thought and research in this highly developed area (see, for example, Braskamp, Brandenberg, & Ory, 1984; Braskamp, 1985). However, we can point out certain basic principles that must be considered in evaluating programs and people with a view to eliciting personal investment.

Explicit Criteria. For the evaluation process to work effectively, there must be some reasonably explicit notions about what is wanted. There are times, of course, when leaders have difficulty stating what they want in performance before the fact and must leave it to the performers to create something that will prove valuable. There are arguments for not being overly specific, especially if employees are expected to be creative and try new things. Such specificity may be quite detrimental to the motivation and performance of faculty in a university or scientists in the research and development section of a firm (McKeachie, 1982). But in many instances, it proves helpful to be rather specific about what is valued before evaluation occurs. The specificity of the criteria to be employed should reflect the overall expectations that an organization has of its employees. For example, a senior-level executive at a medium-sized company that builds ice-cutter ships remarked to us that he hires and rewards people who "are willing to build ships and lick stamps." That is, they have to be creative and able to design, but they also have to be willing to be part of the company team and perform some of the routine tasks. In short, they will be rewarded for being generalists rather than specialists, and it is important to be cooperative rather than competitive. The criteria to reflect this style of accomplishment would be difficult to make specific or measurable in behavioral terms. The point is that the expectations should be made explicit. In any case, the organization should be concerned with the process of establishing evaluation criteria, testing them, and revising them as circumstances dictate.

Effective Communication of Criteria. Only when evaluation criteria are explicit can a manager or supervisor effectively communicate what is expected of those who are to be evaluated. And this knowledge of evaluation criteria is most important for organizing performance to fulfill desired ends.

One of the reasons goal-setting has been demonstrated to be a successful mechanism for fostering productivity in many work settings (Locke & Latham, 1984) rests especially on this major point. Individuals and groups find it possible to produce in accord with expectations only if they know what these expectations are. But a parallel motivational effect also seems to be operative through the setting of goals. Goal-setting not only guides the direction of the behavior but also fosters satisfaction and greater levels of activity. If workers know what they need to do to be compensated and rewarded, they are, overall, more motivated to perform than if performance criteria are lacking. This is not to suggest that all workers will aspire to the same extent, but the evidence indicates that goal-setting has the overall effect of raising the level of performance and productivity. Moreover, employees have been reported to feel positively about goal-setting. As a result, when goal-setting is employed in a work situation, it has been found to be positively associated with greater job satisfaction (Ivancevich & McMahon, 1982).

Although it is useful to know that being very explicit about goals has important positive effects, it is not altogether clear why this should be so. From the point of view of personal investment theory, we suggest one possibility. As we have repeatedly emphasized, the purposes the person has in performing a task are an important feature of the meaning of that task to the person. Thus, goal-setting is primarily a matter of building some meaning into tasks. Moreover, the use of quantitative goals in which performance levels are specified is one way of building meaning into tasks that have very little inherent meaning. That is, goal-setting may foster or be in accord with an external reward or competition orientation, thereby providing a motivational focus and a degree of meaning in what might otherwise be a meaningless task.

To return to the central point: For the evaluation process to be employed in such a manner that it elicits the personal investment of employees, the criteria for recognition and reward must not only be explicit, they must also be effectively communicated. The people in the organization will be most effective when they know what they are about, where they are heading or should be heading, and how they will know when they get there.

Recognition and Rewards. One cannot fully discuss the evaluation process without incorporating recognition and reward into the process. Indeed, all of the points we have been making about evaluation are significantly interrelated, but we wish to stress, especially, the importance of recognition and reward in the work setting. Our research evidence repeatedly emphasizes the role of recognition and reward as motivators in a work setting. We add here that only as recognition and reward are clearly tied to understood evaluation criteria will they have positive effects on personal investment.

Unfortunately, recognition and reward are not always tied to the stated performance or evaluation criteria. Where they are not, problems of morale, motivation, and productivity ensue. We were particularly struck by our own questionnaire and interview results in this regard. Without question, job satisfaction and organizational commitment depended significantly on whether the employees viewed their organization as rewarding and recognizing effective performance in accord with the understood criteria. Fairness in reward and recognition has long been regarded as important for worker investment and performance (Folger, 1984; Greenberg, 1982), but we would add to that general principle by stressing that the perception of fairness is likely to exist in the degree to which recognition and reward are perceived to be administered in terms of explicit criteria communicated to the employees.

Minimizing the Negative Effects of Evaluation. Thus far, we have stressed the positive side of evaluation, but there is also a negative side. People don't always like to be evaluated, and evaluation can reduce motivation and personal investment as well as enhance it. Perhaps it is in regard to evaluation in educational settings that such negative effects have been most systematically documented (Fyans et al., 1981; Hill, 1980; Maehr & Stallings, 1972; Salili et al., 1976), but it is not only in educational settings that such negative effects can be noticed. For example, in Hackman and Oldham's (1980) analyses of jobs, it was found that *autonomy* is a factor in fostering "internal motivation." When people continually have someone looking over their shoulder when they are doing a job, evaluating every step and every process, they do not have autonomy. So it is that a certain kind of evaluation can have negative effects. Indeed, it appears that when the evaluation is excessively controlling, leaving little room for worker autonomy, the worker will be inclined to work only when the control is present, will show little personal initiative, and perhaps will also engage in behavior designed to subvert the system. Thus, an important principle to keep in mind is that as evaluation serves to reduce worker autonomy, one runs the risk that it will reduce what Hackman and Oldham (1980) called "internal motivation" or what we call "continuing motivation" (see chapters 1 and 3).

Negative effects of evaluation on motivation can be reduced, however, by allowing workers to participate in the establishment of evaluation criteria and in the design of the evaluation process.

In summary, then, as one establishes specific criteria, communicates them effectively, and follows them in the evaluation process, one reduces the negative effects of evaluation. Note that we do not claim that one can get rid of the negative side of evaluation completely. So long as evaluation is tied to reward and recognition for some but not for others, some will be happy but others will not. That is probably inevitable. The goal, however, is to reduce these problems, and that can be and is done to a significant extent in well-managed organizations through following the principles we have outlined here.

Organization-Focused Strategies

Leaders of large organizations seldom have a great deal to do with personnel selection and placement or job design—at least directly. They have very little face-to-face contact with the vast majority of the employees who do the work for which the organization was designed. Typically, they do not even see most of their workers at work, and they seldom have an opportunity to assess what the various jobs are like. Basically, they have to hope that something they do at the top will somehow filter down to the levels at which workers are chosen and placed and jobs are designed and supervised. Is this a vain hope?

It is not! This should be evident from a reading of the theory and research discussed in chapter 6, where we reviewed the concept of organizational culture and reported research related to its assessment and possible causes and effects. Generally, we concluded that there is, indeed, something that can be done at the upper levels of management to affect motivation and productivity in the organization as a whole. Leaders can have a pervasive effect on motivation of workers at all levels in the work organization.

First, before developing abstract principles, we should establish the concrete instances we are trying to understand and ultimately control. Therefore, we will present a vignette from a case study of an effective organization to illustrate what commitment in the organization looks like. The vignette will also allow us to anticipate some of the important organizational variables involved in creating personal investment. Second, we will isolate three key factors in creating effective organizations. Finally, we will suggest how leaders can manipulate these variables in creating an effective organizational culture or climate—one that enhances motivation and personal investment.

A Case Study of Organizational Commitment. As we were constructing this chapter, we happened to observe an event in an organization with which we had worked over the years and about which we knew a great deal. By all accounts, the organization was an effective one. It was especially characaterized by a high degree of commitment at all levels of its work force. The vignette on which we will focus involved the retirement of a director of long standing. Such "transition events" are often occasions when one can best observe how the culture operates, and the present case was no exception. As we saw how the organization dealt with this occurrence, we saw something important about the organization—and about the nature of organizations in general.

The organization in question was a multimillion-dollar unit that was in charge of support services involving training and education for a large corporation. This unit provided training materials such as graphics and educational technology on a loan basis, and it provided the evaluation services for the personal appraisal system that was widely used throughout the parent organization. As a service unit, it was particularly important that the people who were involved with clients—in this case, other organizational units within the same corporation—had a philosophy of service to the clients. It was important that they understand their role in the corporation.

Virtually the entire staff was involved in planning the event, using their own skills and interests in developing a program that would be appropriate for honoring the retiring director. Thus, in the months preceding the recognition party, the staff secretly prepared a series of short scenarios describing the various services provided by the unit. What was most interesting was the manner in which they did it. Given the pride they had in their services, they were able to present their organization in a humorous way, poking fun at themselves as well as at the way in which the services were perceived by clients. It was especially interesting to observe that people from a variety of subunits could and did work together to create this dramatic production. They were able to organize their respective skills in such a way that it was truly a joint production of many different facets of the unit. Although their expertise varied, there was a shared unity that allowed for concerted action in a novel circumstance. Moreover, one could sense that the whole undertaking had significance beyond simply doing a task well. It symbolized the organizational life they shared and very obviously valued.

From almost any perspective, the event was highly successful. Given our interest in organizational culture, we viewed it as having symbolic significance in that it reinforced group cohesiveness and reaffirmed the goals of the unit in a simple but nevertheless especially salient fashion. The event was not just a wonderful way to show appreciation for the retiring director; it also served to enhance the commitment of employees. In subsequent days and weeks, the event was referred to repeatedly, and we suspect that it will be for as long as this unit remains a cohesive one with a similar set of shared values. What apparently emerged here was a kind of myth that expressed something deep and basic about the organization.

Organizational Antecedents of Personal Investment. One can summarize the possibilities for managerial effectiveness in influencing personal investment by concentrating on three action domains: communicating the organization's mission, establishing salient incentives, and evidencing concern for the individual.

Establishing and Communicating a Mission. As concluded in chapter 6, an organization is most likely to elicit the personal investment of workers when its goals and values are clear *and* when they are effectively communicated to all concerned. Good companies know what they are about and are able to communicate this across all levels of the organization. When the company can express a clear and integrated set of goals, expectations, and values—a mission—it is most likely to be effective. As employees become aware of this mission, they are likely to be personally invested in the activities and programs that *are* the organization.

Management bears major responsibility in this regard. It falls to the leadership of an organization to establish and communicate a mission. Indeed, it may be that this is the major function of the leaders in an organization in terms of enhancing motivation and personal investment (see Bennis, 1984; Schein, 1985).

Establishing Salient Incentives. If the organization is to elicit the personal investment of employees, it must make it clear that certain opportunities exist within the organization for pursuing selected personal incentives. This course of action may perhaps be considered complementary to the establishment of a mission. However, whereas the mission primarily concerns the relationship of the organization to the world at large—its role in that world—communicating incentive opportunities relates to members of the organization. The two domains are complementary in the sense that only as individuals perceive that they can successfully pursue certain personal incentives within the organization is the overall mission of the organization likely to have motivational effects.

The importance of certain personal incentives within an organization emerges especially in our own research, although it certainly has precedents elsewhere. It may be recalled that organizations that were viewed as concerned with providing (1) interesting and challenging jobs (task dimension), (2) a positive social climate (social dimension), and (3) appropriate recognition and reward (external rewards dimension) were most likely to have satisfied and committed workers. Apparently, these three dimensions of organizational culture are the most crucial in terms of enhancing personal investment.

Concern for the Individual in the Organization. Perhaps it is already evident in the stress on personal incentives within the culture of successful organizations, but it should be stated explicitly that successful companies are characterized by a concern for the individual. That concern includes an interest in the total welfare of the workers, but most important, it is characterized by a focus on enabling all workers to actualize their potential—to do their personal best. Peters and Waterman (1982) emphasized this point, and our research supports their conclusion. The workers' belief that the organization was indeed concerned with the welfare of the individual seemed to play a special role in ensuring job satisfaction and commitment to the organization. Workers apparently want an interesting job, good social relationships in their work place, and appropriate recognition for work well done, but the commitment and the job satisfaction that is engendered by these conditions is enhanced by the underlying perception that the company cares about its workers—cares about their welfare, their personal growth, and the actualization of their potential.

We therefore suggest that corporate leaders not only express a set of goals but also incorporate in these goal statements some clear expression that they care about employees as a most important resource. In other words, the organization's mission is not only "out there"—in corporate successes and achievements—but also resides in the quality of concern for the corporate body. Ideally, the mission should include not only a collection of reasons for existing in the wider society but also an expression of how the organization is to go about fulfilling this mission in society. An organization's concern with the role of individual members in accomplishing organizational goals is a crucial concern.

Organizations that Enhance Personal Investment: How Can They Be Created?
There is little doubt that a strong organizational culture, a sense of mission, and the existence of a certain kind of work climate will encourage personal investment. Our research has confirmed the suggestions of others in making that basic point quite clear. But how does one act to make the organization responsive in this way? Specifically, what can the leadership of the organization do to create an organization that affects the personal investment of employees positively? We have identified four courses of action to be considered in creating an organization that positively influences the personal investment of employees.

Diagnosis/Assessment. The first action involves the establishment of procedures for identifying the culture of the organization. Is it coherent; is it salient; is it desirable? Implicit in this regard is a straightforward and simple piece of advice: Before anything is done, one ought to assess how the organization is perceived by the employees.

If, indeed, the communication of what we have termed mission and the establishment of a certain organizational culture is as important as our research (and that of others) seems to suggest, one would best exercise concern with the overall functioning of the organization by assessing just what that culture and mission are perceived to be by the employees. With the increased research interest in organizational culture, procedures for assessing culture are becoming available. In earlier chapters, we reported our own research in this regard; now we suggest that our methods are applicable beyond simply presenting results of theoretical interest. There is no reason why one cannot use the organizational culture scales of the IPI/IWI to provide a diagnosis of the situation within an organization before deciding what should be changed, if anything.

The overriding point we wish to make in this regard, however, is that a diagnosis/assessment approach to analyzing the character and operation of an organization and its units is desirable and increasingly possible. Thus, even at this early stage of organizational evaluation and assessment, there is good reason to believe in the ultimate worth of a data-based approach in building the organization into a smoothly functioning organism in which the separate parts are truly invested in the overall functions and goals. Data seldom tell a manager specifically what to do, but they are very often the first step and a necessary step in the process (Braskamp & Brown, 1980).

What we suggest, then, is that as managers consider production figures and ledger sheets, they should also view the health of the organizational culture. With increasing evidence that work motivation might be significantly determined by organizational culture, this becomes an increasingly important point to be considered. Moreover, the organizational culture is rightly a concern at the highest levels of the organization.

Having made this first and, we think, very important point regarding the desirability of systematic diagnosis and assessment, we will endeavor also to make a suggestion or two about how leaders might act to affect change in the mission and the overall culture of the organization.

Evaluation. There are few better ways of expressing what is expected than through the evaluation process and the *reward* and *recognition* that accompany this process. In attempting to foster organizational change of almost any type, it is this domain that must be considered extensively. Of course, top-level managers personally evaluate the performance of only a few and certainly do not administer or actualize the evaluation process specifically or directly in many cases. But they do play a major role in establishing *what* is to be valued, and they also set the tone for *how* evaluation is to be accomplished. In these two respects, they can communicate the broad goals and mission of the organization.

To be a bit more concrete: Managers can choose to concern themselves with setting up systematic evaluation procedures and stress criteria. The mere fact that they establish a group to do this and give it some visibility may itself be sufficient to make it clear that there is concern and interest, not only in evaluation but in certain performance criteria. But managers can go even further by, for example, stressing some of the evaluation principles discussed earlier. Most important of all is that managers and their staff must be seen to act in terms of the evaluation information; they must be seen to be taking it seriously.

The Exercise of Power. It is in the exercise of power over the organization's resources that the manager can make an important contribution to the establishment and communication of the organizational mission and to its work climate—its culture. As one makes decisions, one communicates the purposes, goals, and modus operandi of the organization. In this regard, a major issue is how the power will be shared. How are decisions made? To what degree is the decision-making process shared with others?

There is considerable literature on the decision-making process in general and on decision sharing (or the delegation of authority) in particular. For the most part, that literature relates to how worker participation in the decision-making process affects productivity. A review of the research literature shows a somewhat mixed conclusion about the consequences of participatory management (see, for example, Wexley & Yukl, 1984; Yukl, 1981). However, the point we wish to make at this juncture is somewhat broader, relating to how sharing of authority is likely to affect perceptions of the situation or the work context. Here, one general principle must be kept firmly in mind: As one is given responsibility for actions, one is more likely to take initiative in performing them. In other words, the delegation of decison making or the encouragement of broad participation in decision making may create a task and/or excellence personal incentive orientation. It might also increase the feeling in those to whom authority has been delegated that they are important, thus enhancing their sense of competence.

Focusing as we are on the organizational level, the point is that if one desires an organization in which initiative and personal responsibility are encouraged and exercised at all levels of management, one must be clear about sharing or delegating authority. This point has been made often in the management literature. Recently, however, a new perspective on this question has arisen that promises to revise how we view work organizations. Richard Hackman (1985) has argued persuasively for the development of self-mangement systems across the organization as a way to enhance the overall effectiveness of the organization. Increasingly, it is possible for workers to operate somewhat autonomously or to be delegated considerable authority regarding how they will organize and manage their work to reach certain objectives—objectives that are determined by the larger demands of the organization. In such cases, upper-level management articulates goals but leaves the means of attaining them largely to the work unit. Such systems increase the need for upper-level management to be concerned with overall goals and mission and to communicate them to others. But they also enhance the importance of individual work units and workers in determining what must and can be done in their own work domain.

It is in the sharing of authority that leaders perhaps best reflect their respect for others in the organization. Systematic and explicit delegation of responsibility communicates trust. The autonomy that is given to workers will encourage not only their loyalty but also their special commitment to exert their every effort. Of course, delegation can be practiced only to the extent that the delegatee can handle the responsibility. This implies that the delegatee has not only the requisite ability but also the requisite knowledge. As Hackman (1985) has emphasized, self-managed systems most importantly demand a sharing of information—not only information directly related to the specific jobs to be done, but also information on the overall activities, needs, and goals of the organization.

To return to the central point: Only as workers are given an optimal level of autonomy can one expect optimal personal investment. We suggested this principle early on in this volume, and our research evidence has reaffirmed delegation as a general principle. The "art of management" lies in knowing the limits of this principle in a given case.

Symbolizing the Mission. Throughout the organizational culture literature, there is much discussion of the symbols, rituals, and myths that are used in expressing what the organization is about (Bolman & Deal, 1984; Deal & Kennedy, 1982). There is little hard evidence, however, on how slogans, rituals, and myths may influence the development of organizational culture, and there is even less evidence on whether or not leaders and managers can initiate cultural change through slogans, through the initiation of ritual, or through the creation and promotion of myth.

However, there is one action that leaders can take. From our perspective, they are likely to be most influential in affecting organizational culture by identifying, describing, and referring to people who, in the opinion of the leaders, excel. These people are heroes, concrete embodiments of what is worth striving for and what is of value. They represent, in a tangible way, viable and valued options for workers; they model desired behavior. More-over, we conjecture that heroes—human exemplars of values—are what actually communicate to members of an organization what is expected and what is valued. For this reason, heroes are important within an organization.

Earlier, we noted that well-established, successful organizations typically have their own heroes. The effective manager, the true leader, is skillful in referring to the characteristics of these heroes as they reflect what is desired in the organization. Not every organization has a George Steinmetz or a Thomas Watson, but they do have employees who actualize what is desired in the organization. Managers and supervisors have it in their power to identify significant performances of employees in the organization, to interpret these performances in terms of organizational values and goals and to make them widely visible in the organizational community. We suggest that managers should take this opportunity for influencing the organizational culture seriously and handle it skillfully; it is not something to be left to chance. They should identify publicly with these contemporary heroes and use such an identification as an opportunity to express the salient and valued goals of the corporation.

Thus, management's use of reward and recognition not only reinforces the behavior of the employees rewarded and recognized but also symbolizes what is desired throughout the organization. Examples of excellence can be taken from all ranks of the organization. Even in the common practice of singling out an "employee of the month," managers can communicate a great deal about the goals of the organization as a whole.

Summary. Several main points must be considered by leaders of organizations in attempting to affect personal investment. Of special importance, we believe, is the conscious establishment of goals. Leaders should establish the overall purposes of the organization and specify for workers the opportunities that exist for participating in the organization's mission and for fulfilling their own personal incentives. Only as they establish a direction for the organization or work unit and relate it to the individual workers will the leaders be successful. Indeed, we argue that this expression of a direction for the organization is a most important activity for any leader.

Implicit here, also, is a second point about evaluation. Evaluation and assessment are integral particles of the management style we are proposing. Evaluation implies a caring and an interest in what is being accomplished; having no evaluation implies indifference. Evaluation, though sometimes painful and difficult (Rice, 1985), has several important consequences. It provides an occasion for articulating the goals and mission of the organization for specific programs, people, and units. The mere fact that evaluation occurs indicates that the organization cares about what is done. Properly done, evaluation can also reflect a concern for the growth of the individual worker as a contributor to the organization and suggests a stance that is generally growth-oriented rather than static. It is through their concern with evaluation that leaders affect the organizational culture; it is one of the buttons they can press for action in this regard.

A final point relates to the issue of power—particularly the creation of self-managed units within the organization. The creation of a strong task orientation in an organization is important to the effectiveness of the organization, as we have stated repeatedly. Such a task orientation depends significantly on the degree to which the employees are given some degree of responsibility over what is to be done. Thus, one of the more important tasks of leadership is to identify where and under what conditions self-managed systems can be created. More broadly, leaders must create a climate in which self-management can become a part of the organizational culture. Again, evaluation plays a major role here. One cannot supervise too closely if one wants self-management. Also, if one wants self-management to be effective, one must be clear about evaluation criteria. Moreover, self-management interlocks with the establishment of an organizational mission. As Hackman (1985) has pointed out, the establishment and the communication of the purpose are doubly important as authority is delegated.

Conclusion

In this chapter, we have endeavored to do more than organize the many particles of research into a theory of motivation. We have tried to deduce from our framework certain guidelines for practice. We don't presume to have provided a map for action. At best, we have placed a road marker or two to help managers and those in leadership positions find their way toward establishing policies and procedures that can encourage personal investment at a particular time and place. If we have done that, we are satisfied.

10
A Final, Unscientific Postscript

The title for this chapter is borrowed from the dour Dane, Sören Kierkegaard. Although our adaptation of the phrase may not do Kierkegaard—or his concerns—justice, it does serve to introduce a kind of metascientific thinking that ensued as we reflected on the earlier chapters of this book. On the way to writing a fitting conclusion, after spending the better part of five years considering motivation and achievement in the world of work, we chanced to confront the arresting words of "the philosopher" in the Old Testament book of Ecclesiastes:

> It is useless, useless said the Philosopher. Life is useless, all useless. Nothing that I had worked for and earned meant a thing to me, because I knew that I would have to leave it to my successor, and he might be wise, or he might be foolish—who knows? Yet he will own everything I have worked for, everything my wisdom has earned for me in this world. It is useless. So I came to regret that I had worked so hard. You work for something with all your wisdom, knowledge, and skill, and then you have to leave it all to someone who hasn't had to work for it. It is useless, and it isn't right! You work and worry your way through life, and what do you have to show for it? As long as you live, everything you do brings nothing but worry and heartache. Even at night your mind can't rest. It is all useless. (Ecclesiastes 1:2, 2:18–23, *The Good News Bible. The Bible in Today's English Version.* Copyright © American Bible Society, 1966, 1971, 1976)

Whether or not we agree with the ruminations of the philosopher in this passage, we recognize that he is expressing a perspective that cannot be ignored—a perspective that disturbs us a bit as we conclude this volume. In the preceding nine chapters, we have focused on what the philosopher seems to call useless. Worse still, for the past 20 years or so we have been studying "achievement," attempting to encourage and enhance it in people at all age levels. Has this been a useless cause? We cannot conclude without presenting our side of the case alongside that of the philosopher.

In Retrospect

The overarching purpose of this book has been to present a perspective that might be valuable in understanding motivation throughout the adult years. A second, but by no means secondary, purpose has been to specify a theory of personal investment in operational terms. This has involved the description of appropriate instruments for assessing the various constructs. It has also involved the presentation of data to illustrate the validity and usefulness of the theory—and to expand and extend it to an important degree. Finally, we have applied our understanding of personal investment to the world of work.

In retrospect, we believe that a viable perspective for understanding important facets of human behavior has emerged. That perspective is not so much a new theory as it is an integration of research and theory from a variety of domains. Although our own work initially grew out of achievement theory, what has emerged is more than could have been encompassed by that theoretical tradition. The special features of the theory are suggested in the use of the term *personal investment* as a proxy for a general term *motivation.* By using the term *personal investment*, we wished to underscore three characteristics of the theory.

First, the term *investment* implies a special interest in the direction of behavior. Our working assumption was that the choices and decisions people make are among the best indicators of motivation. Implicit here, also, is a working assumption to the effect that all people are motivated, and the real motivational question is *in what way and to what ends* are they motivated. Finally, the term *personal* implies perhaps a more subjective approach to understanding motivation. Indeed, we think we have presented a theory that attempts to understand the world from the *person's* point of view. Actually, the theory builds on current research and theory on social cognition; it also builds on earlier models of decision-making processes. In this regard, we have stressed that personal investment choices are a function of three components: a set of alternatives (perceived options) from which to choose, a set of judgments about self (e.g., sense of competence) in relation to those possible options, and the types of values (personal incentives) held.

As psychologists, we admit to being particularly intrigued at the outset with the last two components. Our own earlier research had focused especially on sense of self and had taken for granted the importance of values, personal goals, and what we now term personal incentives. The research we have reviewed in this book certainly does not rule out the importance of these components of cognitive life in causing personal investment. Yet our research has led us to become increasingly intrigued with the least "psychological" of the components—perceived options. This is an important domain about which we know all too little.

The specific relevance of our theory was illustrated primarily in regard to adults in the world of work. Generally, we endeavored to show that our theoretical perspective was a viable way of considering how a variety of facts about work life can be understood. Moreover, in the preceding chapter, we provided an integrated focus on the problems confronting those who must manage the behavior of others—with the specific goal of encouraging them to work. Is this all quite useless? Of course not!

Vive la Work Ethic!

Few would disagree with the notion that productivity is an important issue of our time. One can hardly pick up a newspaper or turn on the TV without confronting the question of productivity. Even at this moment, a local radio station is reporting a major item: U.S. productivity has apparently slipped this month. Again, our competitive edge with other nations is in jeopardy. At this point, the issue is not the truth of that assertion but the fact that it is so often asserted. The same radio program reports the governor's concern whether the schools are up to the task of reestablishing the industrial viability of the state. Like it or not, productivity and achievement are major issues of our times. Current concerns about industrial productivity underscore the importance of a concern with a personal investment in work. Fostering the pursuit of excellence, motivation to achieve, and a personal investment in work have wider social implications. At times, however, achievement has been thought of as an individualistic, self-serving act. People who invest themselves in their work have been accused of being greedy and selfish.

Clearly, there is another side to this issue. Only as people pursue excellence and achievement and throw themselves wholeheartedly into their jobs is a society likely to have the quality of life it desires. Intertwined with the nature and meaning of work are ultimate questions of singular significance. Concerns about achievement and about managing work effectively are societal and governmental concerns—they are world concerns. As they relate to the most important human concerns, they are rooted not only in a motive of serving oneself but also in the altruistic desire to serve others.

The popular media have pressed upon us an awareness of the plight of starving people in Africa and elsewhere. When we attend our temples or churches—or even our clubs—we are as likely to hear about poverty as we are to hear about moral degradation or theological concerns. There are many facets to these concerns, and productivity certainly is related to them. Productivity or lack of it makes us consider what kind of life is possible not only for ourselves but for others. Solutions to the problems of national health and the care of those who have experienced catastrophe depend, to some degree, on what can be produced—what can be done by people investing their time, talent and energy in the world of work. Republicans and Democrats—and "socialists"—can all reach a measure of agreement on this point.

In short, there is a desirable—indeed, necessary—concern with encouraging individuals and groups to live up to their potential. There is a necessity to encourage productivity in individuals and groups—not just so that they can excel or outdo others, and not at the expense of others, but for the greater good of all. Achievement and productivity are not only nice, they are *essential*. The achieving person and the achieving society are neither interesting curios nor luxuries; they are absolute necessities. Not that *all* people should necessarily become fully absorbed in their work, but clearly some—a substantial number—must.

Perhaps, then, it is not so surprising that work and religion have been intertwined—in both the East (Pascale & Athos, 1981) and the West (McClelland, 1961; Weber, 1904/1930). As Max Weber (1904/1930) reflected on "The Protestant Ethic and the Spirit of Capitalism," he referred specifically and at length to the concept of the individual as *called* to pursue a work role. Within certain traditions, the term *vocation* reflects this perspective on work and the worker. Among the many belief systems people have, there is a prominent notion that one is summoned to one's job by God or that the work one does has meaning of the highest order. Within many traditions, both Eastern and Western, work is a sacred act. Thus, people have not only worked to live but have lived to work. They have viewed themselves as fulfilling a mission or a divine calling through their work. A transcendent goal—a cause beyond themselves and their work—has characterized their involvement, their personal investment.

It was the comments of a highly successful person that put these abstract philosophical concepts in concrete form for us. The person was a highly regarded scholar and author. At the height of her fame, she was asked to reflect on why she had chosen to pursue the course she had. She had gone to college and to graduate school and had become a dedicated scientist at a time when it was not the "feminine thing" to do. Her response was immediate and apparently simple: She was taught that those who had been given talents should not bury them—referring to the New Testament parable. The implicit admonition of that parable was seen as a strong force in her life. It was doubtless part of a larger ideology that has guided her in the pursuit of excellence, as it has likely guided many others. The point is that within the concern focused on achievement and investment in work, there often is a wider social concern. Achievement and an investment in work can and, in our experience, often do fulfill broader purposes—social, religious, and humanitarian.

Thus, we have confronted an important problem in this volume. It is an important problem for those in business and industry—those who manage and govern—but it is ultimately a most important human problem that is of broad relevance to all of us. It is crucial in establishing quality living—even living itself in many critical instances. Although we have not focused specifically on problems of health and human welfare, the problem on which we have focused is arguably an inevitable antecedent to such health and welfare. Productivity is, without question, integrally critical to optimizing human existence. One of our teachers used to counsel his students: "Work is redeeming." At the time, we thought he was merely promoting an old-fashioned ethic—at best. At worst, we surmised that he was a "crypto-capitalist," promoting an ethic that would serve primarily to justify the exploitation of workers. We now see things differently, as do many of our fellow students from that time. Certainly, work has been a redeeming factor in the lives of most of the people we interviewed early in our study—and not just in the lives of the high achievers. Work was redeeming not only in that it gave them daily bread, but also in that it gave them a social life and an identity. We were impressed with how often people identified themselves not just as "Mr. or Ms. So-and-so" but also as "a foreman with the JRQ Company." We were struck by a lively octogenarian—someone very happy in his retirement—who early in our conversation let it be known that he had been a foreman for Ford Motor Company. And he said it with pride! Equally important, it is clear that work has been the instrument whereby individuals have been able to participate in "redeeming" others. As one worker put it: "My work gave me a chance to do good things for my family."

In many ways, the moral issues of the day—"the bomb," starvation—are integrally tied to human survival, and productivity figures strongly in any solution equation. In many cases, only as our productivity goals are achieved can our altruistic goals be pursued. There certainly is the potential for meaning in work, and that meaning can be the very reason for living. If "the philosopher" was, indeed, suggesting the opposite, he was wrong.

Quality of Work Life

Few would question the general value of work and the importance of investing in it. Even if some people personally do not buy into a work ethic, they can hardly deny the personal and societal values that accrue from investing time, talent, and energy in this way. At least some people must invest themselves in productive enterprise if the lives of all people are to be optimized. Thus, although it may be of some value to consider the wider meaning and signficance of personal investment in the world of work, the points of contention in this regard probably revolve more around two other questions. First, does the concern with productivity overwhelm a concern for the producer? Second, what about other personal investments? Are not personal investments in the realms of family, leisure, and the arts deserving of equal prominence? Each of these questions could properly be the subject of another book. Our purpose in this concluding chapter is simply to recognize these concerns as important.

We turn, first, to the question of a possibly overwhelming concern for productivity at the expense of the producer. Although the desirability of productivity is a strong underlying theme in this book, it is by no means the only theme. A study such as we have presented on the preceding pages begins under the assumption that productivity is important. But a careful reading of the book will reveal an equally important theme: One does not have to be inhumane to increase productivity. In fact, the evidence we have presented culminates in a perspective that argues that at the heart of productivity is a "meaningful" job. When the company or the work organization concerns itself with the welfare of the worker, it is most likely to foster personal investment in the tasks to be done. In this regard, we found that a certain organizational culture or work climate was associated with personal investment. When employees felt that managers, supervisors, and the policies and procedures of the company were guided by a concern for the employee, they responded with commitment.

To this general line of thought, we add a complementary one: Delegation of responsibility and autonomy are desirable goals. In this regard, we presented strong arguments for creating self-managed work units. A first reason for this, of course, is that they are likely to enhance worker personal investment. But a self-managed unit also implies a respect for the worker and for his or her potential to make important contributions. Such a respect for and trust in the employee is hardly inhumane. It is fortuitous that it also seems to eventuate in productivity.

To this reminder of the essential thrust of our advice on designing the work place, we would add a more general point that also exists within the basic data for this volume. We were repeatedly impressed by employees' inclinations to seek out meaningful work. When they had it, they expressed pride in belonging to their work organization. When they didn't have it, they expressed a strong interest in finding a job where they would have it. There is certainly more to having a job than producing something. There are also social relationships and chances for fulfillment and the development of identity and self-respect. Effective organizations provide these for workers. The organizations are repaid handsomely for establishing organizational cultures that provide opportunities for workers to enhance their lives through their work by the worker commitment that is given in return. Thus—to stress most emphatically what we have said at various points in this volume—a humane work environment not only has value in itself, it is also very compatible with worker effectiveness.

Beyond the World of Work

There is an old expression that "all work and no play makes Jack a dull boy." It may actually do worse than that, and so the question is inevitable: Are we really suggesting in this book that work, career, or achievement is the predominant force in life? Certainly not! As important as work may be, it is only one phase of life. Although that simple statement masks a host of interesting questions, we will leave the matter there to make a point of theoretical importance.

In the first chapter of this book, we emphasized that the theoretical perspective we intended to propose was, in fact, a theory of human motivation. Thus, although we illustrated the theory and expanded and enhanced it through data gathered in the world of work, it was not our intention that it should be solely a theory of work motivation. Indeed, we suggest that the theory is broadly applicable to almost any human activity. For example, as we write these words, it is being applied to the study of leisure behavior as an extension of the research reported in this book. The point is that we think it important to approach work or any other sphere of human behavior with a broad motivational framework. We contend that the concept of personal investment suggests such a broad framework for viewing the differential choices people make in life—whether we label those choices work, play, leisure, or whatever. Moreover, there is every reason to believe that the same set of constructs (personal incentives, perceived options, and so on) will apply across most, if not all, areas of human social behavior. The validity of this assertion has not been fully tested, but the possibility for doing so is anticipated in this book.

Conclusions

We conclude with the full understanding that we have handled only a few of the pertinent questions and have provided far too few caveats or disclaimers. However, erring in this way might lead to interesting arguments and new lines of inquiry. It is hoped that this concluding chapter, and this book, is but an introduction to books yet to be written and innovative programs yet to be enacted.

Appendix A
Summary of Discriminant Analyses
for Testing Differences among
Selected Vocational Groups

Order of Variable Entering into the Discriminant Functions

| | | Personal Incentives | | | | | | | | Sense of Self | | |
Comparisons	Wilks' Lambda	TA	EX	CO	PW	AF	SC	RC	FN	SR	COMP	GD
College administrators vs. owners, salespersons, executives	.56	3	6		5		4	2	1			7
Middle managers vs. college administrators and faculty	.84		7	4	3			6	1	8	5	2
College faculty vs. owners, salespersons, executives	.84	5										
College faculty vs. schoolteachers	.79	4	5	3	1	7				2		6
Private vs. middle management	.90		5	3	2		6	4		7	1	
Owners, professionals, executives vs. clerical staff	.70		3		1			4			5	2

References

Adams, J.S. (1965). Inequity in social exchange. In L. Berkowitz (Ed.), *Advances in experimental social psychology* (vol. 2). New York: Academic Press.

Allport, G.W. (1955). *Becoming: Basic considerations for a psychology of personality.* New Haven: Yale University Press.

Allport, G.W. (1961). *Pattern and growth in personality.* New York: Holt, Rinehart & Winston.

Allport, G.W., Vernon, P.E., & Lindzey, G. (1960). *A study of values.* Boston: Houghton Mifflin.

Alper, T.G. (1979). Achievement motivation in college women: A now-you-see-it-now-you-don't phenomenon. *American Psychologist, 29,* 194–203.

Alschuler, A.S. (1973). *Developing achievement motivation in adolescents: Education for human growth.* Englewood Cliffs, NJ: Educational Technology.

Ames, R. (in press). Adult motivation in the leadership role: An attribution-value analysis. In D.A. Kleiber & M.L. Maehr (Eds.), *Advances in motivation and achievement, Vol. 4: Motivation in adulthood.* Greenwich, CT: JAI Press.

Ames, R., & Ames, C. (Eds.). (1984). *Research on motivation in education, Vol. 1: Student motivation.* New York: Academic Press.

Andrews, G.R., & Debus, R.L. (1978). Persistence and the causal perception of failure: Modifying cognitive attributions. *Journal of Educational Psychology, 70,* 154–166.

Arnoff, J., & Litwin, G.H. (1971). Achievement motivation training and executive advancement. *Journal of Applied Behavioral Science, 7,* 215–229.

Atkinson, J.W. (1957). Motivational determinants of risk-taking behavior. *Psychological Review 64,* 359–372.

Atkinson, J.W. (Ed.) (1958). *Motives in fantasy action and society.* Princeton, NJ: Van Nostrand.

Atkinson, J.W. (1978). Strength of motivation and efficiency of performance. In J.W. Atkinson & J.N. Raynor (Eds.), *Personality, motivation, and achievement.* Washington, D.C.: Hemisphere.

Atkinson, J.W., & Feather, N.T. (Eds.). (1966). *A theory of achievement motivation.* New York: Wiley.

Atkinson, J.W., & Raynor, J.O. (Eds.). (1974). *Motivation and achievement.* New York: Wiley.

Ausabel, D.P. (1955). Relationship between shame and guilt in the socializing process. *Psychological Review, 62,* 378–390.

Azim, A., & Bosiman, F. (1975). An empirical assessment of Etzioni's topology of power and involvement in a university setting. *Academy of Management Journal, 18*, 680–689.

Azumi, K., & McMillan, C. (1976). Worker sentiment in the Japanese factory: Its organizational determinants. In L. Austin (Ed.), *Japan: The paradox of progress.* New Haven: Yale University Press.

Bandura, A. (1977). Self-efficacy: Toward a unifying theory of behavioral change. *Psychological Review, 84*, 191–215.

Bandura, A. (1982). Self-efficacy mechanism in human agency. *American Psychologist, 37*, 122–147.

Barkow, J.H. (1976). Attention structure and the evolution of human psychological characteristics. In M.R.A. Chance & R.R. Larsen (Eds.), *The social structure of attention.* London: Wiley.

Barry, H. III (1980). Description and uses of the human relations area files. In H.C. Triandis & J.W. Berry (Eds.), *Handbook of cross-cultural psychology, Vol. 2: Basic processes.* Boston: Allyn & Bacon.

Bem, D.J. (1972). Self-perception theory. In L. Berkowitz (Ed.), *Advances in experimental social psychology* (Vol. 6). New York: Academic Press.

Bennis, W. (1984). Transformative power and leadership. In T.J. Sergiovanni & J.E. Corbally (Eds.), *Leadership and organizational culture.* Urbana: University of Illinois Press.

Biddle, B.J. (1979). *Role theory: Expectations, identities, and behaviors.* New York: Academic Press.

Bloom, B.S. (1982a). The role of gifts and markers in the development of talent. *Exceptional Children, 48*, 510–522.

Bloom, B.S. (1982b). The master teachers. *Phi Delta Kappan, 63*, 664–668.

Boje, D.M. Fedor, D.B., & Rowland, K.M. (1982). Myth making: A qualitative step in OD interventions. *Journal of Applied Behavioral Science, 18*, 17–28.

Bolman, L.G., & Deal, T.E. (1984). *Modern approaches to understanding and managing organizations.* San Francisco: Jossey-Bass.

Braskamp, L.A. (1985, July). *Motivating faculty through evaluation: Is it possible?* Paper presented at 11th International Conference on Improving University Teaching, Utrecht, Netherlands.

Braskamp, L.A., Brandenburg, D.C., & Ory, J.C. (1984). *Evaluating teaching effectiveness.* Beverly Hills, CA: Sage.

Braskamp, L.A., & Brown, R.D. (Eds.). (1980). *Utilization of evaluation information.* San Francisco: Jossey-Bass.

Braskamp, L.A., Fowler, D.A., & Ory, J.C. (1984). *Faculty development and achievement: A faculty's view.* Review of Higher Education, 7, 205–222.

Braskamp, L.A., & Maehr, M.L. (1985). *Spectrum: An organizational development tool.* Champaign, IL: Metritech.

Brehm, J.W. (1966). *A theory of psychological reactance.* New York: Academic Press.

Brent, S.B. (1978). Individual specialization, collective adaptation and rate of environmental change. *Human Development, 21*, 21–33.

Brim, O.G., Jr. (1974, September). *Theories of the male mid-life crisis.* Invited address at the meeting of the American Psychological Association, New Orleans.

Brousseau, K.R. (1983). Toward a dynamic model of job-person relationships: Findings, research questions and implications for work system design. *Academy of Management Review, 8,* 33–45.

Bunzel, J.H. (Ed.). (1985). *Challenge to American schools.* New York: Oxford University Press.

Callahan, T. (1985). Masters of their own game. *Time, 125,* 52–60.

Cameron, K. (1981). The enigma of organizational effectiveness. In D. Baugher (Ed.), *New directions in program evaluation: Measuring effectiveness.* San Francisco: Jossey-Bass.

Campbell, J.P., Dunnette, M.D., Lawler, E.E., & Weick, K.E. (1970). *Managerial behavior, performances, and effectiveness.* New York: McGraw-Hill.

Chhokar, J.S., & Wallin, J.A. (1984). A field study of the effect of feedback frequency on performance. *Journal of Applied Psychology, 69,* 524–530.

Chown, S.M. (1961). Age and the rigidities. *Journal of Gerontology, 16,* 353–362.

Chown, S.M. (1977). Morale, careers and personal potentials. In J.E. Birren & K.W. Schaie (Eds.), *Handbook of the psychology of aging.* New York: Van Nostrand Reinhold.

Chuny, K.H. (1977). *Motivational theories and practices.* Columbus, OH: GRID.

Cook, J.D., Hepworth, S.J., Wall, T.D., & Warr, P.D. (1981). *The experience of work.* New York: Academic Press.

Cornelius, E.T., & Lane, F.B. (1984). The power motive and managerial success in a professionally oriented service industry organization. *Journal of Applied Psychology, 69,* 32–39.

Csikszentmihalyi, M. (1975). *Beyond boredom and anxiety.* San Francisco: Jossey-Bass.

Csikszentmihalyi, M. (1978). Intrinsic rewards and emergent motivation. In M.R. Lepper & D. Greene (Eds.), *The hidden costs of reward.* Hillsdale, NJ: Erlbaum.

Csikszentmihalyi, M. (in press). Emergent motivation and the evolution of self. In D.A. Kleiber & M.L. Maehr (Eds.), *Advances in motivation and achievement, Vol. 4: Motivation in adulthood.* Greenwich, CT: JAI Press.

Deal, T.E., & Kennedy, A.A. (1982). *Corporate cultures: The rites and rituals of corporate life.* Reading, MA: Addison-Wesley.

deCharms, R. (1968). *Personal causation.* New York: Academic Press.

deCharms, R. (1972). Personal causation training in the schools. *Journal of Applied Social Psychology, 2,* 95–113.

deCharms, R. (1976). *Enhancing motivation: Change in the classroom.* New York: Irvington.

deCharms, R. (1984). Motivation enhancement in educational settings. In R. Ames & C. Ames (Eds.), *Research on motivation in education, Vol. 1: Student motivation.* New York: Academic Press.

Deci, E.L. (1975). *Intrinsic motivation.* New York: Plenum.

Deci, E.L. (1980). *The psychology of self-determination.* Lexington, MA: Lexington Books, D.C. Heath.

DeVos, G.A. (1973). *Socialization for achievement.* Berkeley: Univeristy of California Press.

Doering, M., Rhodes, S.R., & Schuster, M. (1983). *The aging worker.* Beverly Hills, CA: Sage.

Drake, B., & Mitchell, T. (1977). The effects of vertical and horizontal power on individual motivation and satisfaction. *Academy of Management Journal, 20,* 573–591.

Duda, J. (1980). Achievement motivation among Navajo students: A conceptual analysis with preliminary data. *Ethos, 8*(4), 316–337.

Duda, J. (1981). *A cross-cultural analysis of achievement motivation in sport and the classroom.* Unpublished doctoral dissertation, University of Illinois at Urbana-Champaign.

Dweck, C.S. (1975). The role of expectations and attributions in the alleviation of learned helplessness. *Journal of Personality and Social Psychology, 31,* 674–675.

Edward, A.E., & Wine, D.B. (1963). Personality changes with age: Their dependency on concomitant intellectual decline. *Journal of Gerontology, 18,* 182–184.

Erikson, E. (1950). *Childhood and society.* New York: Norton.

Erikson, E. (1959). Identity and the life cycle: Selected papers. *Psychological Issues* (Whole issue).

Erikson, E. (1968). *Identity, youth and crisis.* New York: Norton.

Farmer, H.S., Maehr, M.L., & Rooney, G.S. (1980). *Attributions and values for personal success, failures, and future goals.* (Measurement instrument available from H.S. Farmer, Department of Educational Psychology, University of Illinois at Urbana-Champaign.)

Farmer, H.S., Vispoel, W., & Maehr, M.L. (1985a). *Effect of achievement context and gender on success goals.* Manuscript submitted for publication.

Farmer, H.S., Vispoel, W., & Maehr, M.L. (1985b). *Variation of attribution patterns with achievement contexts.* Unpublished manuscript, University of Illinois, College of Education, Champaign.

Feather, N.T. (1982). *Expectations and actions: Expectancy-value models in psychology.* Hillsdale, NJ: Erlbaum.

Feldman, D.C., & Arnold, H.J. (1983). *Managing individual and group behavior in organizations.* New York: McGraw-Hill.

Festinger, L. (1957). *A theory of cognitive dissonance.* New York: Harper.

Folger, R. (Ed.). (1984). *The sense of injustice: Social psychological perspectives.* New York: Plenum.

Fyans, L.J., Jr., Kremer, B., Salili, F., & Maehr, M.L. (1981). The effects of evaluation conditions on continuing motivation: A study of the cultural, personological, and situational antecedents of a motivational pattern. *International Journal of Intercultural Relations, 5,* 1–22.

Fyans, L.J., Jr., & Maehr, M.L. (1979). Attributional style, task selection and achievement. *Journal of Educational Psychology, 71,* 499–507.

Fyans, L.J., Jr., Salili, F., Maehr, M.L., & Desai, K.A. (1983). A cross-cultural exploration into the meaning of achievement. *Journal of Personality and Social Psychology, 44,* 1000–1013.

George, L.K. (1980). *Role transitions in later life.* Monterey, CA: Brooks/Cole.

Goodenough, W.H. (1963). *Cooperation in change.* New York: Russell Sage Foundation.

Goodenough, W.H. (1971). *Culture, language, and society.* Reading, MA: Addison-Wesley.

Goodman, P.S., & Pennings, J.M. (Eds.). (1979). *New perspectives on organizational effectiveness*. San Francisco: Jossey-Bass.

Gould, S. (1979). Age, job complexity, satisfaction, and performance. *Journal of Vocational Behavior, 14*, 209–223.

Greenberg, J. (1982). Approaching equity and avoiding inequity in groups and organizations. In J. Greenberg & R.L. Cohen (Eds.), *Equity and justice in social behavior*. New York: Academic Press.

Haas, H.I., & Maehr, M.L. (1965). Two experiments on the concept of self and the reaction of others. *Journal of Personality and Social Psychology, 1*, 100–105.

Hackman, J.R., & Oldham, G.R. (1980). *Work redesign*. Reading, MA: Addison-Wesley.

Hackman, J.R., & Suttle, J.L. (1977). *Improving life at work*. Pacific Palisades, CA: Goodyear.

Hackman, R. (1985, August). *The psychology of self-management in organizations*. Paper presented at APA Master Lecture Series: Psychology and Work, American Psychological Association Convention, Los Angeles.

Hall, D.T., & Nougaim, K.E. (1968). An examination of Maslow's need hierarchy in an organizational setting. *Organizational Behavior and Human Performance, 3*, 12–35.

Harnisch, D., & Maehr, M.L. (1985). *Gender differences in motivation and achievement: A personal investment perspective*. Unpublished manuscript.

Harter, S. (1980). A model of intrinsic mastery motivation in children: Individual differences and developmental change. In W.A. Collins (Ed.), *Minnesota Symposium in Child Psychology* (Vol. 14). Hillsdale, NJ: Erlbaum.

Harter, S., & Connell, J.P. (1984). A structural model of relationships among children's academic achievement and their self-perceptions of competence, control, and motivational orientation in the cognitive domain. In J. Nicholls (Ed.), *The development of achievement motivation*. Greenwich, CT: JAI Press.

Hatvany, N., & Pucik, V. (1981). Japanese management practice and productivity. *Organizational Dynamics, 9*, 5–21.

Havighurst, R.J. (1952). *Developmental tasks and education*. New York: David McKay.

Heckhausen, H. (1967). *The anatomy of achievement motivation*. New York: Academic Press.

Heckhausen, H., & Krug, S. (1982). Motive modification. In A.J. Stewart (Ed.), *Motivation and society*. San Francisco: Jossey-Bass.

Henderson, R. (1980). *Performance appraisal: Theory to practice*. Reston, VA: Prentice-Hall.

Hickman, C.R., & Silva, M.A. (1984). *Creating excellence: Managing corporate culture, strategy, and change in the new age*. New York: New American Library.

Hill, K.T. (1980). Motivation, evaluation, and testing policy. In L.J. Fyans, Jr. (Ed.), *Achievement motivation: Recent trends in theory and research*. New York: Plenum.

Homans, G. (1950). *The human group*. New York: Harcourt, Brace, Jovanovich.

Iaffaldano, M.T., & Muchinsky, P.M. (1985). Job satisfaction and job performance: A meta-analysis. *Psychological Bulletin, 97*, 251–273.

Inkeles, A. (1980). Continuity and change in the American national character. *Tocqueville Review, 2*(2–3), 20–51.

Irvine, S.H., & Carroll, W.K. (1980). Testing and assessment across cultures: Issues in methodology and theory. In H. Triandis & R.W. Brislin (Eds.), *Handbook of cross-cultural psychology* (Vol. 2). New York: Allyn & Bacon.

Ivancevich, J.M., & McMahon, J.R. (1982). The effects of goal setting, external feedback, and self-generated feedback on outcome variables. A field experiment. *Academy of Mangement Journal, 25*, 359–372.

James, L.R., & Jones, A.P. (1974). Organizational climate: A review of theory and research. *Psychological Bulletin, 81*, 1096–1112.

Jelinek, M., Smircich, L., & Hirsch, P. (1983). Introduction: A code of many colors. *Administrative Science Quarterly, 28*, 331–338.

Kelly, J.R. (1981). *Leisure.* Englewood Cliffs, NJ: Prentice-Hall.

Kelly, J.R. (1982a). *Leisure identities and interactions.* London: Allen & Unwin.

Kelly, J.R. (1982b). Leisure in later life: Roles and identities. In N. Osgood (Ed.), *Life after retirement.* New York: Praeger.

Kilman, R.H. (1985, April). Corporate culture. *Psychology Today,* 62–68.

Kirst, M.W. (1982). How to improve schools without spending more money. *Phi Delta Kappan, 64*(3), 6–8.

Kleiber, D.A. (in press). Motivational reorientation in adulthood and the resource of leisure. In D.A. Kleiber & M.L. Maehr (Eds.), *Advances in motivation and achievement, Vol. 4: Motivation in adulthood.* Greenwich, CT: JAI Press.

Kleiber, D.A., & Maehr, M.L. (Eds.). (in press). *Advances in motivation and achievement, Vol. 4: Motivation in adulthood.* Greenwich, CT: JAI Press.

Klein, R. (1972). Age, sex, and task difficulty as predictors of social conformity. *Journal of Gerontology, 27*, 229–236.

Klinger, E. (1977). *Meaning and void: Inner experience and the incentives in people's lives.* Minneapolis: University of Minnesota Press.

Klinger, E., & McNelley, F.W. (1969). Fantasy need achievement and performance: A role analysis. *Psychological Review, 76*, 574–591.

Kluckhorn, F. (1961). *Dominant and variant value orientations.* Evanston, IL: Row, Peterson.

Kluckhorn, F., & Strodbeck, F.L. (1961). *Variations in value orientations.* Evanston, IL: Row, Peterson.

Knox, A.B. (1977). *Adult development and learning: A handbook on individual growth and competence in the adult years for education and the helping professions.* San Francisco: Jossey-Bass.

Knox, A.B. (Ed.). (1980). *Teaching adults effectively: New directions for continuing education* (No. 6). San Francisco: Jossey-Bass.

Knox, A.B. (in press). Adult learning and proficiency. In D.A. Kleiber & M.L. Maehr (Eds.), *Advances in motivation and achievement, Vol. 4: Motivation in adulthood.* Greenwich, CT: JAI Press.

Kornadt, H.J., Eckensberger, L.H., & Emminghaus, W.B. (1980). Cross-cultural research on motivation and its contribution to a general theory of motivation. In H.C. Triandis & W. Lanner (Eds.), *Handbook of crosss-cultural psychology, Vol. 3: Basic processes.* Boston: Allyn & Bacon.

Kuhlen, R.G. (1964). Development changes in motivation during the adult years. In J.E. Birren (Ed.), *Relations of development and aging*. Springfield, IL: Thomas.

Kukla, A. (1978). An attributional theory of choice. In L. Berkowitz (Ed.), *Advances in social psychology* (Vol. 11). New York: Academic Press.

Langer, E.J. (1978). Rethinking the role of thought in social interaction. In J. Harvey, W. Ickes, & R. Kidd (Eds.), *New directions in attribution research* (Vol. 2). Hillsdale, NJ: Erlbaum.

Langer, E.J., & Rodin, J. (1976). The effects of choice and enhanced personal responsibility for the aged: A field experiment in an institutional setting. *Journal of Personality and Social Psychology, 34*, 191–198.

Latham, G.P., & Yukl, G.A. (1975). A review of research on the application of goal setting in organizations. *Academy of Management Journal, 18*, 224–245.

Lawler, E.E., III. (1971). *Pay and organization development*. Reading, MA: Addison-Wesley.

Lawler, E.E., III. (1977). Reward systems. In J.R. Hackman & J.L. Suttle (Eds.), *Improving life at work*. Pacific Palisades, CA: Goodyear.

Lawler, E.E., III, Hall, D.T., & Oldham, G.R. (1974). Organizational climate: Relationship to organizational structure, process, and performance. *Organizational Behavior and Human Performance, 11*, 139–155.

Lawler, E.E., III, & Porter, L.W. (1967). The effects of performance on job satisfaction. *Industrial Relations, 7*, 20–28.

Lefcourt, H.M. (1976). *Locus of control: Current trends in theory and research*. New York: Erlbaum.

Lehman, H.C. (1953). *Age and achievement*. Princeton, NJ: Princeton University Press.

Lepper, M., & Greene, D. (1975). Turning play into work: Effects of adult surveillance and extrinsic rewards on children's intrinsic motivation. *Journal of Personality and Social Psychology, 31*, 479–486.

Lepper, M., & Greene, D. (Eds.). (1978). *The hidden costs of reward: New perspectives on the psychology of human motivation*. Hillsdale, NJ: Erlbaum.

Lepper, M., Greene, D., & Nisbitt, R.E. (1973). Undermining children's intrinsic interest with extrinsic rewards: A test of the "over-justification" hypothesis. *Journal of Personality and Social Psychology, 28*, 129–137.

Levinson, D.J. (1978). *The seasons of a man's life*. New York: Knopf.

Levinson, D.J., Darrow, C.N., Klein, E.B., Levinson, M.H., & McKee, B. (1974). Periods in the adult development of men: Ages 18 to 45. In R.F. Ricks, A. Thomas, & M. Roff (Eds.), *Life history research in psychopathology* (Vol. 3). Minneapolis: University of Minnesota Press.

Lewis, O. (1961). *Children of Sanchez*. New York: Random House.

Litwin, G.H., & Stringer, R.A., Jr. (1968). *Motivation and organizational climate*. Boston: Harvard University Graduate School of Business Administration.

Locke, E.A., & Latham, G.P. (1984). *Goal setting: A motivational technique that works*. Englewood Cliffs, NJ: Prentice-Hall.

Locke, E.A., Staw, K.N., Saari, L.M., & Latham, G.P. (1981). Goal setting and task performance: 1969–1980. *Psychological Bulletin, 90*, 125–152.

Lord, R.G., & Smith, J.E. (1983). Theoretical, information processing, and situational factors affecting attribution theory models of organizational behavior. *Academy of Management Review, 8,* 50–60.

Ludwig, D.J., & Maehr, M.L. (1967). Changes in self-concept and stated behavioral preferences. In J.P. Hill & J. Shelton (Eds.), *Readings in adolescent development and behavior.* Englewood Cliffs, NJ: Prentice-Hall.

Maehr, M.L. (1974a). Culture and achievement motivation. *American Psychologist, 29,* 887–896.

Maehr, M.L. (1974b). *Sociocultural origins of achievement.* Monterey, CA: Brooks/ Cole.

Maehr, M.L. (1976). Continuing motivation. *Review of Educational Research, 46,* 443–462.

Maehr, M.L. (1977). Turning the fun of school into the drudgery of work: The negative effects of certain grading practices on motivation. *UCLA Educator, 19,* 10–14.

Maehr, M.L. (1978). Sociocultural origins of achievement motivation. In D. Bar-Tal & L. Saxe (Eds.), *Social psychology of education: Theory and research.* New York: Hemisphere.

Maehr, M.L. (1983). On doing well in science: Why Johnny no longer excels; why Sarah never did. In S. Paris, G. Olson, & H. Stevenson (Eds.), *Learning and motivation in the classroom.* Hillsdale, NJ: Erlbaum.

Maehr, M.L. (1984a). Meaning and motivation. In R. Ames & C. Ames (Eds.), *Research on motivation in education, Vol. 1: Student motivation.* New York: Academic Press.

Maehr, M.L. (1984b). Maintaining faculty motivation and morale in an era of decline. *Proceedings: 10th Annual International Conference on Improving University Teaching.* College Park: University of Maryland.

Maehr, M.L., & Kleiber, D.A. (1980). The graying of America: implications for achievement motivation theory and research. In L.J. Fyans, Jr. (Ed.), *Achievement motivation.* New York: Plenum Press.

Maehr, M.L., & Kleiber, D.A. (1981). The graying of achievement motivation. *American Psychologist, 36,* 787–793.

Maehr, M.L. & Kleiber, D.A. (Eds.). (in press). *Advances in motivation and achievement, Vol. 5: Enhancing motivation.* Greenwich, CT: JAI Press.

Maehr, M.L., Mensing, J., & Nafzger, S. (1962). Concept of self and the reaction of others. *Sociometry, 25,* 353–357.

Maehr, M.L., & Nicholls, J.G. (1980). Culture and achievement motivation: A second look. In N. Warren (Ed.), *Studies in cross-cultural psychology* (Vol. 2). New York: Academic Press.

Maehr, M.L., & Sjogren, D. (1971). Atkinson's theory of achievement motivation: First step toward a theory of academic motivation? *Review of Educational Research, 41,* 143–161.

Maehr, M.L., & Stake, R.E. (1962). The value patterns of men who voluntarily quit seminary training. *Personnel and Guidance Journal, 40,* 537–540.

Maehr, M.L., & Stallings, W.M. (1972). Freedom from external evaluation. *Child Development, 43,* 177–185.

Maehr, M.L., & Willig, A.C. (1982). Expecting too much or too little: Student freedom and responsibility in the classroom. In H. Walberg & R. Luckie (Eds.),

Improving educational productivity: The research basis of school standards. Chicago: NSSE Series in Contemporary Issues in Education.

Marcuccio, P. (1983). Responding to the economic sputnik. *Phi Delta Kappan, 64*(9), 618–620.

Massie, R.K. (1980). *Peter the Great: His life and work.* New York: Random House.

Mayberry, P. (1984, April). *Analysis of cross-cultural attitudinal scale translation using maximum likelihood factor analysis.* Paper presented at the Annual Meeting of the American Educational Research Association, New Orleans.

Mayberry, P. (1985). *Congruencies among organizational components and their relationship to work attitudes.* Unpublished doctoral dissertation, University of Illinois at Urbana-Champaign.

McClelland, D.C. (1942). Functional autonomy of motives as an extinction phenomenon. *Psychological Review, 49,* 272–283.

McClelland, D.C. (1951). *Personality.* New York: Sloane.

McClelland, D.C. (1961). *The achieving society.* New York: Free Press.

McClelland, D.C. (1965). Achievement motivation can be developed. *Harvard Business Review, 43,* 6–24.

McClelland, D.C. (1975). *Power: The inner experience.* New York: Irvington.

McClelland, D.C. (1976). Power is the great motivator! *Harvard Business Review, 54,* 100–110.

McClelland, D.C. (1978). Managing motivation to expand human freedom. *American Psychologist, 33,* 201–210.

McClelland, D.C. (1985a). *Human motivation.* Glenview, IL: Scott, Foresman.

McClelland, D.C. (1985b). How motives, skills, and values determine what people do. *American Psychologist, 40,* 812–825.

McClelland, D.C., Atkinson, J.W., Clark, R.A., & Lowell, E.L. (1953). *The achievement motive.* New York: Appleton-Century-Crofts.

McClelland, D.C., & Boyatzis, R.E. (1982). The leadership motive pattern and long-term success in management. *Journal of Applied Psychology, 67,* 797–743.

McClelland, D.C., & Winter, D.G. (1971). *Motivating economic achievement.* New York: Free Press.

McGregor, D. (1960). *The human side of enterprise.* New York: McGraw-Hill.

McKeachie, W.J. (1982). The rewards of teaching. In J.L. Bess (Ed.), *Motivating professors to teach effectively.* San Francisco: Jossey-Bass.

Mead, G.H. (1934). *Mind, self, and society.* Chicago: University of Chicago Press.

Mead, M. (1935). *Sex and temperament in three primitive societies.* New York: Morrow.

Messick, S., & Brayfield, A.H. (1964). *Decision and choice: Contributions of Sidney Siegel.* New York: McGraw-Hill.

Miller, A. (1981). Conceptual matching models and interactional research in education. *Review of Educational Research, 51,* 33–84.

Miller, G.A., Galanter, E., & Pribram, K.H. (1960). *Plans and the structure of behavior.* New York: Holt, Rinehart & Winston.

Mischel, W. (1966). Theory and research on the antecedents of self-imposed delay of reward. In B.A. Maher (Ed.), *Progress in experimental personality research* (Vol. 3). New York: Academic Press.

Mitchell, T.R. (1982). Motivation: New directions for theory, research and practice. *Academy of Management Review, 7,* 80–88.

Mobley, W.H., Griffeth, R.W., Hand, H.H., & Meglino, B.M. (1979). Review and conceptual analysis of the employee turnover process. *Psychological Bulletin, 86,* 493–522.

Morris, E. (1979). *The rise of Theodore Roosevelt.* New York: Random House.

Morsbach, H. (1980). Major psychological factors influencing Japanese interpersonal relations. In N. Warren (Ed.), *Studies in cross-cultural psychology* (Vol. 2). London: Academic Press.

Motivation Factor. (1983, May 8). *New York Times,* Business Section, p. 1.

Mowday, R.T. (1975). Equity theory predictions of behavior in organizations. In R.M. Steers & L.W. Porter (Eds.), *Motivation and work behavior.* New York: McGraw-Hill.

Murray, H.A. (1938). *Explorations in personality.* New York: Oxford University Press.

Nadler, D.A. (1977). *Feedback and organization development.* Reading, MA: Addison-Wesley.

Nadler, D.A. (1979). The effects of feedback on task group behavior: A review of the experimental research. *Organizational Behavior and Human Performance, 23,* 309–338.

Nadler, D.A., Hackman,, J.R., & Lawler, EE.E., III. (1979). *Managing organizational behavior.* Boston: Little, Brown.

Neugarten, B.L. (1977). Personality and aging. In J.E. Birren & K.W. Schaie (Eds.), *Handbook of the psychology of aging.* New York: Van Nostrand Reinhold.

Neugarten, B.L., & Datan, N. (1973). Sociological perspectives on the life cycle. In P. Baltes & K.W. Schaie (Eds.), *Life-span developmental psychology: Personality and socialization.* New York: Academic Press.

Nicholls, J.G. (1979). Quality and equality in intellectual development: The role of motivation in education. *American Psychologist, 34,* 1071–1084.

Nicholls, J.G. (1983). Concepts of ability and achievement motivation: A theory and its implications for education. In S.G. Paris, G.M. Olson, & H.W. Stevenson (Eds.), *Learning and motivation in the classroom.* Hillsdale, NJ: Erlbaum.

Nicholls, J.G. (Ed.). (1984a). *The development of achievement motivation.* Greeenwich, CT: JAI Press.

Nicholls, J.G. (1984b). Conceptions of ability and achievement motivation. In R. Ames & C. Ames (Eds.), *Research on motivation in education, Vol. 1: Student motivation.* New York: Academic Press.

Nicholls, J.G., & Miller, A.T. (1984). Development and its discontents: The differentiation of the concept of ability. In J.G. Nicholls (Ed.), *The development of achievement motivation.* Greenwich, CT: JAI Press.

Osgood, C.E., Miron, M., & May, W. (1975). *Cross-cultural universals of affective meaning.* Urbana: University of Illinois Press.

Ouchi, W. (1981). *Theory Z corporations: How American Business can meet the Japanese challenge.* Reading, MA: Addison-Wesley.

Pareek, V., & Rao, T.V. (1980). Cross cultural surveys and interviewing. In H.C. Triandis & J.W. Berry (Eds.), *Handbook of cross-cultural psychology, Vol 2: Methodology.* Boston: Allyn & Bacon.

Pascale, R. (1984). Fitting new employees into the company culture. *Fortune, 28,* 30–34.

Pascale, R.T., & Athos, A.G. (1981). *The art of Japanese management: Applications for American executives*. New York: Simon & Schuster.

Pascale, R., & Maguire, M. (1980). Comparison of selected work factors in Japan and the United States. *Human Relations, 33,* 433–455.

Pascarella, E.T., Walberg, H.J., Junker, C.K., & Haertel, G.D. (1981). Continuing motivation in science for early and late adolescents. *American Educational Research Journal, 18,* 439–452.

Patten, T. (1977). *Pay: Employee compensation and incentive plans.* New York: Free Press.

Pennings, J. (1976). Dimensions of organizational influence and the effectiveness correlates. *Administrative Science Quarterly, 21,* 688–689.

Peters, T.J., & Waterman, R.H., Jr. (1982). *In search of excellence: Lessons from America's best-run companies.* New York: Harper.

Pfeffer, J. (1982). *Organizations and organization theory.* Boston: Pitman.

Plath, D.W. (Ed.). (1983). *Work and life course in Japan.* Albany, NY: SUNY Press.

Pollack, K., & Kastenbaum, R. (1964). Delay of gratification in later life: An experimental analogue. In R. Kastenbaum (Ed.), *New thoughts on old age.* New York: Springer.

Porac, J.F., & Meindl, J. (1982). Undermining overjustification: Inducing intrinsic and extrinsic task representations. *Organizational Behavior and Human Performance, 29,* 208–226.

Porter, L.W., Lawler, E.E., & Hackman, J.R. (1975). *Behavior in organizations.* New York: McGraw-Hill.

Porter, L.W., & Steers, R.M. (1973). Organizational, work and personal factors in employee turnover and absenteeism. *Psychological Bulletin, 80,* 151–176.

Quinn, N. (1977). Anthropological studies on women's status. *Annual Review of Anthropology, 6,* 181–225.

Raynor, J.O. (1969). Future orientation and motivation for immediate activity: An elaboration of the theory of achievement motivation. *Psychological Review, 76,* 606–610.

Raynor, J.O. (1982). A theory of personality functioning and change. In J.O. Raynor & E.E. Entin (Eds.), *Motivational career striving and aging.* New York: Hemisphere.

Rhodes, S.R. (1983). Age-related differences in work attitudes and behavior: A review of conceptual analysis. *Psychological Bulletin, 93,* 328–367.

Rice, B. (1985). Performance review: The job nobody wants. *Psychology Today,* 30–36.

Roberts, G.C. (1984). Achievement motivation in children's sport. In J.G. Nicholls (Ed.), *The development of achievement motivation.* Greenwich, CT: JAI Press.

Roe, A. (1953). *The making of a scientist.* New York: Dodd, Mead.

Rogers, C.R. (1951). *Client-centered therapy.* Boston: Houghton-Mifflin.

Rogers, C.R. (1961). *On becoming a person.* Boston: Houghton-Mifflin.

Rosen, B.C. (1982). *The industrial connection: Achievement and the family in developing societies.* New York: Aldine.

Rosen, B.C., & D'Andrade, R.G. (1959). The psychosocial origins of achievement motivation. *Sociometry, 22,* 185–218.

Salancik, G.R., & Pfeffer, J. (1978). A social information processing approach to job attitudes and task design. *Administrative Science Quarterly 23*, 224–253.

Salili, F., Maehr, M.L., Sorensen, R.L., & Fyans, L.J., Jr. (1976). A further consideration of the effects of evaluation on motivation. *American Educational Research Journal, 13*, 85–102.

Schank, R.C., & Abelson, R.P. (1977). *Scripts, plans, goals, and understanding.* New York: Halsted.

Schein, E.H. (1978). *Career dynamics: Matching individual and organizational needs.* Reading, MA: Addison-Wesley.

Schein, E.H. (1981). SMR Forum: Does Japanese management style have a message for American mmanagers? *Sloan Management Review, 23*, 55–68.

Schein, E.H. (1984). Coming to a new awareness of organizational culture. *Sloan Management Review, 25*, 3–16.

Schein, E.H. (1985). *Organizational culture and leadership.* San Francisco: Jossey-Bass.

Schneider, B., & Snyder, R.A. (1975). Some relationships between job satisfaction and organizational climate. *Journal of Applied Psychology, 60*, 318–328.

Schulz, R. (1976). The effects of control and predictability on the physical and psychological well-being of the aged. *Journal of Personality and Social Psychology, 33*, 563–573.

Schwalb, D., Harnisch, D., & Maehr, M.L. (1985). *A study of motivational orientations in the U.S. and Japan.* Unpublished manuscript.

Sheehy, G. (1981). *Pathfinders.* New York: Bantam.

Sorenson, R.L., & Maehr, M.L. (1976). Toward the experimental anlaysis of "continuing motivation." *Journal of Educational Research, 69*, 319–322.

Spady, W. (1984). Exchanging lessons with corporate America. *Thrust, 6*, 18–22.

Spence, J.T., & Helmreich, R.L. (1978). *Masculinity and femininity.* Austin: University of Texas Press.

Spenner, K.I., & Featherman, D.C. (1978). Achievement ambitions. *Annual Review of Sociology, 4.*

Staw, B.M. (1974). Attitudinal and behavioral consequences of changing a major organizational reward: A natural field experiment. *Journal of Personality and Social Psychology, 29*, 742–751.

Staw, B.M. (1977). Motivation in organizations: Toward synthesis and redirection. In B.M. Staw & G.R. Salancik (Eds.), *New directions in organizational behavior.* Chicago: St. Clair Press.

Staw, B.M. (1983). Motivation research versus the art of faculty management. *Review of Higher Education, 6*, 301–321.

Staw, B.M., Hess, R.K., & Sandelands, L.E. (1980). Intrinsic motivation and norms about payment. *Journal of Personality, 48*, 1–14.

Staw, B.M., & Salancik, G. (Eds.). (1977). *New directions in organizational behavior.* Chicago: St. Clair Press.

Steers, R.M. (1981). *Introduction to organizational behavior.* Santa Monica, CA: Goodyear.

Steers, R.M., & Porter, L.W. (Eds.). (1983). *Motivation and work behavior* (3rd ed.). New York: McGraw-Hill.

Steinkamp, M.W., & Kelly, J.R. (1985a). *Social integration, leisure activity, and life satisfaction in older adults: Activity theory revisited.* Manusript submitted for publication.

Steinkamp, M.W., & Kelly, J.R. (1985b). *Relationship among motivational orientation, leisure activity level, and life satisfaction in older men and women.* Manuscript submitted for publication.

Steinkamp, M.W., & Maehr, M.L. (Eds.). (1984a). *Advances in motivation and
achievement, Vol. 2: Women in science.* Greenwich, CT: JAI Press.

Steinkamp, M., & Maehr, M.L. (1984b). Gender differences in motivational orientation toward achievement in school sciences: A quantitative synthesis. *American
Educational Research Journal, 21*, 39–59.

Stern, G. (1970). *People in context: Measuring person-environment congruence in
education and industry.* New York: Wiley.

Taylor, S.E., & Fiske, S.T. (1978). Salience, attention, and attribution: Top of the
read phenomena. In L. Berkowitz (Ed.), *Advances in experimental social psychology* (Vol. 11). New York: Academic Press.

Terman, L.M. (1954). Scientists and nonscientists in a group of 800 gifted men. *Psychological Monographs: General and Applied, 68*(7, Whole No. 378).

Triandis, H.C., et al. (1972). *The analysis of subjective culture.* New York: Wiley.

Triandis, H.C., & Brislin, R.W. (Eds.). (1980). *Handbook of cross-cultural psychology* (Vol. 2). New York: Allyn & Bacon.

Tyler, R.W. (1983). The contribution of "A study of schooling" to educational research. *Educational Leadership, 40*(7), 33–34.

Uneo, I., Blake, R.R., & Mouton, J.S. (1984). The productivity battle: A behavioral
science analysis of Japan and the United States. *Journal of Applied Behavioral
Science, 20*, 49–56.

Valentine, C.A. (1968). *Culture and poverty: Critique and counterproposal.* Chicago: University of Chicago Press.

Van de Ven, A.H., & Astley, W.G. (1981). Mapping the field to create a dynamic
perspective on organizational design and behavior. In A.H. Van de Ven & W.F.
Joyce (Eds.), *Perspectives on organizational design and behavior.* New York:
Wiley-Interscience.

Veroff, J., Atkinson, J., Feld, S., & Gurin, G. (1960). The use of thematic apperception to assess motivaton in a nationwide interview study. *Psychologiccal
Monographs, 74*(12, Whole No. 499).

Veroff, J., & Veroff, J.B. (1980). *Social incentives: A life-span developmental approach.* New York; Academic Press.

Videbeck, R. (1960). Self-conception and the reaction of others. *Sociometry, 23*,
351–359.

Vroom, V.H. (1964). *Work and motivation.* New York: Wiley.

Wanous, J. (Ed.). (1980). *Organizational entry: Recruitment, selection, and socialization of newcomers.* Reading, MA: Addison-Wesley.

Watts, B.H. (1975). Increasing achievement aspirations and motivation through
teaching. In M.L. Maehr & W.M. Stallings (Eds.), *Culture, child, and school.*
Monterey, CA: Brooks/Cole.

Weber, M. (1930). *The Protestant ethic and the spirit of capitalism* (T. Parsons,
Trans.). New York: Scribner. (Original work published 1904.)

Weiner, B. (1977). An attributional approach for educational psychology. In L.S.
Shulman (Ed.). *Review of research in education* (Vol. 4). Itasca, IL: Peacock.

Weiner, B. (1979). A theory of motivation for some classroom experiences. *Journal
of Educational Psychology, 71*, 3–25.

Weiner, B. (1983). Some thoughts about feelings. In S.G. Paris, G.M. Olson, & H.W. Stevenson (Eds.), *Learning and motivation in the classroom*. Hillsdale, NJ: Erlbaum.

Weiner, B. (1984). Principles for a theory of student motivation and their application within an attributional framework. In R. Ames & C. Ames (Eds.), *Research on motivation in education, Vol. 1: Student motivation*. New York: Academic Press.

Wexley, K.N., & Yukl, G.A. (1984). *Organizational behavior and personnel psychology* (rev. ed.). Homewood, IL: Irwin.

Whetten, D.A. (1984). Effective administration: Good management on the college campus. *Change, 16*, 38–43.

White, R.W. (1959). Motivation reconsidered: The concept of competence. *Psychological Review, 66*, 297–333.

White, R.W. (1960). Competence and the psychosexual stages of development. In M.R. Jones (Ed.), *Nebraska Symposium on Motivation*. Lincoln: University of Nebraska Press.

White, R., & Lippitt, R. (1968). Leader behavior and member reaction in three "social climates." In D. Cartwright & A. Zander (Eds.), *Group dynamics: Research and theory*. New York: Harper & Row.

Whiting, J.W.M. (1959). Sorcery, sin and the superego: A cross-cultural study of some mechanisms of social control. In M.R. Jones (Ed.), *Nebraska Symposium on Motivation*. Lincoln: University of Nebraska Press.

Wigfield, A., & Braskamp, L.A. (in press). Age and personal investment. In D.A. Kleiber & M.L. Maehr (Eds.), *Advances in motivation and achievement, Vol. 4: Motivation in adulthood*. Greenwich, CT: JAI Press.

Wilkins, A.L. (1983). The culture audit: A tool for understanding organizations. *Organizational Dynamics, 11*, 24–38.

Winterbottom, M.R. (1953). *The relation of childhood training in independence to achievement motivation*. Unpublished doctoral dissertation, University of Michigan, Ann Arbor.

Winterbottom, M.R. (1958). The relation of need for achievement to learning experiences in independence and mastery. In J.W. Atkinson (Ed.), *Motives in fantasy, action, and society*. Princeton, NJ: Van Nostrand.

Wylie, R. (1974). *The self-concept* (Vol. I, rev. ed.). Lincoln: University of Nebraska Press.

Wylie, R. (1979). *The self-concept, Vol. 2: Theory and research on selected topics*. Lincoln: University of Nebraska Press.

Yankelowich, D. (1979, August 6). We need new motivational tools. *Industry Week*, 61–65.

Yankelowich, D. (1982, May). The work ethic is underemployed. *Psychology Today*, 5–8.

Yukl, G.A. (1981). *Leadership in organizations*. Englewood Cliffs, NJ: Prentice-Hall.

Zander, A., & Forward, J. (1968). Position in group, achievement motivation, and group aspirations. *Journal of Personality and Social Psychology, 8*, 282–288.

Zeigarnik, B. (1927). Über das Behalten von erledigten und unerledigten Handlungen. [Concerning the retention of finished and unfinished tasks.] *Psychologische Forschung, 9*, 1–95.

Index

Abelson, R.P., 47
Absenteeism, 88, 107
Academics, 41, 103–106
Achievement, 12–13, 19–23, 249–250;
and causal judgments, 37–38; and
competence, 60–61; and culture,
100–101, 193–212; and gender,
197, 199; and managers, 25–26;
and status, 187; and training, 21–23
Achievers, 94–101; and age, 174–
176, 177–178; and competition,
100; and excellence, striving for,
106, 174; and power, 174; and
self-reliance, 100, 105; and training
programs, 226
Achieving Society, The (McClelland),
20, 22, 101, 199
Activity inhibition, 25
Activity level, 5
Adams, J.S., 43
Adolescents, 36–37
Advancement, 82–86, 165, 168–169;
and commitment, 112, 115
Affiliation needs, 19, 24–25, 208–
209; and age, 158, 159; assessment
of, 79; and commitment, 119–121;
and gender, 213; and Japan, 207
Afghanistan-Pashtu, 196
Age: and affiliation, 158, 159; and
assessment, 73; and competence,
69, 158, 164, 175, 180, 230; and
excellence, striving for, 178; and
gender, 212; and job satisfaction,
172–173; and leadership, 158,
163–164; and meaning, 69–70,
160–177; and motivation, 157–
160, 177–178, 181–182; and

options, perceived, 165–172; and
personal incentives, 161–165,
171–172, 181; and personal invest-
ment, 155–182; and power needs,
158, 161, 163–164, 166, 168, 169;
and recognition, 159, 161, 166;
and retraining, 179–181; and self,
sense of, 164, 175; and social concern, 161, 162–163, 175
Aging of population, 155–156
Aggressiveness, 105
Airline company, 136, 138, 145
Allport, Gordon, 42, 50, 60
Alper, T.G., 212
Alschuler, A.S., 225
Ames, C., 73
Ames, R., 35, 38, 73
Andrews, G.R., 227
Argentina, 1
Arnoff, J., 27
Arnold, H.J., 107–108, 218
Artifacts, 191
Assessment procedures, 18–20; and
affiliation, 79; and age, 73; and
cognition, 47; and commitment, 82,
87–90; and competence, 74; and
context, 74–75, 82–86; and fantasies, 19–20, 46; and intensity, 73;
and job opportunity, 82–86; and
job satisfaction, 82, 87–90; and
meaning, 46–47, 71–91; and motivation, 18–19, 46–47, 72–91; and
options, perceived, 76, 82; and
organizational culture, 87, 131–
146, 241–242; and performance,
73, 233–238, 242; and persistence,
73; and personal incentives, 75–76,

Assessment procedures: (*continued*)
78, 82; and personal investment,
71–90; and power, 79; and selec-
tion of motivated people, 271–273;
and self, sense of, 76, 79, 81, 82
Astley, W.G., 29
AT&T managers, 25
Athos, A.G., 30, 126, 207, 250
Atkinson, J.W., 18, 19, 37, 42, 47,
55, 57, 114, 199, 223, 158, 159
Attractiveness of task, 32, 64, 233
Attribution theory, 37–38
Ausabel, D.P., 188
Automobile industry, 179
Autonomy, 65–66, 243, 244, 252
Azim, A., 119
Azumi, K., 203

Baby boom, 155, 162
Bandura, A., 227
Bangkok, 191
Bank tellers, 224, 232–233
Barry, H. III, 193, 204
Behavior: and motivation, 2–6, 45;
and personal incentives, 94
Beliefs, 188–191
Bem, D.J., 36
Benedict, Ruth, 187
Benefits, 54–55, 66
Bennis, W., 234, 240
Biddle, B.J., 30
Bird, Larry, 97
Black English United States, 196
Blake, R.R., 203
Bloom, Benjamin S., 14, 40, 95–96
Boje, D.M., 129
Bolman, L.G., 244
Bosiman, F., 119
Bower, Marvin, 34
Boyatzis, R.E., 25, 223
Brandenberg, D.C., 235
Braskamp, L.A., 42, 45, 100, 160,
178, 223, 228, 235, 242
Brehm, J.W., 41
Brent, S.B., 159
Brim, O.G., Jr., 159
Brislin, R.W., 204
Brousseau, K.R., 151
Brown, R.D., 242
Bunzel, J.H., 185
Burnout, 15, 35, 41, 156, 178

Callahan, T., 97
Cameron, K., 234

Campbell, J.P., 42, 133
Career changes, 3, 35
Career planning, 228
Carol, W.K., 204
Challenge, 57–58, 64
Chhokar, J.S., 65
Chiefs vs. Indians, 105
Children of Sanchez (Lewis), 189
Chown, S.M., 159
Chuny, K.H., 50
Clark, R.A., 18
Cognition, 35–43, 44, 48; assessment,
47
Cognitive dissonance theory, 37
College students and motivation stud-
ies, 71
Child-rearing practices, 21–23, 56–57
Commitment. *See* Organizational com-
mitment
Compensation, 66
Competence, sense of, 36–37, 38–39;
and achievement, 60–61; and age,
69, 158, 164, 175, 180, 230; as-
sessment of, 79; and challenges, 57;
demonstration of, 52–53; and ego
incentives, 55–56; and meaning,
60–61; and options, 41, 116; and
training programs, 227–228
Competition, 79, 112–113, 119, 233;
and age, 159, 163–164; and achievers, 100; cross-cultural meanings,
198; and organizational culture,
143–145; and success, 68
Connell, J.P., 38–39, 53
Consistency theory, 36–37
Consulting firm, 136, 138–139,
145–146
Contexts, 74–75, 82–86
Continuing motivation, 4–5, 73, 218,
237
Control, mechanisms of, 187–188
Cook, J.D., 133
Cooperative work approaches, 30, 33, 68
Cornelius, E.T., 26
Courage, 67–68
Cross-cultural studies, 67–69, 101,
193–212
Culture, 127–130; *see also* Cross-
cultural studies; Organizational
culture; Socio-cultural factors
Csikszentmihalyi, M., 52, 53

D'Andrade, R.G., 21
Darrow, C.N., 156

Datan, N., 159
Deal, T.E., 34, 127, 130, 131–132, 134, 244
Debus, R.L., 227
DeCharms, R., 39, 60
Deci, E.L., 27, 32, 39, 54, 60, 66
Decision making, 33, 227, 243
Decision theory, 39–40, 42
Declining industries, morale in, 40–41
Delayed gratification, 20, 60, 159, 161, 189–190
Delegation of authority, 243–244, 252
Depression, 181
Desai, K.A., 30
Developmental tasks, 156–157
De Vos, G.A., 203, 207
Direction, 3, 5, 45; and goals, 60, 79, 164, 245
Doering, M., 172–173
Drake, B., 119
Dropout rates, 88
Duda, J., 193
Dunnette, M.D., 42
Dweck, C.S., 227
Dynamics of motivation, 10–12

Eckensberger, L.H., 20
Economic growth and achievement needs, 20–23; *see also* Protestant ethic
Edison, Thomas, 45
Education, 179–180, 185, 196–197, 198
Edward, A.E., 159
Ego personal incentives, 53, 55–56, 72, 119; and organizational culture, 146, 152
Emminghaus, W.B., 20
Energy, 8
Equity, 43, 237
Erikson, Erik, 175–176, 157
Ethics, 188–189
Ethnographic studies, 131–133, 147
Evaluation, 233–238, 242, 245
Excellence, striving for, 78, 79; and achievers, 106, 174; and age, 178; and gender, 213; and Japan, 207, 208, 209
Excellers. *See* Achievers
Executives, 143–145
External rewards. 152, 158, 240; *see also* Rewards
Extrinsic personal incentives, 54–55, 56–57

Failure, 67–69, 70
Fairness, 237
Faithfulness, 54, 56
Family, 29, 30, 40, 70
Fantasies and assessment of motivation, 19–20, 46
Farmer, H.S., 76, 193
Fast-food organization, 136–138
Feather, N.T., 37, 42, 57, 73, 114
Featherman, D.C., 27
Fedor, D.B., 129
Feedback, 11, 54–55, 64–65
Feld, S., 158
Feldman, D.C., 107–108, 218
Femininity, 197, 199
Festinger, L., 36, 37
Financial incentives, 161, 207, 208, 209
Fiske, S.T., 47
Folger, R., 237
Forward, J., 31
Fowler, D.A., 42, 45, 100, 178
Freedom, 41, 196–197
Freud, Sigmund, 19, 157
Fyans, L.J., Jr., 4, 30, 34, 61, 68, 101, 193, 199, 201, 237

Galanter, E., 50
Gender differences, 192, 197, 198–199, 212–213
Geneen, Harold, 45
Generativity, 176
George, L.K., 69
Goals, 188–191; and achievers, 100; and age, 164; and direction, 60, 79, 164, 245; and organizational culture, 129, 130, 133–134, 141, 227, 236, 245
Goodenough, W.H., 131
Goodman, P.S., 234
Gould, S., 161
Gray Panthers, 159
Greece, 68
Greenberg, J., 237
Greene, D., 37, 54
Griffith, R.W., 116
Group expectations, 27, 28–31, 44, 59; and meaning, 63–64
Guilt culture, 187–188
Gurin, G., 158

Haas, H.I., 36, 227
Hackman, J.R., 27, 39, 54, 64, 65–66, 71, 75, 147, 218, 233, 237, 243–244, 245

Hall, D.T., 133, 161
Hand, H.H., 116
Harnisch, D., 203, 212, 213
Harter, S., 38–39, 53
Harvard, 18
Hatvany, N., 30
Havighurst, R.J., 156
Heckhausen, H., 20, 21, 27
Helmreich, R.L., 100, 212
Henderson, R., 65
Hepworth, S.J., 133
Heroes, 129, 130, 132, 139, 229, 244
Hess, R.K., 54
Hickman, C.R., 126
High tech industry, 179
Hill, K.T., 237
Hirsch, P., 126
Homans, G., 29, 59

Iaffaldano, M.T., 107
Identity, 59, 64
Incentives. *See* Personal incentives
India, 68, 196
Indians and chiefs, 105
Individualized expectations, 31
Individuals, 151–153, 240–241
Information, 66, 67, 244
Innovators, 60
Insurance salesmen, 96
Intensity, 5, 8, 73
Internal motivation, 218, 237
Interpersonal relationships, 10, 120;
    and meaning, 53; and task, 32–33
Intrinsic motivation, 32, 52
Inventory of Personal Investment (IPI),
    76–81, 93, 228; and achievers, 98–
    101; and Japan, 204–206; and
    meaning/personal investment rela-
    tionship, 93; and organizational
    culture, 241; and selection of per-
    sonnel, 222–223
Inventory of Work Investment (IWI),
    76, 82–91; and career planning,
    228; and commitment, 107; and job
    satisfaction, 108; and meaning/per-
    sonal investment relationship, 93;
    and organizational culture, 135–139,
    241; and personal investment, 108;
    and selection of personnel, 222–223
Iran, 67–68, 196
Irvine, S., 204
Ivancevich, J.M., 65, 236

James, L.R., 133
Japan, 1, 30, 67–68, 202–212; and af-
    filiation needs, 207; and excellence,
    striving for, 207, 208; and financial
    incentives, 207, 208, 209; and United
    States, 192, 202–212, 213–214
Jelinek, M., 126
Job Diagnosis Survey, 75
Job attractiveness, 32, 64, 233
Job criteria, 235–236, 237, 242
Job design, 27, 75, 218, 238
Job opportunities: and age, 165–168,
    171; and assessment, 82–86; and
    job satisfaction, 110, 113, 114–121;
    and organizational culture, 142–
    143, 153; and personal incentives,
    116–121, 225; and task, 166
Job/person matches, 170–172, 223–
    225, 238
Job satisfaction: and age, 172–173;
    and assessment, 82, 87–90; and ex-
    ternal rewards, 152; and job oppor-
    tunities, 110–113, 114–121; and
    marketability, 112–113; and organi-
    zational culture, 117–119, 151–
    152; and perceived options,
    110–113, 115–121; and personal
    incentives, 113–114, 117–119; and
    personal investment, 107; and
    power, 112, 119, 120–121; and
    productivities, 107; and rewards,
    237; and union activity, 107–108
Jones, A.P., 133
Justice. *See* Equity

Kastenbaum, R., 159
Kelly, J.R., 9, 69, 72, 76, 160, 178
Kennedy, A.A., 34, 127, 130, 131–
    132, 134, 147, 244
Kierkegaard, Soren, 247
Kilman, R.H., 126
Kirst, M.W., 185
Kleiber, D.A., 45, 69, 72, 73, 155,
    161, 178, 219
Klein, E.B., 156
Klein, R., 159
Klinger, E., 15, 30, 31, 50, 181
Kluckhohn, Clyde, 187
Kluckhohn, Florence, 189
Knowledge and culture, 184, 197
Knox, A.B., 180
Kornadt, H.J., 20

Krug, S., 27
Kuhlen, R.G., 9, 159
Kuhn, Maggie, 159
Kukla, A., 38, 56, 60, 97

Lane, F.B., 26
Langer, E.J., 47, 181
Latham, G.P., 27, 71, 236
Lawler, E.E., III, 27, 33, 42, 54, 66, 107, 133
Leadership, 25–26, 27; and age, 158, 163–164; characteristics, 105
Lefcourt, H.M., 38–39
Lehman, H.C., 158
Leisure, 71–72, 160, 180, 253
Lepper, Mark, 37, 54
Levinson, Daniel J., 156, 157
Levinson, M.H., 156
Lewis, Oscar, 189
Life-Insurance Round Table, 96–97
Life paths and career, 101–102
Life satisfaction, 14–15
Life stages, 69–70, 167–169; and personal investment, 156–157, 160
Lindzey, G., 42
Litwin, G.H., 27, 34
Locke, E.A., 27, 71, 236
Locus of control, 38–39
Lord, R.G., 38
Lowell, E.L., 18
Ludwig, D.J., 37, 60, 227
Luther, Martin, 3

McClelland, David, 13, 18–27, 30, 42, 47, 51, 55, 60, 96, 97, 101, 114–115, 189, 197, 199, 200, 207, 208, 209–210, 213, 225, 226, 228–229, 250
McGregor, D., 34, 190
McKeachie, W.J., 235
McKee, B., 156
McMahon, J.R., 65, 236
McMillan, C., 203
McNelley, F.W., 30, 31
Maehr, M.L., 4, 8, 13, 27, 29, 30, 32, 33, 36, 37, 40, 42, 45, 50, 51, 54, 56, 59, 60, 61, 67, 68, 69, 72, 73, 76, 95, 100, 101, 114, 127, 155, 158, 159, 161, 181, 193, 197–198, 203, 212, 213, 218, 219, 223, 227, 228, 237
Maguire, M., 203

Managers: and achievement, 25.–26; and affiliation, 25–26, 27; and organizational culture, 126–127, 131–132, 143–144, 239–246; and personal investment, enhancing, 215–246; and power, 25–26, 27, 242–244
Marcuccio, P., 185
Marketability, 112–113, 114–115; and age, 165, 169–170
Masai, 127
Masculinity, 196–197, 199
Massie, Robert, 8
May, W., 67, 193
Mayberry, Paul, 117–118, 151–152, 203, 206
Mead, G.H., 36
Mead, Margaret, 187
Meaning: and age, 69–70, 160–177; antecedents, 62–70, 217–218; assessing, 46–47, 71–91; and competence, 60–61; and context, 74–75; elements of, 48–49; and information, 67; and life stage, 69–70; and motivation, 46, 47–49; and options, 48; and organizational culture, 139–141; and personal investment, 46, 47–49, 76–81, 93–123, 216–217; and personality, 62; and situation, 63–67, 217–218; sociocultural factors, 67–68, 183–214
Meglino, B.M., 116
Meindl, J., 54
Mensing, J., 36, 277
Miller, A.T., 56, 60, 97, 151
Miller, G.A., 50
Miron, M., 67, 193
Mischel, W., 60
Mitchell, T.R., 27, 119
Mobley, W.H., 116
Money, 33, 54–55, 89, 209–210
Morris, Edmund, 8
Morsbach, H., 207, 208
Motivation: and achievers, 96–98; and age, 157–160, 177–178, 181–182; assessment of, 18–19, 46–47, 72–91; and autonomy, 66; and behavior, 2–6, 45; and cognition, 35–43, 44, 48; enhancing, 27, 31, 219–246; evaluation, 233–238; and Japan, 202–212; and meaning, 46,

Motivation: (*Continued*)
47–49; multiple determinants, 26–27; and personal investment, 6–8, 9–12, 46, 216, 240; and personality, 17–27, 43–44; predicting, 26–27, 40–44; as process, 47; situational causes, 27–35, 231–238; and task characteristics, 32–33, 44; and training programs, 225–228
Mouton, J.S., 203
Mowday, R.T., 43
Muchinsky, P.M., 107
Murray, Henry, 19
Mysore, 196
Myths, 129, 130, 132, 191, 229

Nadler, D.A., 65
Nafzger, S., 36, 227
Nature, relationship to, 190
Nesbitt, R.E., 37
Neugarten, B.L., 159
Nicholls, J.G., 27, 38, 45, 50, 56, 60, 67, 68, 69, 73, 97, 101, 193, 199
Norms, 127–130; and expectations, 29–30, 63, 186–187; and training, 227, 230–231
Nougam, K.E., 161

Oldham, G.R., 27, 39, 54, 64, 65–66, 75, 133, 218, 233, 237
Opportunity. *See* Job opportunity
Options, perceived, 39–42, 48, 61–62, 248; and age, 165–172; and assessment, 76, 82; and commitment, 110–113, 115–121; and competence, 41, 116; cross-cultural factors, 198; and gender, 213; and information, 67; and job satisfaction, 110–113, 115–121; and meaning, 48; and personal incentives, 110–113; and personal investment, 109–113
Organizational commitment: and affiliation, 119–121; and age, 173–174; and assessment, 82, 87–90; case study, 238–239; and job advancement, 112, 115; and marketability, 112–113; organizational culture, 149, 151–153, 229–230, 239–240; and perceived options, 110–113, 115–121; and personal incentives, 113–114, 117–119; and personal investment, 107; and power, 115, 119; and rewards, 237–238; and task, 149; and training programs, 226
Organizational culture, 33–34, 121–122, 125–154, 252; assessment, 87, 131–146, 241–242; and commitment, 149, 151–153, 229–230, 239–240; and competition, 143–145; concept of, 126–127; and ego incentives, 146, 152; and executives, 143–145; and goals, 129, 130, 133–134, 141, 227, 236, 241; and individual, 151–153, 240–241; and Inventory of Personal Investment, 241; and Inventory of Work Investment, 135–139, 241; and job opportunities, 142–143, 153; and job satisfaction, 117–119, 151–152; and managers, 126–127, 131–132, 143–144, 239–246; and meaning, 139–141; and mission, 239–240, 244–245; and personal incentives, 133–134, 141; and personal investment, 146–153, 215, 239–245; and position in company, 142; and power, 142, 242–244; saliency of, 87, 134, 136–138, 144, 146–151; and social concern, 146, 147; and socialization, 228–231
Ory, J.C., 42, 45, 100, 178, 235
Osgood, Charles, 67, 193, 200
Ouchi, W., 30, 34, 126

Pareek, V., 204
Pascale, R.T., 30, 126, 203, 207, 229, 231, 234, 250
Pathfinders, 60
Patten, T., 33, 66
Pennings, J.M., 119, 234
Perceived options. *See* Options, perceived
Performance, 5–6; assessment, 73, 233–238, 242
Perquisites, 54–55, 66
Persistence, 3–4, 9; assessment, 73
Personal growth, 13–14
Personal incentives, 48, 121, 248; and academics, 103–106; and age, 161–165, 171–172, 181; assessment, 75–76, 78, 82; and behavior, 94; and challenge, 57–58, 64; and

commitment, 117–119; and context, 74; cross-cultural differences, 196–197; function of, 55–58; and gender, 212–213; and Japan, 205, 206–208, 209–210; and job opportunities, 116–121, 225; and job satisfaction, 113–114, 117–119; and meaning, 48, 49–58; nature of, 50–55; and organizational commitment, 113–114, 117–119, 240; and organizational culture, 133–134, 141; and perceived options, 110–113

Personal investment: and age, 155–182; and antecedents, 217–218, 231–232; assessment of, 71–91; and commitment, 107; and contexts, 74–75, 82–86; defined, 8–12; enhancing, 219–246; and gender differences, 192, 198–199, 212–213; and Japan, 202–212, 213–214; and job satisfaction, 107; and knowledge, 184; and life stages, 156–157, 160; managing for, 215–246; and meaning, 46, 47–48, 76–81, 93–123, 216–217; and motivation, 6–8, 9–12, 46, 216, 248; and options, perceived, 109–113; and organizational culture, 129–131, 146–153, 215, 239–245; outcomes of, 12–15; and personality, 114–115, 217, 220–231; and rewards, 235; and situation, 217–218; and sociocultural context, 67–70, 183–214; theory of, 45, 216–218, 248–249

Personality: and meaning, 62; and motivation, 17–27, 43–44; and personal investment, 114–115, 217, 220–231; and values, 190

Peter the Great, 8

Peters, T.J., 87, 126, 127, 134, 147, 149, 234, 240

Pfeffer, J., 29, 30, 35

Physiological factors, 5, 8

Plateauing, 15, 178

Plath, D.W., 207

Poland, 196

Pollack, K., 159

Porac, J.F., 54

Porter, L.W., 27, 71, 107, 116

Power, 19, 23–24; and achievers, 174; and age, 158, 161, 163–164, 166, 168, 169; and assessment, 79; and gender, 213; and job satisfaction, 112, 119, 120–121; and managers, 25–26, 27, 242–244; and organizational commitment, 115, 119; and organizational culture, 142, 242–244

Preference, 185–186

Pribram, K.H., 50

Product-evaluation cycles, 11–12

Productivity, 13, 243, 249–251, 252; and aging of population, 156, 158; and equity, 43; and job satisfaction, 107; and personal investment, 88

Protestant ethic, 20–21, 68, 201–202, 213; and achievement, 101

Protestant Ethic and the Spirit of Capitalism, The (Weber), 20–21

Pucik, V., 30

Punishment, 68

Quality of work life, 251–252

Quinn, N., 199

Rao, T.V., 204

Raynor, J.O., 42, 55, 57, 158, 159, 161

Recognition, 79, 236–237, 240, 242, 244–245; and age, 159, 161, 166; and Japan, 207, 208–209

Reference groups, 29, 59, 61–62

Reinforcement theory, 54

Religion, 20–21, 250

Retraining, 179–181

Rewards, 9, 27, 54, 89, 235, 244–245; and cognition, 37; and evaluation, 235, 236–237, 242; and information, 66; and job satisfaction, 237; and success, 197

Rhodes, S.R., 161, 172–173

Rice, B., 245

Risk, 97, 158–159, 161

Ritual, 129, 130, 132, 191

Roberts, G.C., 60

Rodin, J., 181

Roe, Ann, 95

Rogers, Carl, 36

Role expectations, 30–31, 64, 69–70, 186–187, 230

Romania, 196

Rooney, G.S., 76

Roosevelt, Theodore, 8

Rosen, B.C., 21
Rowland, K.M., 129

Saari, L.M., 27
Salancik, G.R., 30, 35, 71
Salili, F., 4, 30, 237
Sandelands, L.E., 54
Schank, R.C., 47
Schein, E.H., 34, 101, 126, 131, 190, 229, 231, 240
Schneider, B., 133
Schools, 20, 185, 198, 200
Schulz, R., 181
Schuster, M., 172–173
Schwalb, D., 203–204, 206, 207, 208, 209, 211, 214
Scientists, 95, 96, 97
Seasons of a Man's Life, The (Levinson) 156
Selecting motivated people, 27, 220–223, 238
Self, sense of, 121; and age, 164, 175; assessment, 76, 79, 81, 82; and culture, 192, 196–197, 199–200, 212–213; and gender, 212–213; in Japan, 206–209, 213–214; and job satisfaction, 113–115
Self-concept change, 227
Self-confidence, 37–38, 97, 98, 105
Self-consistency, 36–37
Self-determinatin, 38–39
Self-efficacy, 227
Self-management units, 245
Self-reliance, 59–60, 79; and achievers, 100, 105; and age, 164; and Japan, 208–209
Semantic differential studies, 193–202
Sex roles, 198–199; *see also* Gender differences
Sex and Temperament in Three Primitive Societies (Mead), 187
Shame cultures, 187–188
Sheehy, G., 60
Significant others, 29, 36
Silva, M.A., 126
Simulation games, 226
Situation, 114–115, 121; and cognitive response, 39–43; and meaning, 63–67, 217–218; and motivation enhancement, 231–238; and personal investment, 217–218
Sjogren, D., 53

Skill, 10, 64
Smircich, L., 126
Smith, J.E., 38
Snyder, R.A., 133
Social concern, 79; and achievers, 175–176; and age, 161, 162–163, 175; and commitment, 119, 121; and Japan, 207–208, 209–210; and organizational culture, 146, 147
Social expectations. *See* Group expectations
Social personal incentives, 53–54, 56, 57, 158, 224
Socialization, 171
Sociocultural factors: and achievement, 100–101, 193–212; matrix, 184–193; and meaning, 67–69, 183–214; and options, 42, 213; and personal investment, 67–70, 183–214; and task characteristics, 32, 33–35
Sorensen, R.I., 4
Spady, W., 233, 234
Spence, J.T., 100, 212
Spenner, K.I., 27
Stake, R.E., 42
Stallings, W.M., 4, 237
Status, 69–70, 168, 187
Staw, B.M., 27, 34, 47, 54, 71
Steel industry, 179
Steers, R.M., 1, 31, 71, 116
Steinkamp, M.W., 72, 76, 198, 199, 212
Steinmetz, George, 244
Stringer, R.A., Jr., 34
Strobeck, F.L., 189
Style, 185–186
Success, 67–69, 196–202; and academics, 102–106; definition of, 70, 102–103; *see also* Achievers
Suttle, J.L., 71
Sweden, 196

Tandem Corporation, 130
Task: absorption, 52, 79; and achievers, 100; and age, 161, 169, 178; attractiveness, 32, 64, 233; characteristics, 32–33; and commitment, 149; and gender, 213; and identity, 64; and Japan, 207, 208, 209; and job opportunities, 166–168; and job satisfaction, 120–121, 149;

and motivation, 32–33, 44; and
organizational culture, 143, 146,
147; and personal incentives,
51–54, 55, 56–57, 64–67, 72, 81;
and sociocultural factors, 32,
33–35; and uncertainty, 57
Taylor, S.E., 47
Technology, differences in, 184–185
Tenure in organization, 168, 171, 174
Terman, L.M., 95
Thailand, 67–68
Thematic Apperception Test, 25
Theory X, 34, 190
Theory Y, 34, 190–191
Theory, 34
Theory Z (Ouchi), 34
Thurow, Lester, 1
Time, 97
Time dimension, attitude toward,
189–190
Training program, 225–228
Triandis, H.C., 34, 68, 204
Turnover, 107
Tyler, R.W., 185

Uncertainty, 57
Uneo, I., 203
Union activity and job satisfaction,
107–108
United States, 196; and Japan, 192,
202–212, 213–214

Valentine, C.A., 189
Value. *See* Worth, judgment of
Values, 188–191
Van de Ven, A.H., 29
Vernon, P.E., 42
Veroff, J., 50, 158, 159, 163, 164
Veroff, J.B., 163, 164

Videbeck, R., 36
Vispoel, W., 193
Vroom, V.H., 37, 42, 107

Wages, 66
Wall, T.D., 133
Wall Street Journal, 95
Wallin, J.A., 65
Wanous, J., 116, 225
Warr, P.D., 133
Waterman, R.H., Jr., 87, 126, 127,
134, 147, 149, 234, 240
Watson, Thomas, 23, 244
Weber, Max, 20–21, 68, 101, 197,
200, 201, 209–210, 213, 250
Weick, K.E., 42
Weiner, Bernard, 37–38, 200
Wesleyan University, 18
West Germany, 196
Wexley, K.N., 243
Whetten, D.A., 41, 130
White, Robert, 52, 53
Whiting, J.W.M., 187
Wigfield, A., 160
Wilkins, A.L., 34, 126
Willig, A.C., 60
Wine, D.B., 159
Winter, D.G., 27, 158, 225
Winterbottom, M.R., 21
Work climate, 82
Worth, judgment of, 42–43
Wylie, R., 59

Yankelowich, D., 1, 43
Yukl, G.A., 27, 33, 66, 105, 243

Zander, A., 31
Zeigarnik, B., 4

About the Authors

Martin L. Maehr received his Ph.D. from the University of Nebraska. He has been on the faculty of the University of Illinois, Urbana-Champaign since 1967. During that period, he conducted research on motivation and achievement in the United States and abroad. He has also served in various administrative roles, including that of department chair and associate dean. Currently, he is professor of educational psychology and directs a program of research concerned with organizational effects on motivation. He has authored several books and numerous articles. He is editor of a research annual, *Advances in Motivation and Achievement*. Dr. Maehr is also a regular consultant on motivation and organizational effectiveness.

Larry A. Braskamp received his Ph.D. from the University of Iowa. He serves as associate vice-chancellor of academic affairs at the University of Illinois, Urbana-Champaign. He also holds faculty rank in the departments of educational psychology and business administration. He has served on the faculty of the University of Illinois Executive M.B.A. Program, and as acting director of the Executive Development Center. He is currently director of the Office of Instructional and Management Services.

Professor Braskamp's research interests are in the area of program and personnel evaluation with an emphasis on the uses of evaluative information in organizational decisionmaking. He has coedited or written three books and numerous articles. He often conducts workshops and seminars for various business groups and serves as a consultant to public and private organizations.